absolute **tao**

OSHO

Extemporaneous talks given by Osho
at the OSHO International Meditation Resort, Pune, India

absolute **tao**

Subtle is the way to love,
happiness and truth

ON THE *TAO TE CHING* BY LAO TZU

OSHO

OSHO is a registered trademark of OSHO International Foundation
www.osho.com/trademarks

Previously published as *Tao: The Three Treasures,* Vol. 1.

This book is a series of original talks by Osho, given to a live audience. All of
Osho's talks have been published in full as books, and are also available as
original audio recordings. Audio recordings and the complete text archive can
be found via the online OSHO Library at www.osho.com/library

Osho comments in this work on excerpts from *The Wisdom of Laotse,* edited by
Lin Yutang, copyright © 1948 by Random House, Inc. Used by permission of
Modern Library, a division of Random House, Inc.

OSHO MEDIA INTERNATIONAL
New York • Zurich • Mumbai
an imprint of
OSHO INTERNATIONAL
www.osho.com/oshointernational

Distributed by Publishers Group Worldwide
www.pgw.com

Library of Congress Catalog-In-Publication Data is available

Printed in India by Manipal Technologies Limited, Karnataka

ISBN: 978-0-9836400-0-4
Also available as eBook ISBN: 978-0-88050-209-2

contents

preface

Tao is another name for God, far more beautiful than God because God, the word God, has been exploited too much by the priests. They have exploited in the name of God for so long that even the word has become contaminated – it has become disgusting. Any man of intelligence is bound to avoid it because it reminds him of all the nonsense that has happened on the earth down the ages in the name of God, in the name of religion. More mischief has happened in the name of God than in any other name.

Tao in that sense is tremendously beautiful. You cannot worship Tao because Tao does not give you the idea of a person. It is simply a principle, not a person. You cannot worship a principle – you cannot pray to Tao. It will look ridiculous; it will be utterly absurd, praying to a principle. You don't pray to gravitation, you cannot pray to the theory of relativity.

Tao simply means the ultimate principle that binds the whole existence together. Existence is not a chaos; that much is certain. It is a cosmos. There is immense order in it, intrinsic order in it, and the name of that order is Tao. Tao simply means the harmony of the whole. No temples have been built for Tao; no statues, no prayers, no priests, no rituals – that's the beauty of it. Hence I don't call it a doctrine, nor do I call it a religion, it is pure insight.

Osho
Tao: The Golden Gate, Vol.1

CHAPTER 1

on the absolute tao

Lao Tzu says, on the Absolute Tao:

The Tao that can be told of is not the Absolute Tao...

And on the rise of relative opposites, he says:

*When the people of the Earth all know beauty as beauty,
there arises the recognition of ugliness.
When the people of the Earth all know the good as good,
there arises the recognition of evil.*

*Therefore:
being and non-being interdepend in growth;
difficult and easy interdepend in completion;
long and short interdepend in contrast;
high and low interdepend in position;
tones and voice interdepend in harmony;
front and behind interdepend in company.*

Therefore the Sage:

manages affairs without action;
preaches the doctrine without words.
All things take their rise, but he does not turn away from them;
he gives them life, but does not take possession of them;
he acts, but does not appropriate;
accomplishes, but claims no credit.

It is because he lays claim to no credit
that the credit cannot be taken away from him.

I speak on Mahavira as a part of my duty – my heart is never with him. He is too mathematical. He is not a mystic, he has no poetry of being. He is great, enlightened, but like a vast desert; you cannot come across a single oasis in him. But because I was born a Jaina I have to pay some debts. I speak on him as my duty but my heart is not there; I speak only from the mind. When I speak on Mahavira I speak as an outsider. He is not inside me and I am not inside him.

The same is true about Moses and Mohammed. I don't feel like speaking on them; I have not spoken on them. If I had not been born a Jaina I would never have spoken on Mahavira either. Many times my Mohammedan disciples or my Jewish disciples come to me and ask, "Why don't you speak on Mohammed or Moses?" It is difficult to explain to them. Many times, just looking at their faces, I decide that I will speak; many times I look again and again into the words of Moses and Mohammed, then again I postpone it. No bell rings in my heart. It would not be alive – if I spoke it would be a dead thing. I don't even feel a duty toward them as I feel toward Mahavira.

They all belong to the same category: they are too calculative, extremist; they miss the opposite extreme. They are single notes, not harmonies, not symphonies. A single note has its beauty – an austere beauty – but it is monotonous. Once in a while it is okay, but if it continues you feel bored; you would like to stop it. The personalities of Mahavira, Moses and Mohammed are like single notes: simple, austere, beautiful even, once in a while. But if I meet Mahavira, Moses or Mohammed on the road I will pay my respects and escape.

I speak on Krishna. He is multidimensional, superhuman, miraculous, but looks more like a myth than a real man. He is so extraordinary that he cannot be. On this earth such extraordinary persons cannot exist, they exist only as dreams. And myths are nothing but collective dreams. The whole of humanity has been dreaming them – beautiful, but unbelievable. I talk about Krishna and I enjoy it, but I enjoy it as one enjoys a beautiful story and the telling of a beautiful story. But it is not very meaningful – a cosmic gossip.

I speak on Jesus Christ. I feel deep sympathy for him. I would like to suffer with him and I would like to carry his cross a little while by his side. But we remain parallel, we never meet. He is so sad, so burdened – burdened with the miseries of the whole of humanity. He cannot laugh. If you move with him too long you will become sad, you will lose laughter. Gloominess surrounds him. I feel for him but I would not like to be like him. I can walk with him a little while and share his burden, but then we part. Our ways are different ways. He is good, but too good, almost inhumanly good.

I speak on Zarathustra – very rarely, but I love the man as a friend loves another friend. You can laugh with him. He is not a moralist, not a puritan; he can enjoy life and everything that life gives. A good friend; you could be with him forever, but he is just a friend. Friendship is good, but not enough.

I speak on Buddha – I love him. Down through the centuries, through many lives, I have loved him. He is tremendously beautiful, extraordinarily beautiful, superb. But he is not on the earth, he does not walk on the earth. He flies in the sky and leaves no footprints. You cannot follow him, you never know his whereabouts. He is like a cloud. Sometimes you meet him but that is accidental. And he is so refined that he cannot take roots on this earth. He is meant for some higher heaven. In that way he is one-sided. Earth and heaven don't meet in him. He is heavenly but the earthly part is missing. He is like a flame, beautiful – but there is no oil, no container. You can see the flame but it is going higher and higher, nothing holds it on the earth. I love him, I speak on him from my heart, but still a distance remains. It always remains in the phenomenon of love; you come closer and closer and closer, but even in closeness there is a distance. That is the misery of all lovers.

I speak on Lao Tzu totally differently. I am not related to him because even to be related a distance is needed. I don't love him, because how can you love yourself? When I speak on Lao Tzu I speak as if I am speaking on my own self. With him my being is totally one. When I speak on Lao Tzu it is as if I am looking in a mirror: my own face is reflected. When I speak on Lao Tzu, I am absolutely with him. Even to say "absolutely with him" is not true – I am him, he is me.

Historians are doubtful about his existence. I cannot doubt his existence because how can I doubt my own existence? The moment I became possible, he became true to me. Even if history proves that he never existed it makes no difference to me; he must have existed because I exist – I am the proof. During the following days when I speak on Lao Tzu, it is not that I speak on somebody else. I speak on myself – as if Lao Tzu is speaking through a different name, a different *nama-roop*, a different incarnation.

Lao Tzu is not like Mahavira, not mathematical at all, yet he is very, very logical in his madness. He has a mad logic! When we penetrate into his sayings you will come to feel it; it is not so obvious and apparent. He has a logic of his own: the logic of absurdity, the logic of paradox, the logic of a madman. He hits hard.

Mahavira's logic can be understood even by blind men. To understand Lao Tzu's logic you will have to create eyes. It is very subtle. It is not the ordinary logic of the logicians; it is the logic of a hidden life, a very subtle life. Whatsoever he says is on the surface absurd; deep down there lives a very great consistency. One has to penetrate it; one has to change his own mind to understand Lao Tzu. You can understand Mahavira without changing your mind at all; as you are, you can understand Mahavira. He is on the same line. Howsoever ahead of you he may have reached the goal, he is on the same line, the same track.

When you try to understand Lao Tzu, he zigzags. Sometimes you see him going toward the east and sometimes toward the west, because he says east is west and west is east, they are together, they are one. He believes in the unity of the opposites. And that is how life is.

So Lao Tzu is just a spokesman of life. If life is absurd, Lao Tzu is absurd; if life has an absurd logic in it, Lao Tzu has the same logic. Lao Tzu simply reflects life. He doesn't add anything to it, he doesn't choose out of it. He simply accepts whatsoever it is.

It is simple to see the spirituality of Buddha, very simple; it is impossible to miss it, he is so extraordinary. But it is difficult to see the spirituality of Lao Tzu. He is so ordinary, just like you. You will have to grow in understanding. Buddha passes by you – you will immediately recognize that a superior human being has passed you. He carries the glamour of a superior human being around him. It is difficult to miss him, almost impossible to miss him. But Lao Tzu may be your neighbor. You may have been missing him because he is so ordinary, he is so extraordinarily ordinary. And that is just the beauty of it.

To become extraordinary is simple: only effort is needed, refinement is needed, cultivation is needed. It is a deep inner discipline. You can become very, very refined, something absolutely unearthly. But to be ordinary is really the most extraordinary thing. No effort will help; effortlessness is needed. No practice will help, no methods, no means will be of any help, only understanding. Even meditation will not be of any help. To become a Buddha, meditation will be of help. To become a Lao Tzu, even meditation won't help – just understanding. Just understanding life as it is, and living it with courage; not escaping from it, not hiding from it, facing it with courage, whatsoever it is, good or bad, divine or evil, heaven or hell.

It is very difficult to be a Lao Tzu or to recognize a Lao Tzu. In fact, if you can recognize a Lao Tzu, you are already a Lao Tzu. To recognize Buddha you need not be a buddha, but to recognize Lao Tzu you need to be a lao tzu – otherwise it is impossible.

It is said that Confucius went to see Lao Tzu. Lao Tzu was an old man, Confucius was younger. Lao Tzu was almost unknown, Confucius was almost universally known. Kings and emperors used to call him to their courts; wise men used to come for his advice. He was the wisest man in China in those days. But by and by he must have felt that his wisdom might be of use to others, but he was not blissful, he had not attained to anything. He had become an expert, maybe helpful to others, but not helpful to himself.

So he started a secret search to find someone who could help him. Ordinary wise men wouldn't do, because they used to come to him for his advice. Great scholars wouldn't do; they used to come to ask him about their problems. But there must be someone somewhere – life is vast. He tried a secret search.

He sent his disciples to find someone who could be of help to him, and they came with the information that there lived a man – nobody knew his name – he was known as The Old Guy. Lao Tzu means "the old guy." The word is not his name, nobody knows his name. He was such an unknown man that nobody knows when he was born, nobody knows to whom; who his father was or who his mother was. Because nobody knew... He had lived for ninety years but only very rare human beings had come across him, very rare, who had different eyes and perspectives with which to understand him. He was only for the rarest. So ordinary a man, but only for the rarest of human minds.

Hearing the news that there exists a man known as The Old Guy, Confucius went to see him. When he met Lao Tzu he could feel that here was a man of great understanding, great intellectual integrity, great logical acumen, a genius. He could feel that there was something there, but he couldn't catch hold of it. Vaguely, mysteriously, there was something; this man was no ordinary man although he looked absolutely ordinary. Something was hidden; he was carrying a treasure.

Confucius asked, "What do you say about morality? What do you say about how to cultivate good character?" – because he was a moralist and he thought that if you cultivate a good character that is the highest attainment.

Lao Tzu laughed loudly, and said, "If you are immoral, only then does the question of morality arise. And if you don't have any character, only then do you think about character. A man of character is absolutely oblivious of the fact that anything like character exists. A man of morality does not know what the word *moral* means. So don't be foolish! And don't try to cultivate. Just be natural."

The man had such tremendous energy that Confucius started to tremble. He couldn't stand him. He escaped. He became afraid – as one becomes afraid near an abyss. When he came back to his disciples who were waiting outside under a tree, they could not believe it. This man had been going to emperors, the greatest emperors, and they had never seen any nervousness in him. He was trembling, and cold perspiration was coming, pouring out from all over his body. They couldn't believe it; what had happened? What had this man Lao Tzu done to their teacher? They asked him and he said, "Wait a little. Let me collect myself. This man is dangerous."

And about Lao Tzu he said to his disciples: "I have heard about great animals like elephants, and I know how they walk. And I have heard about hidden animals in the sea, and I know how they swim. And I have heard about great birds who fly thousands of miles away from the earth, and I know how they fly. But this man is a dragon. Nobody knows how he walks. Nobody knows how he lives. Nobody knows how he flies. Never go near him; he is like an abyss. He is like a death."

That is the definition of a master: a master is like a death. If you come near him, too close, you will feel afraid, a trembling will take over. You will be possessed by an unknown fear, as if you are going to die. It is said that Confucius never came again to see this old man.

Lao Tzu was ordinary in a way. And in another way he was the most extraordinary man. He was not extraordinary like Buddha; he was extraordinary in a totally different way. His extraordinariness was not so obvious – it was a hidden treasure. He was not miraculous like Krishna, he did not do any miracles, but his whole being was a miracle: the way he walked, the way he looked, the way he was. His whole being was a miracle.

He was not sad like Jesus; he could laugh, he could laugh a belly laugh. It is said that he was born laughing. Children are born crying, weeping. It is said about him that he was born laughing. I also feel it must be true; a man like Lao Tzu must be born laughing. He is not sad like Jesus. He can laugh, and laugh tremendously, but deep down in his laughter there is a sadness, a compassion – a sadness about you, about the whole existence. His laughter is not superficial. Zarathustra laughs but his laughter is different, there is no sadness in it.

Lao Tzu is sad like Jesus and not sad like Jesus; Lao Tzu laughs like Zarathustra and doesn't laugh like Zarathustra. His sadness has a laughter to it and his laughter has a sadness to it. He is a meeting of the opposites. He is a harmony, a symphony.

Remember this: I am not commenting on him. There exists no distance between me and him. He is talking to you through me – a different body, a different name, a different incarnation, but the same spirit.

Now we will take the sutra:

The Tao that can be told of
is not the Absolute Tao.

Let me first tell you the story of how these sutras came to be written, because that will help you to understand them. For ninety years Lao Tzu lived – in fact he did nothing but live. He lived totally. Many times his disciples asked him to write, but he would always say: "The Tao that can be told is not the real Tao, the truth that can be told becomes untrue immediately." So he would not say anything, he would not write anything. Then what were the disciples doing with him? They were only being with him. That's what *satsang* is – being with him. They lived with him, they moved with him, they simply imbibed his being. Being near him they tried to be open to him. Being near him they tried not to think about anything. Being near him they became more and more silent. In that silence he would reach them, he would come to them and he would knock at their doors.

For ninety years he refused to write anything or to say anything. This is his basic attitude: that truth cannot be told and truth cannot be taught. The moment you say something about truth, it is no longer true, the very saying falsifies it. You cannot teach it. At the most you can indicate it. And that indication should be your very being, your whole life – it cannot be indicated by words. He was against words. He was against language.

It is said that he used to go for a morning walk every day, and a neighbor used to follow him. Knowing well that he didn't want to talk, that he was a man of absolute silence, the neighbor always kept silent. Even a "hello" was not allowed, even to talk about the weather was not allowed. To say "How beautiful a morning!" would be too much chattering. Lao Tzu would go for a long walk, for miles, and the neighbor would follow him.

For years it went on, but once it happened that a guest was staying with the neighbor and he also wanted to come, so the neighbor brought him. He did not know Lao Tzu or his ways. He started feeling suffocated because his host was not talking, this Lao Tzu was not talking, and he couldn't understand why they were so silent – and the silence became heavy on him.

If you don't know how to be silent, it becomes heavy. It is not that by saying things you communicate – no. It is by saying things that you unburden yourself. In fact, through words communication is not possible; just the opposite is possible – you can avoid communication. You can talk, and you can create a screen of words around you so that your real situation cannot be known by others. You clothe yourself through words.

The man started feeling naked and suffocated and awkward; it was embarrassing. So he simply said, when the sun was rising, "What a beautiful sun. Look! What a beautiful sun is born, is rising! What a beautiful morning!"

That's all he said. But nobody responded because the neighbor, the host, knew that Lao Tzu wouldn't like it. And of course Lao Tzu wouldn't say anything, wouldn't respond.

When they came back, Lao Tzu told the neighbor, "From tomorrow, don't bring this man. He is a chatterbox." And he had only said this much: "What a beautiful sun," or "What a beautiful morning." That much in a two or three-hour-long walk. But Lao Tzu said, "Don't bring this chatterbox again with you. He talks too much, and talks uselessly – because I also have eyes, I can see that the sun is being born and it is beautiful. What is the need to say it?"

Lao Tzu lived in silence. He always avoided talking about the truth that he had attained and he always rejected the idea that he should write it down for the generations to come.

At the age of ninety he took leave of his disciples. He said good-bye to them, and he said, "Now I am moving toward the hills, toward the Himalayas. I am going there to get ready to die. It is good to live with people, it is good to be in the world while you are living, but when one is getting nearer to death it is good to move into total aloneness, so that you move toward the original source in your absolute purity and loneliness, uncontaminated by the world."

The disciples felt very, very sad, but what could they do? They followed him for a few hundred miles, then by and by Lao Tzu persuaded them and they went back. Alone he was crossing the border, and the guard imprisoned him. The guard was also a disciple and he said, "Unless you write a book, I am not going to allow you to move beyond the border. This much you must do for humanity. Write a book. That is the debt you have to pay, otherwise I won't allow you to cross." So for three days Lao Tzu was imprisoned by his own disciple.

It is beautiful. It is very loving. He was forced – and that's how this small book, the book of Lao Tzu, *Tao Te Ching*, was born. He had to write it because the disciple wouldn't allow him to cross. He was the guard and he had the authority, he could create trouble, so Lao Tzu had to write the book. In three days he finished it.

This is the first sentence of the book: *The Tao that can be told of is not the Absolute Tao.* This is the first thing he has to say: that whatsoever can be said cannot be true. This is the introduction for the book. It simply makes you alert: now words will follow, don't become a victim of the words. Remember the wordless. Remember that which cannot be communicated through language, through words. The Tao can be communicated, but it can only be communicated from being to being. It can be communicated when you are with the

master; just with the master, doing nothing, not even practicing anything. Just being with the master it can be communicated.

Why can't the truth be said? What is the difficulty? The truth
cannot be said for many reasons. The first and the most basic reason
is: truth is always realized in silence. When your inner talk has
stopped, then it is realized. And that which is realized in silence, how
can you say it through sound? It is an experience. It is not a thought.
If it was a thought it could be expressed, there would be no trouble in
it. Howsoever complicated or complex a thought may be, a way can
be found to express it. The most complex theory of Albert Einstein,
the theory of relativity, can also be expressed in a symbol. There is
no problem about it. The listener may not be able to understand it;
that is not the point. It can be expressed.

It was said when Einstein was alive that only twelve persons, a
dozen, in the whole world understood him and what he was saying.
But even that is enough. If even a single person can understand, it
has been expressed. And even if not a single person can understand
right now, maybe after many centuries there will come a person who
can understand it. Then too it has been expressed. The very proba-
bility that somebody can understand it, and it has been expressed.

But truth cannot be expressed because the very reaching to
it is through silence, soundlessness, thoughtlessness. You reach it
through no-mind, the mind drops. And how can you use something
which as a necessary condition has to drop before truth can be
reached? The mind cannot understand, the mind cannot realize; how
can the mind express? Remember it as a rule: if the mind can attain
to it, the mind can express it; if the mind cannot attain to it, the mind
cannot express it. All language is futile. Truth cannot be expressed.

Then what have all the scriptures been doing? Then what is Lao
Tzu doing? Then what are the Upanishads doing? They all try to say
something which cannot be said in the hope that a desire may arise
in you to know about it. Truth cannot be said but in the very effort of
saying it a desire can arise in the hearer to know that which cannot
be expressed. A thirst can be provoked.

The thirst is there, it needs a little provocation. You are already
thirsty – how can it be otherwise? You are not blissful, you are not
ecstatic – you are thirsty. Your heart is a burning fire. You are seeking
something which can quench the thirst, but not finding the water, not
finding the source, by and by you have tried to suppress the thirst

itself. That is the only way, otherwise it is too much, it will not allow you to live at all. So you suppress the thirst.

A master like Lao Tzu knows well that truth cannot be said, but the very effort to say it will provoke, will bring the suppressed thirst in you to the surface. And once the thirst surfaces, a search, an inquiry starts. And he has moved you.

The Tao that can be told of is not the Absolute Tao. At the most it can be relative. For example, we can say something about light to a blind man knowing well that it is impossible to communicate anything about light because he has no experience of it. But something can be said about light, theories about light can be said. Even a blind man can become an expert about the theories of light; he can become an expert about the whole science of light – there is no problem in it – but he will not understand what light is. He will understand what light consists of. He will understand the physics of light, the chemistry of light, he will understand the poetry of light, but he will not understand the facticity of light, what light is. He will not understand the experience of light. So all that is said to a blind man about light is only relative: it is something about light, not light itself. Light cannot be communicated.

Something can be said about godliness, but godliness cannot be said; something can be said about love, but love cannot be said. That "something" remains relative. It remains relative to the listener, his understanding, his intellectual grip, his training, his desire to understand. It depends on, it is relative to the master – his way of expressing, his devices to communicate. It remains relative, relative to many things, but it can never become the absolute experience. This is the first reason why truth cannot be expressed.

The second reason that truth cannot be expressed is because it is an experience. No experience can be communicated – leave truth aside. If you have never known love, when somebody says something about love, you will hear the word, but you will miss the meaning. The word is in the dictionary; even if you don't understand you can look in the dictionary and you will know what it means. But the meaning is in you. Meaning comes through experience. If you have loved someone then you know the meaning of the word *love.* The literal meaning is in the dictionary, in the language, in the grammar. But the experiential meaning, the existential meaning is in you. If you have known the experience, immediately the word *love* is no longer empty; it contains something. If I say something, it is empty unless you bring your experience to it. When your experience comes to it, it becomes significant; otherwise it remains empty – words and words and words.

How can truth be expressed when you have not experienced it? Even in ordinary life an unexperienced thing cannot be told. Only words will be conveyed. The container will reach you but the content will be lost. An empty word will travel toward you; you will hear it and you will think you understand it because you know the literal meaning of it, but you will miss. The real, authentic meaning comes through existential experience. You have to know it, there is no other way. There is no shortcut. Truth cannot be transferred. You cannot steal it, you cannot borrow it, you cannot purchase it, you cannot rob it, you cannot beg it – there is no way. Unless you have it, you cannot have it. So what can be done?

The only way – and I emphasize it – the only way is to live with someone who has attained to the experience. Just being in the presence of someone who has attained to the experience, something mysterious will be transferred to you. Not by words, it is a jump of energy: just as a flame can jump from a lit lamp to an unlit lamp, you bring the unlit lamp closer to the lit lamp and the flame can jump. The same thing happens between a master and a disciple: a transmission beyond scriptures; a transmission of energy, not of message; a transmission of life not of words. *The Tao that can be told of is not the Absolute Tao.* Remember this condition.

Now enter the sutras:

When the people of the Earth all know beauty as beauty,
there arises the recognition of ugliness.
When the people of the Earth all know the good as good,
there arises the recognition of evil.

Lao Tzu is the absolute anarchist. He says: "The moment you start thinking of order, disorder arises." The moment you think of God, the Devil is already present, because thinking can only be of the opposites; thinking can be only of the duality. Thinking has a deep dichotomy in it, thinking is schizophrenic, it is a split phenomenon. That's why there is so much insistence on attaining to a non-thinking state – because only then will you be one. Otherwise you will remain two, divided, split, schizophrenic.

In the West schizophrenia has become by and by more and more common because all the Western religions are deep down schizophrenic – they divide. They say God is good. Then where to put all the evil? God is simply good and he cannot be bad, and there is much that is bad in life – where to put that badness? So a Devil is created. The moment you create a God, you immediately create a Devil.

I must tell you – Lao Tzu never talks about God, never. Not even a single time does he use the word *God*, because once you use the word *God*, the Devil immediately enters through the same door. Open the door, they both come in together. Thinking is always in opposites.

When the people of the Earth all know beauty as beauty, there arises the recognition of ugliness. The world will be beautiful when people have forgotten about beauty, because then there will be no ugliness. The world will be moral when people have completely forgotten the word *moral*, because then there will be no immorality. The world will be in order when there is nobody to enforce it, nobody who is trying to create order. All those who try to create order are the mischief-makers – they create disorder. But it is difficult to understand. It is difficult because our whole mind has been trained, trained by these schizophrenic thinkers. They say: "Choose God and reject the Devil; be good, don't be bad." And the more you try to be good the more you feel your badness inside.

Have you ever observed that saints who are trying to be absolutely virtuous are too conscious of their sins? Then read Augustine's *Confessions*. A whole life trying to be a saint, then there arises the recognition of sin. The more you try to be a saint the more you will feel you are encircled by sins. Try to be good and you will feel how bad you are. Try to be loving and you will come across hatred, anger, jealousy, possessiveness. Try to be beautiful and you will become more and more aware of how ugly you are.

Drop the dichotomy. Drop the schizophrenic attitude. Be simple. And when you are simple you don't know who you are – beautiful or ugly.

There is a Sufi story:

A master was traveling, and he came to an inn for an overnight stay with his disciples. The innkeeper told him that he had two wives, one beautiful, another ugly.

"But the problem is," said the innkeeper, "that I love the ugly one and I hate the beautiful one."

The master asked, "What is the matter? What is the reason for it?"

The man said, "The beautiful one is too conscious of her beauty; that makes her ugly" – when you are too conscious of beauty certainly you will become ugly – "and the other is too conscious of her ugliness. That makes her beautiful."

The one who was beautiful thought continuously that she was beautiful – she had become arrogant, very proud. How can you be beautiful with arrogance? Arrogance is ugliness. She had become very egoistic. And have you ever come across any ego which is beautiful? How can the ego be beautiful? The other, who was ugly and was conscious of her ugliness, had become humble, and humility has a beauty of its own. Humbleness, without any pride, without any ego, creates beauty.

So the man said, "I am puzzled. I love the ugly one and I hate the beautiful one. And I am asking you to solve the puzzle. What is the matter? Why is it happening?"

The master called all his disciples and said, "You also come, because this is really something to be understood."

And he said exactly what Lao Tzu is saying. To his disciples he also said, "Don't be proud that you know. If you know that you know, you are ignorant. If you know that you don't know, you are wise. An absolutely simple man does not know either way, whether he knows or doesn't know. He lives completely unselfconsciously."

Now, I would like to prolong the story a little longer. It stops there; as Sufis have told it, it stops there. But I would like to give it a deeper turn. I would like to tell you that after this master's visit, I also visited the inn, after many years, of course. And the man, the innkeeper, came to me and said, "There is a puzzle. Once a Sufi master visited me and I put this problem before him and he solved it. But since then everything has turned. The ugly woman has become proud about her humbleness, and now I don't love her. Not only is her body ugly, now her being, her whole being, has become ugly. And the beautiful woman, knowing that the consciousness that she is beautiful was destroying her beauty, has dropped that consciousness. Now I love her. Not only is her body beautiful, her being has become beautiful." So he said to me, "Now tell me what the matter is."

But I told him, "Please keep quiet. If I say something, then again, the story will take a turn. Keep quiet!"

Self-consciousness is the disease; in fact, to be *unselfconscious* is to become realized. That's what enlightenment is all about: to be *unselfconscious*. But between the dichotomy, between the two, between the dilemma, how can you be *unselfconscious*?

You always choose: you choose to be beautiful, and ugliness becomes your shadow; you choose to be religious, and irreligious-ness becomes your shadow; you choose to be a saint, and sin becomes your shadow. Choose and you will be in difficulty, because the very choice has divided life. Don't choose, be choiceless. Let life flow. Sometimes it looks like God, sometimes it looks like the Devil – both are beautiful. Don't choose. Don't try to be a saint; otherwise your saintliness will not be real saintliness – a pride in it will make everything ugly. So I say that many times sinners have reached the divine and saints have missed. Because sinners are always humble; thinking themselves sinners, they cannot claim.

I will tell you another story. Once it happened...

A saint knocked at the doors of heaven, and at the same time, just by his side, a sinner knocked too. And the saint knew the sinner very well. He had lived in his neighborhood, in the same town, and they had died on the same day.

The doors opened. The gatekeeper, St. Peter, didn't give even a look at the saint. He welcomed the sinner. The saint was offended. This was not expected, that a sinner should be welcomed.

He asked St. Peter, "What is the matter? You offend me. You insult me. Why am I not received when the sinner has been received with such welcome?"

St. Peter said, "That's why. You expect. He does not expect. He simply feels grateful that he has come to heaven. You feel that you have earned it. He feels the grace of God; you think it is because of your efforts that you have achieved it. It is an achievement to you, and all achievements are of the ego. He is humble. He cannot believe that he has come to heaven."

It is possible that a sinner can reach and a saint can miss. If the saint is too filled with his saintliness, he will miss.

Lao Tzu says:

When the people of the Earth all know beauty as beauty,
there arises the recognition of ugliness.
When the people of the Earth all know the good as good,
there arises the recognition of evil.

Therefore:
being and non-being interdepend in growth...

Use both – don't choose. Life is an interdependence. Use sin
also, it exists there for a purpose; otherwise it wouldn't exist. Use
anger also, it exists there for a purpose; otherwise it wouldn't exist.
Nothing exists without any purpose in life. How can it exist without
any purpose? Life is not a chaos; it is a meaningful cosmos. *...being*
and non-being interdepend in growth... So be and not-be together.

...difficult and easy interdepend in completion;
long and short interdepend in contrast;
high and low interdepend in position;
tones and voice interdepend in harmony;
front and behind interdepend in company.

Lao Tzu is saying that opposites are not really opposites but
complementaries. Don't divide them, division is false; they are one,
they *interdepend*. How can love exist without hate? How can compassion exist without anger? How can life exist without death? How
can happiness exist without unhappiness? How is heaven possible
without hell?

Hell is not against heaven, they are complementary, they exist
together; in fact, they are two aspects of the same coin. Don't
choose. Enjoy both. Allow both to be there. Create a harmony
between the two; don't choose. Then your life will become a symphony of the opposites, and that is the greatest life possible. It will be
most ordinary in a way, and most extraordinary in another way.

That's why I say Buddha moves in the sky, he has no earth part
in him. Lao Tzu is both earth and heaven together. Buddha, even in
his perfection seems to be incomplete; Lao Tzu, even in his incom-
pletion is complete, perfect.

You understand me? Try to dig it! Buddha in his perfection is still incomplete, the earth part is missing. He is unearthly like a ghost, the body part is missing; he is unembodied, a tree without roots.

You are roots, but only roots; it has not sprouted, the tree has not come to bloom. Buddha is only flowers, and you are only roots – Lao Tzu is both. He may not look as perfect as Buddha, he cannot, because the other is always there – how can he be perfect? But he is complete. He is total. He may not be perfect but he is total. And these two words have to be remembered always: don't try to be perfect, try to be total. If you try to be perfect you will follow Buddha, you will follow Mahavira, you will follow Jesus. If you try to be total only then can you have the feeling of what it means to be near Lao Tzu, what it means to follow Tao.

Tao is totality. Totality is not perfect, it is always imperfect because it is always alive. Perfection is always dead – anything that becomes perfect is dead. How can it live? How can it live when it has become perfect? – it has no need to live. It has denied the other part. Life exists through the tension of the opposites, the meeting of the opposites. If you deny the opposite you can become perfect but you will not be total, you will miss something. Howsoever beautiful Buddha is, he misses something. Lao Tzu is not so beautiful, not so perfect.

Buddha and Lao Tzu are both standing before you: Lao Tzu will look ordinary and Buddha extraordinary, superb. But I tell you, thousands of buddhas exist in Lao Tzu. He is deeply rooted in the earth – he is rooted in the earth, and he is standing high in the sky; he is both heaven and earth, a meeting of the opposites.

There are three words to be remembered: one is *dependence*, another is *independence*, the third is *interdependence*.

Buddha is independent. You are dependent: a husband dependent on his wife, a father dependent on his son, an individual dependent on society – thousands of dependencies. You are dependent. Buddha stands like a peak, independent. He has cut all the ties with the world: with the wife, with the child, with the father; he has cut everything. He has renounced all – a pillar of independence. You are part; Buddha is part, the other part. You may be ugly, he is beautiful. But his beauty exists only because of your ugliness. If you disappear Buddha will disappear. He looks wise because of your stupidity; if you become wise he will no longer be wise.

Lao Tzu is the phenomenon of interdependence because life is interdependent. You cannot be dependent, you cannot be independent – both are extremes. Just in the middle, where life is a balance, is interdependence. Everything exists with everything else, everything is interconnected. Hurt a flower and you hurt a star. Everything is interconnected, nothing exists like an island. If you try to exist like an island, it is possible, but it will be an unearthly phenomenon, almost a myth, a dream. Lao Tzu believes in interdependence. He says: "Take everything as it is, don't choose."

It seems to be simple and yet the most difficult thing, because the mind always wants to choose. The mind lives through choice. If you don't choose the mind drops. This is the way of Lao Tzu. How to drop the mind? – don't choose! That's why he never prescribes any meditation, because then there is no need for any meditation.

Don't choose. Live life as it comes – float. Don't make any effort to reach anywhere. Don't move toward a goal; enjoy the moment in its totality and don't be bothered by the future or the past. Then a symphony arises within your soul, the lowest and the highest meet in you, and then – then you have a richness.

If you are only the highest you are poor, because you are like a hill which has no valleys: it is a poor hill. Valleys give depth and valleys give mystery; in valleys abides the very poetry. The peak is plain, arithmetical. In the valley move the shadows, the mysteries. Without a valley a peak is poor. And without a peak a valley is poor, because then there is only darkness. The sun never visits it; it is damp and gloomy and sad. The richest possibility is to be a peak and a valley together.

Somewhere Nietzsche says – Nietzsche had one of the most penetrating minds that has ever been possessed by any human being. Because of that penetration he became mad; it was too much, his mind was too much, he couldn't contain it. He says that a tree that wants to reach to the sky has to go to the deepest earth. The roots have to go to the very hell, deep down; only then can the branches, the peak, reach heaven. The tree will have to touch both: hell and heaven, both the height and the depth.

And the same is true for the being of man: you have, somehow, to meet the Devil and the divine both in your innermost core of being. Don't be afraid of the Devil, otherwise your God will be a poorer God. A Christian or a Jewish God is very poor. The Christian or Jewish or Mohammedan God has no salt in it – tasteless, because the salt has been thrown away, the salt has become the Devil. They have to become one. An organic unity exists in existence between the opposites: being and nonbeing, difficult and easy, long and short, high and low.

...tones and voice interdepend in harmony;
front and behind interdepend in company.

Therefore the Sage:
manages affairs without action...

This is what Lao Tzu calls *wu wei*: the sage manages affairs without action. There are three possibilities – one: be in action and forget inaction. You will be a worldly man. The second possibility: drop action, move to the Himalayas and remain inactive. You will be an otherworldly man. The third possibility: live in the market but don't allow the market to live in you. Act without being active, move but remain unmoving inside.

I am talking to you and there is silence inside me – I am talking and not-talking together. Move and don't move. Act and don't act. If inaction and action can meet, then the harmony arises. Then you become a beautiful phenomenon – not beautiful against ugliness, but beautiful which comprehends ugliness also.

Go to a rosebush. See the flower and the thorns. Those thorns are not against the flower, they protect it. They are guards around the flower: security, safety measures. In a really beautiful person, in a really harmonious person, nothing is rejected. Rejection is against existence: everything should be absorbed. That's the art. If you reject, that shows you are no artist. Everything should be absorbed, used. If there is a rock in the way don't try to reject it, use it as a stepping stone.

Therefore the Sage: manages affairs without action... He does not escape to the Himalayas. He remains in the world. He manages affairs, but without any action. He is not active inside, the action remains on the outside. At the center he remains inactive. That is what Lao Tzu calls *wu wei* – finding the center of the cyclone. The cyclone is on the outside but in the center nothing moves, nothing stirs.

...preaches the doctrine without words.

Here I am preaching to you a doctrine without words. You will say I am using words. Yes, I am preaching without words, because deep inside me no word arises. It is for you, not for me; the word is for you, it is not for me. I use it; I am not used by it, it does not fill me. The moment I am not talking to you I am not talking at all. I never talk to myself, there is no inner talk. When I am not talking I am silent, and when I am talking the silence is not disturbed, the silence remains untouched.

...preaches the doctrine without words.
All things take their rise, but he does not turn away from them...

He never escapes. He never rejects. He never renounces. And that is the meaning of my sannyas. The word sannyas means renunciation, but I don't preach renunciation. Then why do I call you sannyasins? I call you sannyasins in the Lao Tzu'an sense: renounce and yet don't renounce, remain in the world but yet out of it – this is the meeting of the opposites.

So I don't tell you to move, to drop, to leave your families. There is no need. Be there, be totally there, but deep down something remains above, transcendental – don't forget that. When you are with your wife, be with your wife, and also be with yourself. That's the point. If you forget yourself and you are just with your wife, you are a worldly man. Then sooner or later you will escape, because it will create so much misery in life that you will want to leave and renounce and go to the hills. Both are extremes. And the truth is never in the extreme, the truth comprehends the extremes. It is in both and in neither.

All things take their rise, but he does not turn away from them;
he gives them life, but does not take possession of them...

Love your children, but don't possess them. Love your wife and your husband, but don't possess them. The moment you possess... You don't know: deep down you have been possessed. The moment you possess you have been possessed. The possessor is the possessed. Don't possess – because the possession tries to destroy the center of the other, and the other won't allow you to. And if you destroy the center of the other, in the very effort your own center will be destroyed. Then there will be only the cyclone and no center. Be in the world and yet not in it. Something deep in you transcends, remains floating in the sky – roots in the earth, branches in the sky.

...he gives them life, but does not take possession of them;
he acts, but does not appropriate;
accomplishes, but claims no credit.

He simply lives, as part of the whole – how can he claim any credit? He simply lives as a part of this organic unity, this existence, this thusness. He is part of it; how can he claim? How can a wave claim anything? The wave is just a part of the ocean.

...he acts, but does not appropriate;
accomplishes, but claims no credit.

It is because he lays claim to no credit
that the credit cannot be taken away from him.

This is the absurd logic of Lao Tzu. He is absolutely logical, but he has a logic of his own. He says: *It is because he lays claim to no credit that the credit cannot be taken away from him.*

If you claim, the claim can be disproved; if you don't claim, how can the claim – which has not been claimed at all – be disproved? If you try to be somebody in the world, may be it can be proved that you are nobody. It will be proved, because everybody is trying to be somebody and everybody is a competitor in that claim. But if you don't claim, you remain a nobody; how can this be disproved? In your nobodiness you become somebody, and nobody can disprove it and nobody can compete with it.

If you try to be victorious you will be defeated. Ask the Alexanders and the Napoleons and the Hitlers: if you try to be victorious you will be defeated. Lao Tzu says: "Don't try to be victorious, then nobody can defeat you." A very subtle logic, the logic of life itself: don't claim, and your claim is absolutely fulfilled; don't try to be victorious, and your victory is absolute; don't try, just be, and all that you can try for will come to you by itself, on its own accord.

A man who has not asked for anything, who has not been trying to be successful in any way, who has not been striving for any ambition to be fulfilled, suddenly finds that all is fulfilled. Life itself comes to him to share its secrets, to share its riches because a man who remains without claim becomes emptiness; into that emptiness life goes on pouring its secrets and riches.

Life abhors a vacuum. If you become empty everything will come on its own accord. Trying, you will fail; non-trying, success is absolutely certain. I am not saying that if you want to be successful don't try – no, I am not saying that. It is not a result, it is a consequence. And you have to understand the difference between a result and a consequence. When you listen to Lao Tzu or to me, of course you understand the logic that if you try to be victorious, you will be defeated because there are millions of competitors. How can you succeed in this competitive world? Nobody ever succeeds. Everybody fails. And everybody fails absolutely, there is no exception. And then Lao Tzu says that if you don't try to succeed you will succeed. Your mind becomes greedy, and your mind says: "That's right! So this is the way to succeed! I will not claim, I will not be ambitious so that my ambition can be fulfilled." Now this is asking for a result. You remain the same – you have missed Lao Tzu completely.

Lao Tzu is saying that if you really remain without any claim, without asking for any credit, fame, name, success, ambition, then as a consequence success is there, victory is there. The whole existence pours down into your emptiness; you are fulfilled. This is a consequence, not a result. A result is when you desire it; a consequence is when you were not even thinking about it, there was no desire, no thinking about it. It happens as part of the inner law of existence. That law is called Tao.

It is because he lays claim to no credit that the credit cannot be taken away from him. Understand Lao Tzu. And understand your inner greed because the greed can say... It happens every day; almost every day people come to me and I tell them, "Meditate, but don't ask for results." They say, "If we don't ask for results, will they happen?" I say, "Yes, they will happen, but don't ask for them." So they say "Okay." Then after a few days they come and they say, "We have been waiting and they have not happened up to now."

You miss the point. You cannot wait. You can wait for a result; you cannot wait for a consequence. Consequence has nothing to do with you or your waiting. It is part of the innermost law. It happens on its own accord. You are not needed even to wait, because even in the waiting – the desire. And if the desire is there, the consequence will never happen. Don't desire and it happens. Don't ask and it is given. Jesus says: "Ask, and it shall be given. Knock and the door shall be opened." Lao Tzu says: "Ask not, and it shall be given. Knock not, and the door has always remained open" – just look!

And I say to you Lao Tzu goes the deepest anybody has ever gone. Lao Tzu is the greatest key. If you understand him, he is the master key; you can open all the locks that exist in life and existence. Try to understand him. It will be easy for you if you don't ask for any results out of the understanding. Just enjoy the understanding. Just enjoy the fact that you are on a journey with this old guy. This old guy is beautiful – not against ugliness; this old guy is wise – not against stupidity; this old guy is enlightened – not against unenlightenment or unenlightened persons. This old guy is total. You exist in him, and buddhas also exist in him. He is both. And if you can understand him, nothing is left to be understood. You can forget Mahaviras, Buddhas, Krishnas – Lao Tzu alone is enough. He is the master key.

Enough for today.

CHAPTER 2

ordinariness

The first question:

Osho,
Have I come to the wrong place? I just want to be ordinary and
happy. I want a woman to love, and to love me; friends to spend
time with and enjoy. I don't want enlightenment. Have I come to
the wrong place?

Centuries of wrong upbringing have completely confused
your mind about enlightenment. The very word seems to be
unearthly, otherworldly; the very word seems to be something which is after death or for those who are already dead. This is
absolutely wrong.

If you want to be happy there is no other way than enlightenment. If you want to be ordinary nobody has ever been ordinary
without enlightenment. If you want to love and be loved it is impossible without enlightenment. So you will have to understand my
concept of enlightenment. It is just to be ordinary, healthy, aware,
whole, total.

Every mind is seeking some extraordinariness. That is what the ego is: always trying to be somebody in particular, always afraid of being nobody, always afraid of emptiness, always trying to fill the inner void with everything and anything. Every human being is seeking extraordinariness and that creates misery. It is not possible. Nobodiness is your very nature, nonbeing is the very stuff you are made of. Howsoever you try you will never succeed; even Alexanders fail. You cannot be somebody because that is not possible in the nature of things. You can only be nobody.

There is nothing wrong in being nobody; in fact, the moment you accept your nobodiness, immediately bliss starts flowing from you in all directions because misery disappears. Misery is the shadow of the ego, the shadow of the ambitious mind. Misery means you are doing something impossible and because you are failing in it you are miserable. You are doing something unnatural, trying to do it and failing, so you feel frustrated, miserable. Hell is nothing but the end result of an impossible, unnatural effort. Heaven is nothing but to be natural.

You are nobody. You are born as a nobodiness with no name, no form. You will die as a nobody. Name and form are just on the surface, deep down you are just a vast space. And it is beautiful, because if you are somebody you will be limited. It is good that existence doesn't allow anybody to be somebody; if you are somebody you will be finite, limited, you will be an imprisoned being. No, existence doesn't allow that. It gives you the freedom of nobodiness – infinite, nonending. But you are not ready.

To me, enlightenment is all about this phenomenon: to recognize, to realize, to accept the fact that one is a nobody. Suddenly you stop trying the impossible. Suddenly you stop pulling yourself up by your shoelaces. You understand the absurdity of it and you stop. And laughter spreads over your being. Suddenly you are calm and collected. The very effort of wanting to be somebody is creating trouble.

When you try to be somebody, you cannot love. An ambitious mind cannot love. It is impossible, because he has first to fulfill his ambition. He has to sacrifice everything for it. He will go on sacrificing his love. Look at ambitious people – if they are after money they always postpone love. Tomorrow when they have accumulated a lot of money then they will be in love. Right now it is impossible, it is not in any way practical; right now they cannot afford it. Love is a relaxation and they are running after something to achieve – a goal. Maybe it is money, maybe it is power, prestige, politics. How can they love now?

They cannot be here and now and love is a phenomenon of here and now. Love exists only in the present, ambition exists in the future. Love and ambition never meet.

You cannot love. And if you cannot love, how can you be loved by anybody else? Love is a deep communion of two beings who are ready to be together this moment, not tomorrow, who are ready to be total in this moment and forget all past and future. Love is a forgetfulness of the past and the future and a remembrance of this moment, this throbbing moment, this alive moment. Love is the truth of the moment.

The ambitious mind is never here, it is always on the go. How can you love a running man? He is always in a race, in a competition; he has no time. Or he thinks that somewhere in the future, when the goal is achieved, when he has attained the power he seeks, the riches he desires, then he will relax and love. This is not going to happen, because the goal will never be achieved.

Ambition will never be fulfilled. It is not the nature of it to be fulfilled. You can fulfill one ambition, immediately a thousand other ambitions arise out of it. Ambition never stops. If you follow it, if you understand, it can stop right now. But if you give energy to it, how can you love? That's why people are so miserable trying to be somebody – miserable because they are not getting love, miserable because they cannot love.

Love is an ecstasy: ecstasy of a no-mind, ecstasy of the present, ecstasy of a non-ambitious state, ecstasy of emptiness. Wherever lovers are there is nobody, only love exists. When two lovers meet they are not two. They may appear two to you, from the outside. But the inside story is totally different; they are not two. The moment they meet the two-ness disappears, only love exists and flows. How is it possible unless you are an emptiness within, a nothingness, so that there is no barrier, nothing between you and your lover? If you are somebody and your lover or beloved is also somebody, then two persons are not meeting but four. Two real nobodies who are standing in the background and two somebodies – false egos shaking hands, caressing, making gestures of love. It is a drama to look at, ridiculous! Whenever lovers meet there is nobody, and two nobodies cannot be two. How can two nothingnesses be two? Nothingnesses have no demarcation line – a nothingness is a vastness. Two nothingnesses become one. Two somebodies remain two.

That's why love becomes such an ugly affair – the love which is called love by you, not by me. Your love is an ugly affair, the ugliest. It has to be so. It could have been the most beautiful phenomenon in the world but it has become the ugliest: lovers constantly fighting, quarreling, creating misery for each other. Sartre says, "The other is hell." He is saying something about your love. Whenever you are alone you feel relaxed, whenever you are with the lover a tension arises. You cannot live alone because the deepest nobodiness hankers; it has a thirst, a deep hunger. So you cannot remain alone. You have to move. You seek togetherness, but the moment you are together it is a misery. All relationships create misery and nothing else. Unless you are enlightened, love becomes just a conflict, a quarrel. By and by one gets adjusted to it. That means by and by one gets dull, insensitive. That's why the whole world looks so dead, so stale. It stinks. All relationships have gone stale, they have become ugly.

So if you really want to love and be loved, that is not possible right now as you are. You have to disappear. You have to leave, so that a clean nothingness is left, a fresh nothingness is left behind. Only then can the flower of love bloom. The seeds are there but the ego is like a rock, and the seeds cannot sprout on it.

And you say you want to be ordinary? And you want to love? And you want friends? And you want to enjoy? – Exactly! This is what enlightenment is all about. But if you go to the priests and to the preachers and to the organized religions and the churches, their enlightenment is different: they are against love, they are against ordinariness, they are against friendship, they are against enjoyment, they are against everything that your nature naturally seeks. They are the great poisoners.

But if you have come to me you have come to the right person – the right person in the sense that my enlightenment is of this world. I'm not saying that there is no other world. I am not saying that the earthly existence is the only existence – no. Don't misunderstand me. But the other depends on this, the other world depends on this world, and the sky depends on this earth. If you want to move higher you have to be rooted deeper here in this earth. You need roots in this life, then flowers will come in the other life. The other life is not against this life; in fact, the other life is just the flowering of this life. God is not against the world, he is not outside it; he is in it, hidden in it. You need not go against the world to seek him – if you go you will never find him. He is hidden here and now. You have to seek, you have to go deep into this existence – and that is the only way to find him. This whole life, this whole existence is nothing but a temple, and he is hiding inside it. Don't escape from it.

I am not against this life; in fact I am not against anything. I am for everything, because if it exists there must be a purpose to it. God cannot create things without any purpose – he is not mad. Existence is very purposeful, meaningful; if this life exists it means the other life cannot exist without it. It is the base.

But you carry your notions when you come to me. When you come to me and I talk about enlightenment, you understand me in terms of what you have been taught about enlightenment. When you come to me and I talk about renunciation, sannyas, you understand something else; not what I am saying. I have to use your language, and the words are all contaminated. They have been used millions of times by millions of people with different connotations, different meanings. I am giving them different dimensions of meaning.

Enlightenment is a man who is fully aware of his inner emptiness and is not fighting it; rather, he enjoys it, it is blissful. Through the enjoyment of his own emptiness he becomes available to others; others can enjoy, others can come and participate in his mystery. His doors are open, he invites friends, lovers, and he is ready to share, he is ready to give. When you give out of your emptiness you are never afraid of giving because you cannot exhaust the emptiness. You go on giving, you go on giving, you go on giving – it is always there, you cannot exhaust it. Only finite things can be exhausted, that's why they create miserliness – you are afraid to give. A man who feels he is empty, why should he be afraid to give? He can give himself totally, and unless that is possible love is not possible. Love is a holy phe-nomenon, love is not profane. Every love worth the name is sacred. And when you enter into love you enter into the world of purity, inno-cence. When you love you enter the temple of the divine.

Enjoy! I am not for sadness and long faces. I am not here to make you more miserable – you are already too miserable. I am not here to give you more sadness. I am here to awaken you to the bliss that is your birthright, that is naturally available to you. But you have for-gotten how to approach it, and you are going in wrong directions: you seek it somewhere where it is not; you seek it outside and it is inside, you seek it far away and it is near; you seek it in the distant stars and it is just in front of you.

In English there are two beautiful words. One is: *obvious*. *Obvious* means just in front of you. It comes from a Latin root meaning just in front of you. And then there is another word: *problem*. It comes from a Greek root which also means just in front of you. The root meaning of *obvious* and *problem* is the same. The obvious is the problem, that which is just in front of you is the problem – because you cannot see it, your eyes are wandering into distant lands. The obvious has become the problem. And enlightenment is to become aware of the obvious, and when you become aware of the obvious the problem disappears.

To live a life of no problems is to live an enlightened life. It is a totally different way of being: it has nothing to do with achievement, it has nothing to do with learning, it has nothing to do with effort, practice. The only thing that is needed is to be a little more alert so that you can look at, see, watch, that which is in front of you. The solution is closer, very, very much closer to you than you can imagine. Don't seek it far away; it exists within you. Once you are settled inside, centered, rooted, I give you all freedom – go and love. Go and be in the world; now you will be able to enjoy it, you will be able to taste it, you will be able to penetrate into its deepest possibilities. And wherever you go into the realm of depth, you will always find the divine there. In love, go deep and you will find godliness; in food, eat well with alertness, awareness and you will find godliness.

The Upanishads say, "*Annam brahma* – food is God." And the Upanishads say that sex is just a brother, a twin brother, of the final ultimate bliss. A twin brother of the ultimate final bliss – sex! You have condemned it too much. It may be the lowest rung of the ladder but it belongs to the ladder. The highest rung belongs as much as the lowest; in fact, everything belongs to existence and is divine.

This is enlightenment: to be able to see in everything the sacred throbbing. Religion is not against anything, religion is the search to find the holy everywhere. And it is there, waiting for you.

You have come to the right place. Your mind may like to escape from here because this is going to be a death to your mind. It is the right place for you, but the wrong place for the mind. It is absolutely the right place for your being – but for your ambitions, your ego, your pride, your stupidities, it is the most wrong place you can find anywhere on the earth at this moment.

So you decide. If you want to be stupid, escape. Then the mind will go on befooling you that you are in love and enjoying – and you know you are not enjoying, and you know that you are not in love. Then the mind may go on befooling you that you are indulging – you cannot indulge. You are not even there to indulge. You don't exist. You don't have an integrated being in any way. You may wander around and deceive yourself but if you really want to be loved by a woman and you want a woman to love, and you want friends, and you want to enjoy life, I am giving you the keys to it.

The second question:

Osho,
You say that Lao Tzu is for the rarest of seekers. Then how do you call him total?

He is for the rarest of seekers because he is total. The mind is afraid of totality, the mind is always searching for perfection. The mind is a perfectionist.

Try to understand these two dimensions: the dimension of perfection and the dimension of totality. With perfection the ego can exist perfectly; in fact, it cannot exist without the dimension of perfection. The ego is always trying to be more and more perfect, and when you want to be perfect you have to choose – you cannot be total. If you want to be wise you have to choose: you have to drop foolishness, you have to fight against ignorance. And if you want to be perfectly wise you have to cut out all the possibilities of ignorance, of foolishness, of madness.

But a total man is totally different. He is wise in his foolishness; he is foolish in his wisdom. He knows that he is ignorant – that is his wisdom. In him opposites meet. Lao Tzu says, "Everybody seems to be wise except me. I appear to be a fool."

Everybody is trying to be wise, trying to be knowledgeable, trying to be intelligent – cutting out, hiding, suppressing foolishness. But foolishness has a beauty of its own, if it can be joined together with wisdom. Then wisdom is total. And the greatest wise men in the dimension of totality are always fools also. They are so simple and so innocent that they look foolish. Lao Tzu must have looked foolish to many people. He was, he was both. And that is the difficulty: mind seeks perfection. Who will go to Lao Tzu? Nobody wants to be both foolish and wise. And you cannot even understand how one can be both. How can one be both?

It is reported that a Sufi mystic was traveling and came to a town. And his name had reached there before him, his fame was already known. So people gathered together and said, "Preach something to us."

The mystic said, "I am not a wise man, because I am a fool also. You will be confused by my teachings, so better let me keep quiet." But the more he tried to avoid it, the more they insisted, the more they became intrigued by his personality.

Finally he yielded and he said, "Okay. This coming Friday I will come to the mosque" – it was a Mohammedan village – "and what do you want me to talk about?"

They said, "About God of course."

So he came. The whole village gathered, he had created such a sensation. He stood at the pulpit and asked a question: "Do you know anything about what I am going to say about God?"

The villagers of course replied, "No, we don't know what you are going to say."

"Then," he said, "it is useless, because if you don't know at all, you will not be able to understand A little preparation is needed, and you are absolutely unprepared. It is going to be futile and I will not speak." He left the mosque.

The villagers were at a loss: what to do? They persuaded him again the next Friday. The next Friday he again came. He asked the same question; all the villagers were ready. He asked, "Do you know what I am going to talk to you about?"

They said, "Yes, of course."

So he said, "Then there is no need to talk. If you already know – finished. Why unnecessarily bother me and waste your time?" He left the mosque.

The villagers were completely puzzled: what to do with this man? But now their interest was going mad. He must be hiding something! So they again persuaded him somehow.

He came, and again he asked the same question: "Do you know what I am going to talk about?"

Now the villagers had become a little wiser. They said, "Half of us know, and half of us don't know."

The mystic said, "Then there is no need. Those who know can tell those who don't know."

This is a wise and foolish man. He looks foolish but he is very wise in his foolishness; he looks very wise but he is behaving like a fool. If you understand life, the deeper you go the deeper you will understand that the whole is worth choosing. That means there is no need to choose. Choice will dissect the whole and whatsoever you get will be fragmentary and dead. Wisdom and foolishness are together in life; if you dissect them then wisdom will be separate and foolishness will be separate, but both will be dead. The greatest art of life is to let them grow together in such a balance that your wisdom carries a certain quality of foolishness, and your foolishness carries a certain quality of wisdom. Then you are total.

That's why rarest are the seekers who will go to Lao Tzu. He will seem to be absurd because sometimes he will behave like a wise man and sometimes he will behave like a foolish man. You cannot rely on him, he is not predictable. Nobody knows what he is going to do the next moment – he lives moment to moment. And you cannot make a doctrine out of him, he is not a wise man. You cannot make a doctrine out of him, he is foolish also. That foolishness will disturb you. And he is always inconsistent – on the surface.

Of course, deep down exists a consistency, absolute consistency: he is so consistent that his wisdom and foolishness are also consistent. But for that you will have to go deeper into this man. Just a surface acquaintance won't do, just familiarity won't do; you will need *satsang*. You will have to be in a deep participation with his being, only then will you be able to understand the totality.

Buddha is wise, Mahavira is wise. You cannot find a single bit of foolishness in them, they are perfection. Lao Tzu is not, Chuang Tzu is not, Lieh Tzu is not. They are contradictory, paradoxical, but that is where their beauty is. Buddha is monotonous. If you understand Buddha today you have understood his yesterday and you have understood his tomorrow also. He is a consistent thing – clean, logical, moving in a line, linear.

But Lao Tzu is zigzag, he runs like a madman. You will understand, as we go into his sayings; you will understand that he runs like a madman. His assertions don't make sense on the surface. They are the most sensible utterings, but to know the sensibility you will have to change completely. Buddha is on the surface – logical, rational. You can understand him without becoming a meditator; without flowing into his being you can understand him. He is understandable, not Lao Tzu. This totality – Lao Tzu accepts this world and the other, and he accepts totally. He is not bothered about the other world; he knows that the other is going to grow out of this – *that* is going to grow out of this, so why bother about it? Live this as beautifully as possible, as totally as possible, and the other will come out of it naturally. It is going to be a natural growth.

If you meet Lao Tzu he will be puzzling. Sometimes he will say something, another time he will say something else; he will assert a sentence and in the next sentence he will contradict it. That's why only very rare seekers reach to him, that's why there exists no organized religion for Lao Tzu. It cannot exist. Only individual seekers can reach him because organized religion has to be perfectionist: has to be according to the mind, has to be according to you; because organized religion means a religion more interested in the crowd, more interested in the mob. It has to exist with the mob and with the crowd.

Lao Tzu can remain uncontaminated, pure. He does not compromise. His totality becomes incomprehensible – that's why rare seekers reach him, because he is total.

The more total a person is, the more incomprehensible he becomes because he becomes more like existence. He is not clear-cut. He is not like a garden made by man; he is a wilderness, a forest, with no rules, no plans, unplanned, a wild growth. That is the beauty. Howsoever beautiful a garden planted by man is – the man is too apparent there, the hand of man is too apparent there. Everything is planned, cut, planted by man; the symmetry and everything. But in a wild forest you don't have any symmetry, you don't see any logic. If God is the gardener, he must be mad. Why does he grow such a forest? Buddha is like a garden, a garden of a royal palace. Lao Tzu is like a wild forest, you can be lost in it. You will feel fear and danger will lurk at every step and every shadow will scare you to death. That's why Confucius said, "Don't go near him. No one knows his ways. Either he is mad or he is the most wise man. But nobody knows who he is."

The third question:

Osho,
I have a strong desire to merge with the universe, but I remain
separated, anxious, homeless – why? What holds me back, and
what is to be done?

The very desire is holding you back. The intense desire to merge
with the universe is keeping you separate. Drop the desire and there
is a merging.

You cannot merge by an intense desire, because the very desire
will keep you separate. Who is this who is desiring? To whom does this
intense desire belong? An intense desire creates an intense ego – and
a suppression. And who told you that you are separate and you need
to be merged? You have never been separate, so why are you chasing
yourself? You are merged.

Look at the difference of the point of view. Lao Tzu says, "You are
merged in existence, you are not separate. You have never been, you
can never be separated." How is it possible? You exist in the ocean of
the divine, or Tao, or whatsoever you name it. How can you be separate? So first a wrong notion that "I am separate," then another wrong
notion comes out of the first – that "I have to merge." And if you try to
merge you will remain separate. Just look and watch and see: you
have never been separate. Who breathes in you? You think you? Who
lives in you? You think you? Who is born in you? Have you got any
notion? That which is born in you, that which is living in you, that
which is breathing in you, is the whole. And these are just thoughts:
"How to merge?" – then you will never be able to merge. Just look at
the state of affairs. You are already in it.

It is said that when Lin Chi approached his master, crying and
weeping with tears flowing from his eyes, and asked how to become
a buddha, the master hit him hard on the face, slapped him hard.

He was shocked and he said, "What are you doing? Have I asked
anything wrong?"

The master said, "Yes. This is the most wrong thing that one
can ever ask. Ask again and I will hit you harder. How foolish! You
are a buddha and you ask how to become a buddha?"

Once you get into the trap of how to become a buddha, for
millions of lives you will miss the whole point. You have always
been a buddha.

It happened in Buddha's own life. In his past life he heard about a man who had become a buddha. So he went and touched his feet. But he was completely surprised, because when he touched the feet of the buddha, the buddha immediately touched his feet.

So he said, "This is puzzling. I touch your feet because I am an ignorant man, searching and seeking. But why do you touch my feet? You are already enlightened."

The buddha laughed and he said, "You may not know. I see you don't know yet who you are. But I know you well. Once I realized who I am, I realized what this whole existence is. But you may not be aware yet. It may take a little time for you to become aware of who you are."

Buddhahood is not an achievement. It is just a recognition of who you are, it is just a remembrance. So don't ask me how to merge. And if you have an intense desire to merge, the more intense the desire the more difficult will be the merger. Desire is the barrier. Please drop the desire and just look all around. Who are you? God exists, not you. You are a false notion, an idea, a bubble in the head – an air bubble, nothing more. And if there is too much intense desire, nothing happens – only the air becomes hot, a hot air bubble, that's all. Cool down a little and just look around; you have always been in the ocean, you have never been anywhere else. You cannot be, because nothing else exists. There is no space except existence or Tao. So the sooner you realize the foolishness of desire, of merging, the better. You are already that which you are seeking.

This is the message of all the awakened ones: you are already that which you are seeking. You are already the goal. You have never left home.

There is a beautiful story – it looks a little profane, but only Zen Buddhists can do that. They love their master so much, they love Buddha so much, that they can even afford profanity.

There is a story that a monkey came to Buddha. Monkey represents man, monkey means the mind. The mind is a monkey. Charles Darwin came to know it very, very late – but we have always been aware that man must have come from monkeys, because he is still monkeyish. You just watch the mind, its constant chattering, and then watch a monkey in the tree. You will feel a similarity.

A monkey came to Buddha, and he was no ordinary monkey. He

was a king, a king of monkeys – that means absolutely a monkey.

The monkey said to Buddha, "I would like to become a buddha."

Buddha said, "I have never heard of anybody having ever become a buddha while remaining a monkey."

The monkey said, "You don't know my powers. I am no ordinary monkey." No monkey thinks that he is ordinary, all monkeys think that they are extraordinary; that is part of their monkeyness. He said, "I am no ordinary monkey. What are you talking about? I am a king of monkeys."

So Buddha asked, "What exceptional or extraordinary powers do you have? Can you show me?"

The monkey said, "I can jump to the very end of the world." He had been jumping all along in the trees. He knew how to jump.

So Buddha said, "Okay. Come onto the palm of my hand and jump to the other end of the world."

The monkey tried and tried, and he was really a very powerful monkey, a very intense monkey. He went like an arrow; he went and he went and he went. Months and – the story says – years passed. And then the monkey came to the very end of the world.

He laughed, he said, "Look! The very end!" He looked down. It was an abyss: five pillars were standing there to mark the boundary. Now he had to come back. But how would he prove that he had been to these five pillars? So he pissed near a pillar – a monkey! – to mark it.

Years passed and he came back. When he reached Buddha he said, "I have been to the very end of the world, and I have left a mark."

But Buddha said, "Just look around."

He had not moved at all. Those five pillars were the five fingers of Buddha and they were stinking! He had been there with closed eyes – must have been dreaming.

Mind is a monkey with closed eyes, dreaming. You have never gone anywhere, you have always been here and now – because nothing else exists. Just open the eyes. Just open the eyes and have a look around, and suddenly you will laugh. You have always been rooted in the ultimate being, there is no need to merge. The only need is to become alert about where you are, who you are.

And drop that stupidity of intense desire. Desire is a barrier; intense desire is of course a greater barrier. Desire clouds the mind.

Desire makes smoke around you, a smokescreen, and then you cannot see what is in fact the case.

The fourth question:

Osho,
You talked about the harmony of the opposites. I feel that hate kills love and anger kills compassion. The extremes are fighting inside me. How can I find the harmony?

You are completely wrong. If hate kills love and anger kills compassion then there is no possibility – there is no possibility of there ever being love or ever being compassion. Then you are caught, then you cannot get out of it. You have lived with hate for millions of lives – it must have killed love already. You have lived with anger for millions of lives – it must have murdered compassion already. But look, love is still there. Hate comes and goes; love survives. Anger comes and goes; compassion survives. Hate has not been able to kill love; night has not been able to kill the day and darkness has not been able to murder light. No, they still survive.

So the first thing to understand is they have not been killed. That is one thing. And the second thing will be possible only later on, when you really love. You have not really loved; that is the trouble, not hate. Hate is not the trouble – you have not really loved. Darkness is not the trouble; you don't have light. If light is there, darkness disappears. You have not loved. You fantasize, you imagine, you dream – but you have not loved.

Love. But I'm not saying that just by loving hate will immediately disappear – no. Hate will fight. Everybody wants to survive. Hate will struggle. The more you love, the stronger hate will come. But you will be surprised: hate comes and goes. It doesn't kill love; rather, it makes love stronger. Love can absorb hate also. If you love a person, in some moments you can hate. But that doesn't destroy love; rather, it gives a richness to love.

What is hate in fact? – it is a tendency to go away. What is love? – a tendency to come closer. Hate is a tendency to separate, a tendency to divorce. Love is a tendency to marry, to come near, to become closer, to become one. Hate is to become two, independent. Love is to become one, interdependent. Whenever you hate, you go away from your lover, from your beloved. But in ordinary life going away is needed to come back again.

It is just like when you eat: you are hungry so you eat, then hunger goes because you have eaten. When you love a person it is like food. Love is food – very subtle, spiritual – but it is food, it nourishes. When you love a person the hunger subsides; you feel satiated, then suddenly the movement to go away starts and you separate. But then you will feel hungry again; you would like to come nearer, closer, to love, to fall into each other. You eat, then for four, five, six hours you forget about food; you don't go on sitting in the kitchen, you don't go on sitting in the mess. You go away; after six hours suddenly you start coming back, hunger is coming.

Love has two faces to it: hunger and satiety. You misunderstand love for hunger. Once you understand that there is no hate but only a situation to create hunger, then hate becomes part of love. Then it enriches love. Then anger becomes part of compassion, it enriches compassion. A compassion without any possibility of anger will be impotent, it will have no energy in it. A compassion with the possibility of anger has strength, stamina. A love without the possibility of hate will become stale. Then the marriage will look like an imprisonment, you cannot go away. A love with hate has a freedom in it – it never becomes stale.

In my mathematics of life, divorces happen because every day you go on postponing them. Then divorce goes on accumulating and one day the marriage is completely killed by it, destroyed by it. If you understand me, I would suggest to you not to wait; every day divorce and remarry. It should be a rhythm just like day and night, hunger and satiety, summer and winter, life and death. It should be like that. In the morning you love, in the afternoon you hate. When you love you really love, you totally love; when you hate you really hate, you totally hate. And suddenly you will find the beauty of it: the beauty is in totality.

A total hate is also beautiful, as beautiful as total love. A total anger is also beautiful, as beautiful as total compassion. The beauty is in totality. Anger alone becomes ugly, hate alone becomes ugly – it is just the valley without the hill, without the peak. But with the peak the valley becomes a beautiful scene – from the peak the valley becomes lovely, from the valley the peak becomes lovely.

You move; your life river moves between these two banks. And by and by, the more you understand the mathematics of life, you won't think that hate is against love; it is complementary. You won't think that anger is against compassion; it is complementary. Then you don't think that rest is against work; it is complementary – or that night is against day, it is complementary. They make a perfect whole.

Because you have not loved, you are afraid of hate – you are afraid because your love is not strong enough, hate could destroy it. You are not certain really whether you love or not, that's why you are afraid of hate and anger. You know that it may completely shatter the whole house. You are not certain whether the house really exists or is just imagination, an imaginary house. If it is imagination the hate will destroy it; if it is real the hate will make it stronger. After the storm a silence descends. After hate lovers are again fresh to fall into each other – completely fresh, as if they are meeting for the first time again. Again and again they meet, again and again for the first time.

Lovers are always meeting for the first time. If you meet a second time, the love is already getting old, stale. It is getting boring. Lovers always fall in love every day, fresh, young. You look at your woman and you cannot even recognize that you have seen her before – so new. You look at your man and he seems to be a stranger – you fall in love again.

Hate does not destroy love, it only destroys the staleness of it. It is a cleaning, and if you understand it you will be grateful to it. And if you can be grateful to hate also, you have understood; now nothing can destroy your love. Now you are for the first time really rooted; now you can absorb the storm and can be strengthened through it, can be enriched through it.

Don't look at life as a duality, don't look at life as a conflict – it is not. I have known – it is not. I have experienced – it is not. It is one whole, one piece, and everything fits in it. You have just to find out how to let them fit, how to allow them to fit. Allow them to fit into each other. It is a beautiful whole.

And if you ask me, if there were a possibility of a world without hate I would not choose it; it would be absolutely dead and boring. It might be sweet, but too sweet – you would hanker for salt. If a world were possible without anger I would not choose it, because just compassion without anger would have no life in it. The opposite gives the tension, the opposite gives the temper. When ordinary iron passes through fire it becomes steel; without fire it cannot become steel. And the higher the degree of temperature, the greater will be the temper, the strength of the steel. If your compassion can pass through anger, the higher the temperature of the anger the greater will be the temper and the strength of the compassion.

Buddha is compassionate. He is a warrior. He comes from the kshatriya race, a samurai. He must have led a very angry life – and then suddenly, compassion. Mahavira comes from a kshatriya clan. In fact, this looks absurd but it has a certain consistency to it: all the great teachers of nonviolence have come from the kshatriya race. No brahmin has preached nonviolence. We know of only one brahmin who is known as one of the *avataras*, Parusharam. He was the most violent man the world has ever known – a brahmin, the most violent! The twenty-four *tirthankaras* of the Jainas are all kshatriyas, Buddha is a kshatriya. They talk about non-violence, compassion; they have lived violence, they know what violence is, they have passed through it. Even if a brahmin tries to be nonviolent, his nonviolence cannot be more than skin deep. Only a kshatriya, a warrior, who has lived through fire, has a strong compassion or the possibility for it.

So remember, if inside your heart extremes are fighting, don't choose. Allow them both to be there. Be a big house, have enough room inside. Don't say, "I will have only compassion, not anger; I will have only love, not hate." You will be impoverished.

Have a big room; let both be there. And there is no need to create a fight between them; there is no fight. The fight comes from your mind, from your teachings, upbringing, conditioning. The whole world goes on saying to you: Love, don't hate. How can you love without hate? Jesus says, "Love your enemies." And I tell you, "Hate your lovers also" – then it becomes a complete whole. Otherwise Jesus' saying is incomplete. He says, "Love your enemies." You hate only; he says love also. But the other part is missing.

I tell you, "Hate your friends also; hate your lovers also. And don't be afraid." Then by and by you will see there is no difference between the enemy and the friend, because you hate and love the enemy and you love and hate the friend. It will be only a question of the coin upside down or downside up. Then the friend is the enemy and the enemy is the friend. Then distinctions simply disappear.

Don't create a fight inside, allow them both to be there. They both will be needed – both will give you wings; only then can you fly.

The last question:

Osho,
Lao Tzu may be superb, he may be the very peak of truth, but his
very height renders him useless for ordinary people like us. Can't it
be said, on the other hand, that Mahavira and Moses and
Mohammed are much more practical and helpful?

They are. They are much more practical, much more helpful.
But they are helpful because they don't change you completely; they
compromise, they don't transform you totally. They look helpful;
they are practical, that's certain – Mohammed or Moses – absolutely
practical because they fit with your mind. That's why they look practical. Whatsoever you think is practical they also think is practical.

Lao Tzu is totally different from your mind and that is the possibility of transformation. With Mohammed you will not be transformed.
You may become a Mohammedan, you may become a good man, you
may become virtuous even, but you will remain on the same track.
The dimension will not change. With Mahavira you will remain the
same: better but the same; modified, but the same, refined, painted,
renovated, but the same. With Lao Tzu you will be destroyed completely and will be reborn. He is death and resurrection.

Try to understand why it is so. You can understand Mahavira; his
calculation is of your mind, his logic is not beyond you. That's why
he looks practical. And it is not coincidence that all his followers
became businessmen: calculating, mathematical, practical people. It
is not coincidence that all Jainas became businessmen; they are
more mathematical, more clever, calculating. And it is not coincidence that Jews are the most calculating men on the earth, the most
calculating community – clever. Jainas and Jews are almost the
same; Jainas are the Jews of India. Why is it so? Moses is practical,
Mahavira is also practical.

I am reminded of an anecdote; it belongs to the very beginning
of the world.

God was in search of a community that would take his ten commandments. The world was going a little chaotic, and morality and
ethics were needed. So he approached many communities, but
nobody accepted.

He reached the Hindus and said, "I have ten commandments to
offer to you. This is a whole philosophy of life."

And the Hindus asked: "For instance? Just tell us about one commandment?"

God said, "Be true. Be honest."

The Hindus said, "It will be difficult in the world of *maya*. In this illusion, one needs untruth also. Sometimes, in this world of dreams – how can one be always true? It will be difficult, and why create unnecessary difficulties?"

He asked other races. Some people said that it would be too much not to be adulterous, because life would lose all interest. Adultery gives life interest, a fantasy. It would be too much, then life wouldn't be worth living.

God became frustrated. From everywhere he was rejected.

It is said then he approached Moses and he said: "I have got ten commandments for you." Now he was afraid because this was the last race. "Would you like to have them?"

He was expecting that Moses would ask, "What are these commandments?" But he never asked. He asked: "What is the price? How much does it cost?"

God said, "They are free of charge."

And Moses said, "Then I will have two sets of them."

Calculating, mathematical, clever, intelligent – Jews are only two percent of the people in the world, but they get eighteen percent of the Nobel Prizes. Two percent of the people and eighteen percent of the Nobel Prizes! It is a very, very difficult phenomenon. Two percent of the people but they run almost the whole world, and everywhere they are rejected, everywhere condemned. But they are so practical and so clever. The three persons who have ruled the whole twentieth century are all Jews: Marx, Freud, Einstein.

Three persons who have ruled the whole world – they are all Jews. Why does it happen so? Simple. They are not impractical. Lao Tzu is impractical. Lao Tzu in fact praises impracticalness.

There is a story:

Lao Tzu was passing with his disciples and they came to a forest where hundreds of carpenters were cutting trees, because a great palace was being built. So almost the whole forest had been cut, but only one tree was standing there, a big tree with thousands of branches – so big that ten thousand persons could sit under its shade.

Lao Tzu asked his disciples to go and inquire why this tree had not been cut yet when the whole forest had been cut and was deserted. The disciples went and they asked the carpenters, "Why have you not cut this tree?" The carpenters said, "This tree is absolutely useless. You cannot make anything out of it because every branch has so many knots in it. Nothing is straight. You cannot make pillars out of it. You cannot make furniture out of it. You cannot use it as fuel because the smoke is so dangerous to the eyes – you almost go blind. This tree is absolutely useless, that's why."

They came back. Lao Tzu laughed and he said, "Be like this tree. If you want to survive in this world be like this tree – absolutely useless. Then nobody will harm you. If you are straight you will be cut, you will become furniture in somebody's house. If you are beautiful you will be sold in the market, you will become a commodity. Be like this tree, absolutely useless. Then nobody can harm you. And you will grow big and vast, and thousands of people can find shade under you."

Lao Tzu was passing through a town. All the young men of the town were forced to be enlisted in the military.

They came across a hunchback. Lao Tzu said, "Go and inquire why this man has been left and not enlisted into the military."

The hunchback said, "How can I be enlisted? You see, I am a hunchback. I am of no use."

The disciples came and Lao Tzu said, "Remember. Be like this hunchback. Then you will not be enlisted to murder or to be murdered. Be useless."

Lao Tzu has a logic altogether different from your mind. He says: "Be the last. Move in the world as if you are not. Remain unknown." Don't try to be the first, otherwise you will be thrown. Don't be competitive, don't try to prove your worth. There is no need. Remain useless and enjoy.

Of course he is impractical. But if you understand him you will find that he is the most practical on a deeper layer, in the depth – because life is to enjoy and celebrate, life is not to become a utility. Life is more like poetry than like a commodity in the market. It should be like poetry; a song, a dance, a flower by the side of the road, flowering for nobody in particular, sending its fragrance to the winds, without any address, being nobody in particular, just enjoying itself, being itself.

Lao Tzu says: "If you try to be very clever, if you try to be very useful, you will be used." If you try to be very practical, somewhere or other you will be harnessed, because the world cannot leave the practical man alone. Lao Tzu says: "Drop all these ideas." If you want to be a poem, an ecstasy, then forget about utility. Remain true to yourself. Be yourself. Hippies have a saying: "Do your thing." Lao Tzu is the first hippie in the world. He says: "Be yourself and do your thing and don't bother about anything else." You are not here to be sold. So don't think of utility, just think of your bliss. Be blissful, and if something flows out of your bliss it is okay – share it. But don't force yourself just to be a utility because that is how suicide happens. One kills oneself. Don't be suicidal.

All the teachers of the world will be more practical than Lao Tzu, that's why they have much appeal. That's why they have great organizations: Christians – almost half the world has become Christian – Mohammedans, Hindus, Jainas, Sikhs; they are all utilitarians. Lao Tzu stands alone, aloof. Lao Tzu stands in a solo existence.

But Lao Tzu is rare and unique. If you can understand him you can also become rare and unique. And the way is to be ordinary – then you become extraordinary. The way is to be just the last, and then suddenly you find you are the first. The way is not to claim, not to claim the credit, and then nobody can take it from you. The way is to exist as a nonbeing, as a nobody, and then, in a subtle and mysterious way, you and only you become somebody – somebody the whole existence feels blessed with, feels blessed by; somebody with whom the whole existence celebrates.

Enough for today.

on the character of tao

Lao Tzu says, on the character of Tao:

Tao is a hollow vessel, and its use is inexhaustible! Fathomless!

And on the spirit of the valley, he says:

The Spirit of the Valley never dies.
It is called the Mystic Female.
The door of the Mystic Female
is the root of Heaven and Earth.

Continuously, continuously,
it seems to remain.
Draw upon it
and it serves you with ease.

The world of Lao Tzu is totally different from the worlds of philosophy, religion, ethics. It is not even a way of life. Lao Tzu is not teaching something – he is that something. He is not a preacher, he is a presence. He has no doctrine for you, he has only himself to offer and share.

Had he been a philosopher, things would have been easy; you could have understood him. He is a mystery because he is not a philosophy. He is not even an anti-philosophy, because both depend on logic. He is absurd. Philosophies depend on logic, anti-philosophies also depend on logic – so the anti-philosophies are also nothing but philosophies. Nagarjuna, a great anti-philosopher, is still a philosopher. He talks, he argues, he discusses in the same way as any philosopher. He discusses against philosophy, argues against philosophy, but the argument is the same. And logic is a whore.

There is a story: one of Lao Tzu's greatest disciples, Lieh Tzu, reports it. Lao Tzu, Chuang Tzu and Lieh Tzu are the three pillars of the world of Tao. Lao Tzu goes on talking in epigrams, maxims; he does not even elaborate. But Lieh Tzu and Chuang Tzu, being disciples of Lao Tzu, cannot argue. They go on telling parables, stories, analogies. This word has to be continuously remembered: Tao cannot be explained, only analogies can be given – indications. Tao cannot be discussed, it can only be shown. So a deep sympathetic heart is needed, it is not a question of the mind at all.

Lieh Tzu reports a story that happened once in his town:

The richest man of the town was crossing the river and the river was in flood. And there arose a great storm and just in midstream the boat overturned. Somehow the boatman escaped, but he couldn't save the rich man; the rich man was drowned. A great search was made.

A fisherman found the body – the dead body – and he asked a fantastic price for it and would not give it up for less. The family was not willing to give so much just for a dead body so they went to a logician, a lawyer, a legal adviser, to ask what to do. Could something legally be done?

The lawyer said, "Don't be worried. First give me my fee and then I will show you the way." So the lawyer took his fee and then said, "Hold on. He cannot sell the dead body to anybody else; he will have to yield, because nobody will purchase that body – so just hold on."

Two, three days passed. The family followed the advice. The fisherman became worried because now the body was stinking, and he started feeling that it was better now to yield and accept whatsoever they gave. It had become a problem, nobody else would purchase the body – he also felt it. So how could he bargain? But before deciding anything, he also went to the legal adviser – the same man.

He said, "First give me the fee and then I will give you the advice." He took his fee and said, "Hold on! The family cannot purchase the body from anywhere else – they will have to yield."

Logic is a whore, a prostitute. It can be for, it can be against. It belongs to nobody. So logic can be for philosophy and logic can be against philosophy.

Lao Tzu is not an anti-philosopher because he is not a logician at all. Buddha is anti-philosophic: he argues against it. Nagarjuna is anti-philosophic: he argues against it. Not Lao Tzu. He does not argue at all, he simply states. He is not after you to convince you – no, not Lao Tzu. Everybody else seems to be in some way trying to convince you, but not Lao Tzu. He simply states and does not bother whether you are convinced or not.

But his seduction is great. He seduces. He persuades. Not trying to convince, he convinces you deep down in the heart and you cannot refute him because he gives no argument. That's the beauty and that's his power. He simply states a fact. And he is not seeking converts, and he is not ready to make you a follower – no. Even if you are ready he will not accept you. But he seduces. His seduction is very subtle and indirect. His seduction is non-aggressive. His seduction is feminine.

There are two types of seduction. When a man seduces a woman, he is aggressive. He tries in every way, takes the initiative, sets a trap; he makes all the efforts that he can make. A woman seduces in a totally different way. She does not take the initiative, she does not set any trap, she does not go after the man; in fact, she pretends that she is not much interested. The man can fail, but the woman never fails – that is the feminine seduction. Her trap is very subtle. You cannot get out of it; it has no loopholes. And without chasing you, she chases you. She haunts you in your dreams – never knocks on your door, but haunts you in your dreams; never shows any interest but becomes the deepest fantasy in your being. That is the feminine trick. And Lao Tzu is a great believer in the feminine mind. We will come across it.

So remember, Lao Tzu's world is not of logic but analogy. Logic is apparent, direct: either you have to be convinced or you have to convince the opponent; either you have to follow it, become a follower, or you become the enemy. You have to choose. With logic your mind has to be active. It is easy, nothing is difficult about it. Everybody argues. More or less everybody is a logician; good or bad, everybody is a philosopher.

If you want to understand Lao Tzu that old way won't help. You will have to put your logic aside because he is not chasing you as a logician, he is not arguing against you – if you argue against him, it will be ridiculous because he has not argued at all. He simply gives an analogy.

What is analogy? If I have a certain experience that you don't have, then how am I to describe it to you? The only way is an analogy: some experience that you have – it is not exactly the same as one that I have, but some similarity exists. So I say that it is like the experience you have – not exactly like it, not exactly the same, but a small similarity exists. That small similarity understood will become the bridge.

That's why those who have come to the ultimate ecstasy say it is like two lovers in deep embrace, it is like two lovers in deep orgasm, it is like when the sex act comes to a peak. This is analogy. They are not saying that it is this. No. They are not saying anything like that. They are simply saying that your experience has nothing else which can become a bridge.

Jesus says, "God is love." This is an analogy. In your life the highest is love. In God's being the lowest is love. The lowest of the divine and the highest of the human meet; that is the boundary. The highest that humanity can reach is love; it is lowest for the divine, just the feet of the divine. But from there, if the feet are found, you can find the whole God. That's why Jesus says, "Love is God." Not that love is God, but in your experience nothing else exists through which an analogy can be made.

So don't take Lao Tzu verbally and literally; these are all analogies. If he says "The spirit of the valley," this is an analogy. He is saying something – not exactly about the valley, because the valley you know. Through the valley he is giving you a feeling of something that you don't know. From that which you know he is bringing you to that which you don't know. Analogy means a reference to the known to explain the unknown. When he says "The spirit of the valley," he means many things.

An analogy is always very pregnant. Logic is always narrow, analogy wide, infinite. The more you search in it, the more you can find through it. Logic is exhaustible, analogy never. That's why you can go on reading and reading and reading books like *Tao Te Ching* or *Bhagavadgita* or Jesus' "Sermon on the Mount" – they are inexhaustible. You can go on finding more and more because they are analogies. The more you grow the more you can see in them; the more you can see in them the more you grow; the more you grow the more you can see again. So these books are not books: they have a life of their own, they are alive phenomena. And you cannot read them once and be finished with them – no, that is not the way. A logical book can be read once and be finished, understood, you can throw it in the rubbish. But a book of analogy is poetry: it changes with your moods, it changes with your insight, it changes with your growth. It gives you different visions in your different states of mind.

The analogy remains the same, for example: "Love is God." A man who has never known anything except sex and who has thought that sex is love...

In the West it is happening too much. Now for the sexual act they say "lovemaking." This lovemaking or making love is absolutely foolish – you cannot make love, love is not an act. Sex is an act. Love is not an act, it is a state of being – you can be in it but you cannot make it. You fall in it, it is not an effort. Sex can be made, not love. A prostitute can give you sex, not love – because how can you make love on order for money? Impossible! How can you make love for money? It comes on its own. It has its own mysterious ways. You cannot control it, you can only be controlled by it. You cannot possess it, you can only be possessed by it. Sex can be done, not love. You can make sex, but you cannot make love – you can only be in love. So a man or a woman who has thought that sex is love and the sexual act is the act of love will think, when Jesus says, "Love is God" – and of course there is no other way for them to think because this is their analogy – that sex is God.

In Sweden they are making a film now on the love life of Jesus because they think that a man who says, "Love is God" must mean that sex is God. And this film is going to be one of the most profane of acts, the unholiest possible, because in the film they are trying to depict a Jesus making love in their sense – moving into sexual acts. Now no country is ready to allow them to make the film. But they will make it, it is difficult now to stop them. The love life of Jesus to them means just sex life.

You understand an analogy from your standpoint. The analogy

can give you only as much as you can put into it. A man who has
loved not only sexually, but totally – because sex is a local phenomenon, physical. There is nothing wrong in it, but it is not total. When
it becomes total and you love a person in totality, not only sexually –
the attraction is not only physical but spiritual also, not only bodily;
not that the body is denied in it, but the attraction is greater, and
bodily attraction is just a smaller circle in it – then you will understand "love is God" in a different way. The analogy will become
deeper for you.

If you have known love which is beyond sex, in which sex simply
disappears and the whole sexual energy is transformed into ecstasy –
if you have known that love, then "love is God" will have a different
meaning for you.

So analogy depends on you. And a book of analogy like Lao Tzu's
has to be read again and again – it is a life work. You cannot simply
read it in a paperback and throw it away. It is a treasure to be carried;
it is a lifelong work; it is a lifelong discipline to enter the analogy.

Logic is superficial. You can understand Aristotle, there is nothing
much in it. But when you come to Lao Tzu – the first time you may
even miss that there is something, but by and by Lao Tzu will haunt
you. His attraction is feminine. By and by he will catch hold of your
being, you have only to allow him. In logic you have to fight; in analogy
you have to be sympathetic, you have to allow it, only then can the
analogy flower. So only in deep sympathy and reverence, in deep faith
and trust, can Lao Tzu be understood. There is no other way.

If you come to Lao Tzu through your mind you will never come
to him. You will go round and round and round – you will never touch
his being. Come to him through the heart. Analogy is for the heart,
logic is for the mind.

Lao Tzu is more a poet. Remember that. You don't argue with a
poet – you listen to the poetry, you absorb the poetry, you chew it,
you let it move inside your being, you let it become a part of your
blood and bones, you digest it. You forget the words, you forget the
poetry completely, but the fragrance becomes part of you. You may
not remember what that poet was singing but the song has been
retained: the flavor of it, the fragrance, the significance has entered
you; you have become pregnant.

Lao Tzu can be understood only if you become pregnant with
him. Allow him. Open the doors. He will not even knock, because he

is not aggressive. He will not try to argue because he does not believe in argument. He is not a mind-being at all, he is absolutely a heart-being. He is simple, his analogies are that of a villager – but alive, radiant, vital. If you allow him, suddenly you will be trans- formed – just an understanding, a heart-understanding, and you will be transformed by him.

The second thing to remember is that Lao Tzu is not a religious man in the ordinary sense. He is not a theologian. He is not a reli- gious man at all in the way you understand the word. He has never gone to the temple, never worshipped, because he found that the whole existence is the temple and all of life is the worship. He is not a fragmentary being. He does not divide life, he lives it as an undi- vided river.

You divide; one hour for the temple, every week you go to church. Sunday is the religious day and by and by religion becomes a Sunday affair – the six working days are not touched by it. You are very cun- ning! – Sunday the holiday, Sunday the religious day, when you are not working. You can be honest easily when you are not working, you can be honest easily when you are not in the shop, you can be honest easily when you are resting in the sun, you can be honest easily when you are listening to the sermon in the church. That is nothing, no problem. The six working days create the real problem – you cannot be religious then. So this is a trick. This Sunday is a trick to avoid reli- gion. You have made airtight compartments in your life. Religion has its own place on Sunday, and then, then you are free for six days to be as irreligious as possible.

Hindus have their own ways, Mohammedans their own, Christians their own: how to avoid religion. And these people you call reli- gious! They are the avoiders. They go to the temple and they pray. When they pray look at them, at their faces. They look so beautiful. But when they come out of the church or the temple they are no longer the same. They are different.

Tolstoy has written a small story, not a story really. It is a fact, it happened, an incident.

Tolstoy went one day into the church, early in the morning. It was dark and he was surprised to find that the richest man of the town was praying and confessing before God and saying that he was a sinner. Of course Tolstoy became interested. And he was relating his sins; how he had deceived his wife and had been unfaithful, and how he had been in love relationships and affairs with other women, others' wives.

Tolstoy became intrigued. He came nearer and nearer. And the rich man was relating with much gusto, confessing to God: "I am a sinner and unless you forgive me there is no way for me. And how I have been exploiting! And how I have been robbing people! I am a sinner and I don't know how to change myself. Unless your grace descends there is no possibility for me." And tears were flowing.

Then suddenly he became aware that there was somebody else there. He looked. He recognized – by this time the day was dawning – and he became very angry and he said to Tolstoy: "Remember! These things I have said to God, not to you. And if you say these things to anybody I will drag you to the court for defaming me. So remember that you have never heard these things. This was a personal dialogue between me and God and I was not aware that you were here."

One face before God and a totally different face before the world. Religion is a compartment – airtight. This is a trick to avoid it; this is a way to be religious without being religious at all – a deception.

Lao Tzu is not religious in that way at all. He is a simple man. He is not even aware that he is religious – how can a religious man be aware that he is religious? Religion is like breathing to him. You become aware of breathing only when something goes wrong, when it is hard to breathe, when you have asthma or some other type of breathing trouble. Otherwise you never know, never become aware that you breathe. You simply breathe, it is so natural.

Lao Tzu is naturally religious, he is not even aware of it. He is not like your saints who are practicing religion. No, he doesn't practice: he has allowed the total to take possession. He lives it, but he does not practice it. Religion is not a discipline for him, it is a deep understanding. It is not something imposed from the outside, it is something that flows from within. There is not a bit of distance between him and religion.

He is not religious in the sense that you understand. He is not a saint because he has never practiced saintliness. He has not forced it; it is not his character. A real religious man has no religious character – cannot have it because character is a device of the irreligious. Try to understand it: you develop a character because you are afraid of your being; you develop morality because you are afraid of inner immorality, you force yourself into a certain way of life because you know that if you live spontaneously and naturally you will become a sinner, not a saint. You are afraid of your being, you impose a character all around you. Character is an armor; it protects you from others and it protects you from yourself. It is a citadel, you move in it. You speak truth not because you have come to know the bliss of it; you speak truth because you have been taught that if you don't, you will be thrown into hell.

Your theologians have tried to picture your God as the greatest sadist possible – throwing people into hell, into burning fire, into boiling oil. This God seems to be a sadist. He needs a great psychological treatment, he seems to be the greatest torturer.

You are afraid of hell and you are ambitious for heaven – the carrot of heaven is hanging in front of you continuously. And your character is just a device between heaven and hell – a protection against hell and an effort to achieve the ambition: heaven. How can you be religious if you are so afraid and so ambitious?

A religious man is not ambitious at all. Ambition is the first thing that drops from a religious man, because ambition means to be in the future and a religious man is always here and now. He exists in the present, he has no future to bother about. And he is not in any way afraid. He lives so totally, how can he be afraid? The fear comes because you live fragmentarily. You have not lived at all, that's why the fear.

Just try to understand the point. A man is afraid of death – why? Do you know that death is bad? How can you know unless you die? Do you know that death is going to be worse than life? How can you know? It may be better than life. Why are you afraid of death without knowing? How can one be afraid of the unknown? It seems to be impossible. You can be afraid only of the known. How can you be afraid of the unknown, the unfamiliar that you don't know at all? No, you are not afraid of death. You have wrongly placed your fear in death. You are really afraid of death because you have not been able to live – the fear is concerned with the unlived life. You are afraid that you have not been able to live, love, and death is coming near, which will finish everything. You will be no more, and you have not been able to love.

You are like a tree which has not flowered and the woodcutter is coming. The tree feels afraid, not knowing what is going to happen. The fear is not coming from death, the fear is coming from something which has not happened. The tree knows well that the fruits have not come, the flowers have not come, it has not bloomed. The tree has not known the spring yet; it has not danced with the winds, it has not loved, it has not lived. This unlived life creates fear, and the woodcutter is coming. And the woodcutter will come and there will be no future. Death means no future. Past is gone, and no future – and the present is so narrow. Fear takes over, you tremble.

Fear is always of the unlived. If you live totally you are unafraid of anything. If death comes to me right now I am ready. I have lived. Everything is complete, nothing is incomplete. Death cannot destroy. If something were incomplete then I would like death to wait a little, but everything is complete. I have taken my bath this morning, I have talked to you, whatsoever was to happen has happened. I am completely ready. If death comes I am ready, I will not even look back once because there is nothing to look at, everything is complete. Whenever anything is complete you are free of it. A life really lived; one becomes free of it. A life not lived; you can never be free of it. You can go to the caves, to the Himalayas, to Tibet – you can move anywhere, but you will never be free, and fear will always be there.

Fear and freedom cannot exist together. When freedom comes – and freedom comes only when you have lived, bloomed, everything complete and finished – then for what do you hanker to live longer? Not even a single moment is needed. Then fear disappears.

Your religion is based on fear. It is not in fact religion. It is pseudo, it is false, it is just a deception. Lao Tzu is not religious in the sense that you are religious or you feel other people are religious. Lao Tzu is religious in a totally different way. His quality is different. He is simple, he lives innocently moment to moment. He also does not talk about God – because what is the use? God is not a word. How can you talk about him? He lives him, he does not talk about him. He enjoys him, he celebrates him, it is not a cerebral phenomenon. He dances. He drinks him. He lives him. So what is the point of talking about him?

This is my observation: that people always talk about things which they don't know.

There is a Sufi story:

A great king used to come to a fakir, a mystic beggar. But he was surprised, because whenever he came the mystic would talk about money, kingdom, politics, and he was there to talk about God, meditation, religion.

So one day he said, "Forgive me, but this I cannot understand. I come here to talk about God, religion, meditation, *samadhi*. This is ridiculous that I, a man of the world come to talk about *samadhi*, enlightenment and you a religious man – supposedly religious because now I have become suspicious – whenever I come you always talk about the kingdom and politics and money and thousands of things, but always of the world. How do you explain it?"

The fakir laughed. He said, "There is nothing to explain. It is simple. You talk about things you don't know. I talk about things I don't know. It is simple. Why should I talk about God? I know. Why should you talk about kingdoms? You are a king. You know."

Lao Tzu doesn't talk about God, doesn't even mention him, not even once. Has he forgotten him? Is he against him? No. He lives him so totally that even to remember would be a sacrilege. To talk about God would be talking about such a deep phenomenon, it would be a betrayal.

It would be a betrayal, I say to you, to talk about God. It is such an intimate phenomenon; it is between him and the whole. It is just like lovers don't like to talk about their love. And people who talk about their love – you can be certain they have no love life. Love is such an intimate phenomenon nobody wants to talk about it. Poets talk about it because they don't know it. They go on writing poems, that is their fantasy, but they have not known. Lovers keep quiet. Lovers don't talk about love at all. There is nothing to talk about, they know it. And by knowing it they know also that it cannot be talked about, it would be a betrayal.

Lao Tzu is religious in a totally different way.

Now, try to enter this sutra with me:

Tao is a hollow vessel, and its use is inexhaustible! Fathomless!

Hollowness is one of the key words in Lao Tzu. He talks about hollowness again and again. *Hollowness* means space; *hollowness* means vastness; *hollowness* means inexhaustibleness.

You live in a house, but your concept of the house is the walls. Lao

Tzu's concept of the house is the space within, not the walls. He says: "Walls are not the house." How can you live in the walls? You live in the emptiness, not in the walls. The hollowness, that is the real house. But when you think about the house you think about the structure that is around the hollowness. That's why a palace and a hut look different to you. Not for Lao Tzu because the hollowness is the same. If you look at the walls then of course a hut is a hut and a palace is a palace. But if you look at the innermost hollowness, which is the real house – because only hollowness can house you, not the walls – then there is no difference between a hut and a palace. There is no rich hollowness and no poor hollowness: all hollownesses are the same, they are equal. But there are rich walls and poor walls.

Once you understand this, then many things will become possible because this is an analogy with infinite potentiality and meaning. When you look at a person do you look at the body? Then you are looking at the walls. That is not the real man, the real man is the inner hollowness. A body can be beautiful, ugly, ill, healthy, young, old, but the inner hollowness is always the same. Then you don't look at the bodies, then you look at the hollowness within.

Everywhere Lao Tzu finds the analogy. You go to the market to purchase an earthen pot or a golden pot. The golden pot differs from the earthen pot – just the walls differ – but the inner hollowness is the same. And when a poor man goes to the well and a rich man goes to the well; the rich man with a golden pot and the poor man with an earthen pot, they go with the same hollownesses. They carry the same water and when they fill their pots, the walls are not used but the inner hollowness, the inner emptiness.

Lao Tzu says: "Look at the inner, don't look at the outer." And the inner hollowness is your being; the inner hollowness, the inner emptiness is your being. That means your being is a nonbeing, because the word *being* gives you a feeling that something is there inside. No, there is nobody inside – all somebodiness is on the outside. Inside is nobodiness, hollow. All ego is just on the surface, inside is egolessness. Who is there inside? Once you know you will laugh, you will say that the question is irrelevant.

There is nobody, exactly nothingness. That's why you are vast, that's why you are of the quality of Brahma. That's why you cannot find God anywhere because he is the hollowness of the whole and you go on looking for the body. Somebody is looking for Krishna, somebody is seeking Christ, somebody is seeking Mahavira – all looking for bodies. Nobody is in search of the hollowness; otherwise where do you need to go? The space surrounds you from everywhere. This is godliness – the space: the space in which you are born, the space in which you live, the space in which you will dissolve.

A fish is born in the sea; the fish lives in the sea, the fish dies and dissolves in the sea. The fish is nothing but seawater. You are exactly the same. The hollowness is all around and the same hollowness is within. How can there be two types of hollownesses? Impossible. Emptiness is always the same. The same hollowness exists in a sinner as in a saint. The sinner has a label on the outside of being a sinner, and the saint has a label on the outside of being a saint. You are too attached to the walls, you don't see that walls are not meaningful.

Why do you call a man a saint? – because he does something which you call good. Why do you call a man a sinner? – because he does something you call bad. But all doing is on the outside, all actions are on the outside, they are just paintings on the walls. But the inner hollowness, can the inner hollowness become impure by your acts? Can you make emptiness impure? Can you make emptiness pure? Emptiness is simply emptiness. How can you make it pure or impure? Emptiness remains untouched. If you cut me with a sword, you cut my body but not me, because *me* means the inner emptiness. If I do something I do it with the walls, but the inner emptiness is a nondoer. Remember this analogy. It is a key word in Lao Tzu.

Tao is a hollow vessel, and its use is inexhaustible! Fathomless! If Tao or God were not empty then their use could not be inexhaustible, then some day they would be exhausted. And what God can be called God who is exhaustible? One day that God will be dead, it will be exhausted. But in your minds the concept of God has been created as a person sitting somewhere in the skies and controlling. He is not controlling. He is not a person. In fact he is not a he, and he is not a she also.

All our words are irrelevant because Tao is a vast hollowness, a vast space, emptiness. Your logic will immediately arise in the mind: then how are things there? Ask the physicists; now they have come to the same understanding as Lao Tzu. Now they say that as we enter deeper and deeper into matter, matter disappears. Finally it disappears completely. Now we don't know. Inside, it is a hollowness.

They were searching for the substance of matter; they searched hard but now it has escaped completely, out of vision – they cannot see where it has gone. They searched for it first in the molecules, then they went deeper into the atoms, then they divided the atom and went deeper into electrons. Now matter has completely disappeared – nothingness. Matter is hollow. Even these walls of stone are hollow. That's why Hindus call the world of matter illusion: it looks very solid and substantial and inside everything is hollow.

Whenever you are silent, sitting with closed eyes watching inside, you will feel a hollowness. Don't get scared. Physicists were chasing matter and they came to hollowness, and the people who have really been seekers of a spiritual dimension have also come to the hollowness. Then you become scared. If matter is hollow it doesn't matter, but if you are also hollow, a hollow bamboo inside nothing but emptiness, you become afraid. If you become afraid you will cling to the wall, and in the final analysis the wall is also hollow. This existence is a vast emptiness, and that's the beauty of it.

In the night you go to sleep – dreams arise out of nothing: beautiful dreams, ugly dreams, nightmares which scare you to death. Dreams arise out of nothing and they look so real. They look so authentically real, but when your eyes open in the morning you cannot find them anywhere. From where did they come? From where did they arise? And now where have they gone? You never think about the phenomenon of the dream. If it can happen in the night, why not in the day?

One of the disciples of Lao Tzu, Chuang Tzu, dreamed one night that he had become a butterfly, fluttering, flying amidst flowers. And the next morning when he awoke he was very sad.

His disciples asked, "What is the matter, master? We have never seen you so sad. What has happened?"

He said, "I am in such a quandary. I am in such a dilemma that it seems now it cannot be solved."

The disciples said, "We have never seen any problem that you cannot solve. Just say, what is the problem?"

Chuang Tzu said, "Last night I dreamed that I had become a butterfly, flying in the garden, moving from one flower to another flower."

The disciples laughed. They said, "This is a dream, master!"

Chuang Tzu said, "Wait, let me tell you the whole story. Now I am awake and I am puzzled. A doubt has arisen. If Chuang Tzu can dream that he can become a butterfly, why not otherwise? A butterfly could dream that she had become a Chuang Tzu. Now who is who? Am I a butterfly dreaming that I have become a Chuang Tzu?"

If it can happen that you can become a butterfly in a dream, then what is the problem? A butterfly sleeping there this morning, resting, may be dreaming that she is you. And how do you know who you are? If Chuang Tzu can become a butterfly, why can't a butterfly become a Chuang Tzu? There seems to be no impossibility about it.

Night dreams come out of nothingness and they look real; in the day dreams come out of nothingness and they look real. The only difference between the night and the day is, the night dream is private and the day dream is public. That is the only difference. In the night dream you cannot invite your friends to be there – it is private. In the day dream you can invite friends – it is public. The house in which you live in the day is public. If there is a possibility of private dreaming there is a possibility of public dreaming. We are here. If we all go to sleep there will be as many dreams as there are people here: private. Nobody's dream will enter into anybody else's dream. They will not clash with anybody, and everybody will forget about everybody else; he will live in his dream and in his own dream-reality. Then you are awake. You look at me and I am talking to you. This is a public dream, you are all dreaming together. That is the only difference.

There is a possibility of a greater awakening – when you awake out of the public dream also. That is what enlightenment is. Then suddenly the whole world is *maya*. This is what Lao Tzu is saying.

Tao is a hollow vessel, and its use is inexhaustible! Fathomless! It is a vast emptiness and everything arises out of it and goes back to it, falls back into it. And it is inexhaustible because it has no limits.

You may not be aware that the concept of zero was invented, discovered in India. India became aware that everything comes out of nothingness, zero, and everything falls back into nothingness, to zero. The whole journey is from zero to zero. So India coined the concept of zero, *shunyam*. And that is the basis of all mathematics – zero is the basis of all mathematics. If zero is taken away the whole structure of mathematics falls down. With zero the whole game starts – you add one zero to the figure one, then the value of the zero is nine because immediately one becomes ten, nine is born out of zero immediately.

You add two zeroes to one, the value is ninety-nine, immediately one has become a hundred – out of zero the whole structure builds up. Without zero, mathematics disappears, and without mathematics the whole of science disappears.

So if you ask me, zero is the root of all mathematics and of all science; you cannot conceive of an Einstein without the concept of a zero. No, it is not possible. All computers would stop immediately if you drop the concept of zero, because without the zero they cannot work. Zero seems to be the most substantial thing in the world. And what is a zero? A zero is simply zero, nothing – it is inexhaustible. You can take as many things out of it as you want. It can become nine, it can become ninety-nine, it can become nine hundred and ninety-nine. Go on and on and it can become anything you like; it is bottomless, fathomless. You cannot fathom it. One is limited. It has a limitation, it has a fixed value to it. Two is limited – all the nine digits are limited, only the zero is an unlimited phenomenon. In fact the nine digits cannot work without it. They come out of it, they grow out of it. This whole existence comes out of zero, a hollowness.

Why this emphasis on hollowness? It is not a philosophical doctrine, remember, it is simply an analogy – Lao Tzu is trying to show you something. He is trying to show you that unless you become hollow you will suffer, because hollowness is your reality. With unreality you will suffer.

And that is the meaning of meditation: to become hollow, to be empty inside. Not even a thought flutters – no content, just space. Suddenly all misery has disappeared because misery exists in thoughts. Death has disappeared because death exists in thoughts. The past has disappeared because the whole burden is carried through thoughts. Ambition disappears because how can you be ambitious without thoughts? How can you be mad without thoughts? Have you ever seen a madman who has no thoughts? In fact a madman is a madman because he has too many thoughts and he cannot hold them together: a whole crowd – too much to bear. A madman is a great thinker. That is his trouble. He thinks too much, and he thinks in many dimensions together. In his cart, in all directions, horses are harnessed and he goes on in all directions, and he cannot stop because he is not. He is so divided, so fragmentary, that he is not.

Only a hollowness can be undivided. Can you divide a hollowness?

Everything can be divided – anything that is substantial can be divided. Self can be divided, only no-self cannot be divided. That's why when Buddha reached to his ultimate enlightenment he coined a word that was his invention: the word *anatta*. It never existed before him. *Anatta* means no-self. *Anatta* means *anatma*. *Anatta* means you are not. *Anatta* means not is, you are not. *Anatta* means nothingness, hollowness.

The analogy is to indicate certain things: become hollow, be hollow. But the whole teaching, the conditioning of society is against it. In the West they say that if you are empty you will become the Devil's workshop. An empty mind is the Devil's workshop. This is foolishness, extreme foolishness because an empty mind can never be the Devil's workshop. If it is really empty, suddenly only God is there and nothing else, because God is hollow. The Devil is full of thoughts, he is never empty. The Devil has a mind; God has no mind. You can become the Devil's workshop – the more you think the more you can become one. If you don't think at all how can you become the Devil's workshop? The Devil cannot enter a hollowness, he will be afraid of death because to enter into emptiness is to die. He can enter you only if there are many thoughts – then he can hide in the crowd, then he can also become a thought in you.

An empty mind is God's mind – it is no-mind. Become hollow, sit as a hollow bamboo. Move as a hollowness, live as a hollowness, do whatsoever you have to do but do it as if you are hollow inside. Then karmas will not touch you at all; then your actions will not become a burden to you; then you will not be entangled because a hollowness cannot be entangled.

The Spirit of the Valley never dies.

The Spirit of the Valley... is the spirit of hollowness. What is a valley? – it is a hollow thing. Go to the hills. You will find two things: peaks full of rocks – filled; and valleys – empty. *The Spirit of the Valley...* is the spirit of emptiness. Peaks come and go, valleys remain – you cannot destroy nothingness. Something can always be destroyed. If you are something you will have to be born and die again and again. If you are nothing then how can you be destroyed? How can you be created? You simply disappear out of the world of forms to the formless; a valley means the world of the formless.

The Spirit of the Valley never dies.
It is called the Mystic Female.

These are all analogies. A woman is a valley, a man is a peak. A man enters the woman, the woman simply allows. A man is an aggression, a woman is a receptivity. A man tries to do, a woman simply waits for things to happen.

It is called the Mystic Female. These words have to be understood: *...the Mystic Female* because for Lao Tzu that is the ultimate. Lao Tzu feels that the nature of existence is more like a woman than like a man because man comes out of woman, woman comes out of woman. Man can even be discarded but woman cannot be discarded. Woman seems to be a basic element. Man is a growth out of it. Woman seems to be more elemental, more natural; man has something unnatural about him. If you ask the biologists they say that man has a deep imbalance in his biology; woman is symmetrical, balanced. That's why she looks more beautiful and round. Man has corners, woman has no corners.

A woman is a more balanced phenomenon, that's why she never tries to invent something, to create something, to do something, to be on the go – no, she is never on the go. Man is always on the go. He has to do something to prove that he is; he cannot simply accept himself. He cannot simply be and enjoy. He has to go to the moon, and he has to go to the top of Everest, and he has to do something. A deep imbalance is there, he cannot simply sit and be. He becomes an adventurer, a scientist. A woman simply enjoys being, she is happy with small things, she does not hanker for the moon. And every woman thinks what foolishness it is: "Why are you going to the moon?" You ask the wives of the astronauts, they simply cannot believe it. Why? Why move in danger and death unnecessarily? What is wrong in being here?

Man is a vagabond, a gypsy. If the world were left to man there would be no houses, only tents at the most. And he would be moving and moving from one place to another. He cannot stay in one place, something deep inside him forces him to move. He is not balanced; this imbalance is his madness. Look at a woman. She is balanced. Her needs are small: somebody to love, somebody to be loved by, food, shelter, a little warmth around, a home – finished. Then she is not worried about anything. No woman has created any science, no woman has founded any religion. People come to me and ask why all religions were created by man. Because man is tense, he has to do something or other. If he becomes frustrated with this world he starts doing something with the other world, but he has to do. He is never here and now, he cannot be here and now.

Lao Tzu has this analogy that the nature of existence is more feminine, it is more balanced. Look at the trees, look at the birds singing, look at the rivers flowing, look all around and watch – you will find more feminineness everywhere. Everything seems to be perfect at this moment. The trees are not worried about the future, the birds are not worried about the future, the rivers are simply moving so lazily, so silently – as if they are not moving at all. Nothing seems to be in a hurry.

That's why it happens every day: the man is honking the horn on the street and the woman goes on saying from the window, "I'm coming. Just wait a minute." Women have no time sense. They have watches, but they are ornamental – they are not watches really. They don't have any time sense because they are not in a hurry. Time sense arises out of hurry and haste – everything is trembling and everything is at stake, as if one minute late and everything will be lost. And if you ask the man, "Where are you going?" he will shrug his shoulders – just to the pictures, but honking the horn as if something great, a life experience was going to be missed. And the woman goes on saying...

I have even heard one woman once... I was sitting with the husband in the car and we were getting really late and the husband was very worried. In fact he need not have worried, he should not have worried, because it was my appointment not his. I was getting late. But he was honking, and he was very worried and perspiring and swearing at his wife.

And two or three times the wife said, "I am coming" – but her makeup was not complete. It is never complete. She always comes somehow but it is incomplete, much could have been done. She is so at ease with the mirror, with herself – she is so at ease. That is her world. Then the wife got angry, and she looked down from the window and said, "I have told you one thousand times that I am coming in a minute!" One thousand times! You cannot even say "I am coming" one thousand times in one minute. And "I am coming in one minute!"

No time sense! The world moves without any time sense. Clocks and watches don't exist with trees and rivers and mountains – it is a timeless world.

Man exists with time, with a worry. Deep down the worry seems to be sexual: the worry about achieving a sexual orgasm. Whenever a man is making love to a woman he is worried whether he will be able to make it or not, worried whether he will be able to satisfy the woman or not, worried whether he will be able to prove that he is a man or not. The worry: an inner trembling, in a hurry somehow to prove, and that's why he misses. Ejaculation is there, but orgasm – no. Orgasm is a different phenomenon. It happens only when you are not worried, it happens only when you are not an achiever, it happens only when you are not reaching for something, it happens in a deep relaxation, it happens only when you are not in control – but nature takes control. Then your whole body throbs with an unknown bliss. Then every cell of your body celebrates in a total ecstasy; then it is divine.

But man is worried, and that sexual worry is the root cause of all worries. Then everywhere he is trying to prove himself.

There is no need to prove yourself. You are. You are perfect. No woman is worried about proving; she takes it for granted that she is perfect. She lives in a very relaxed way. Many husbands come to me and always their complaint is that their wives are lazy. They are not lazy; they are enjoying! Whatsoever is the case, they are not in a hurry. But comparatively they look lazy.

Lao Tzu says, "The nature of existence is more like the female, more feminine." And the analogy is beautiful. He is not saying that existence is female – remember this. This is not logic, he is not trying to prove that existence is female. He is not for the "lib" movement – no. He is simply giving an analogy.

A man can also be feminine. A Buddha is feminine, a Lao Tzu is feminine, a Jesus is feminine. Then he lives, he lives in the moment, unhurried; he enjoys the moment unhurried. Jesus says to his disciples, "Look at the lilies in the field. How beautiful they are. Even Solomon in all his glory was not so beautiful."

But what is the secret of the lilies? – they are just flowering here and now. What will happen the next moment is not a worry; the next moment has not entered into their consciousness yet.

A man can live a feminine existence – then he becomes a mystic.

That is the only way. So all mystics become in a certain way feminine. And they are the real religious men, not the founders of religion.

Remember, this is a difference. Buddha is not the founder of Buddhism – no. His disciples are the founders. Jesus is not the founder of Christianity – no. His apostles are the founders. Mahavira is not the founder of Jainism. Gautam, his disciple, who was a scholar and great pundit, was. These are the men.

Jesus himself is feminine. To show this in India we have never painted *avataras, tirthankaras,* buddhas, with beards and mustaches – no – just to show that they are feminine. Have you ever seen Rama with a mustache? Krishna with a beard? It is not that they were somehow lacking in hormones. They were not the third sex. They were men; beards existed. But this is just an analogy. We have dropped the beards to show that they have become feminine: the feminine mystic has come into being. They existed without any hurry, they existed not as a tense man but as a non-tense woman, and you can feel around them the feminine warmth, the roundness of a buddha.

> *The Spirit of the Valley never dies.*
> *It is called the Mystic Female.*
> *The door of the Mystic Female*
> *is the root of Heaven and Earth.*

The door of the Mystic Female is the root of Heaven and Earth. And if you can find the key to open the door of ...*the Mystic Female...* you have opened the door of existence. Everybody has to enter that door non-tense, balanced, satisfied, content – that's the secret of the feminine being.

When I say this there are two possibilities of misunderstanding: women can misunderstand and think that they have nothing to do; men can misunderstand and think that this Lao Tzu is not for them. No, it is for you both. But remember: women are not pure women, they have lost the feminine mystique themselves. They have to gain it again. It will be easier for them of course to gain it than men, because man has gone farther away. And don't think that if you are a man Lao Tzu is not for you – he is particularly for you, otherwise you will go farther and farther away from existence and life's ecstasy. Everybody has to come back to the mother; that is the feminine mystique.

You are born out of the mother's womb, and you have to find the womb again in existence. If you can find the womb again in existence, the same warmth, the same life, the same love, the same care in existence – then existence becomes your home, your mother.

Hindus are better – when they call their God "mother," mother Kali – than Christians and Mohammedans and Jews, who go on calling their God "father." Those three religions are man-oriented, that's why they have been so violent. Mohammedans and Christians have killed so many, they have been a catastrophe on the earth. They have been murderers. In the name of religion they have been only killing and doing nothing else. This is man-oriented religion.

Buddhism has not killed, Jainism has not killed, Hinduism has not killed, because they are more and more inclined toward the feminine mystique. And you cannot complain against Lao Tzu at all, with him there exists no organized religion. Once a religion becomes organized, violence enters into it. Organization is going to be violent, it has to fight its way, it is bound to become male. Organization is male; religion is female.

I have heard an anecdote that a few disciples of the Devil came to him very worried and told him, "Why are you sitting here? Our whole business is at stake. A man has again become a buddha, enlightened. We have to do something, otherwise he will transform people and our world will be deserted, then who will come to hell? Do something immediately! No time should be lost. A man has again become a buddha!"

The Devil said, "Don't worry. I work through the disciples. I have sent some already, the disciples are on the way. They will surround him. They will create an organization. No need to worry: the organization will do everything that we cannot do, and they always do it better. I have learned it through history. I will create a church, and I will not be involved in it at all. In fact, they do it on their own. I just simply encourage and help."

Once the pope is there, Christ is forgotten; once the church is there, the buddha is killed and murdered. It is always on the corpse of a buddha that a religion stands.

These are analogies. Women can attain to their feminine mystique easily; that is the reason more women become attracted toward religion. They don't create religion – but more women, almost four times more than men, become interested in religion. Among Mahavira's disciples, forty thousand were women and ten thousand men; and the proportion was the same with Buddha's disciples. Go to any church and any temple and just count – you will always find four women to one man, and that one may have come just because the wife has come; he may not be really there.

Women can become more easily attuned; they are mothers, they are nearer nature. Man will find it a little difficult to come back; he has involvements, commitments, investments in his anxiety and tension. Even if he comes he will create an anxiety around religion.

This is my everyday observation: women come to me – if they surrender, they surrender totally. If they meditate at all, they meditate totally. Then they simply start growing.

Men come to me – if they surrender they cannot surrender totally, they always save a part. And when you surrender half-heartedly it is not a surrender at all. Then they meditate, but then meditation becomes an anxiety. And they come and they say, "Now this meditation is creating anxiety. I cannot sleep. I am constantly thinking about it – how it is going to happen, how I am to manage it."

It is not a management. You cannot manage it. You have to be in a let-go, a great let-go. It is difficult for man; he is so disciplined for anxiety, so trained to be tense. From the very childhood, the society forces men to become men – aggressive, violent, always reaching for something, trying to achieve something, ambitious. If they start playing with dolls the parents say, "Why? What are you doing? Are you being a sissy? This is for girls, not for boys. Home is for girls; to play with dolls is for girls, not for boys. They have to go out, and fight their way into life. They have to struggle – that is for them."

If home is for girls then at-homeness will also be for girls. Then you are never at home and at-homeness is meditation.

Continuously, continuously,
it seems to remain.
Draw upon it
and it serves you with ease.

The feminine mystique, the valley spirit, the hollowness. *Continuously, continuously, it seems to remain.* It is always there.

Draw upon it and it serves you with ease. And it makes you total, it fills you with ease, at-homeness. A relaxation comes to you.

Look at existence not as a struggle, but as an enjoyment. Look at existence not as a war, conflict, but as a celebration. And infinite is the celebration. Infinite is the possibility of bliss – bliss upon bliss. *Continuously, continuously, it seems to remain. Draw upon it and it serves you with ease.*

Enough for today.

CHAPTER 4

emptiness

The first question:

Osho,
Do you know who I am?

No sir, not at all. Because you are not. You are an emptiness – *anatta*. No sir. On the surface you may be somebody, but I am not concerned with your surface. In the deepest core you are simply a nobodiness, not even a nobody – nobodiness. How can I know you?

And that's the beauty, because if I can know you I have defined you, I have made you limited by my knowledge. If you can be known, immediately you become an object, you are no longer a consciousness. If you can be known you cannot be infinite, and you are infinite in your emptiness. How can I know you? Even you yourself cannot know. There exists nothing like self-knowledge. When you come to realize it, it is a no-self-knowledge. When you come to settle with it, suddenly you become aware that the knower and the known have disappeared: there is only emptiness, a vast space, with no beginning, no end – an infinity. That's what you are – how can it be known?

There is no possibility of knowledge. And it is good that you cannot be known, otherwise science will know you, and once known you are an object, a thing. Then the mystery is lost. That's why I say again and again that science will never be able to know the inner-most core of being, because the innermost core is a nonbeing. You are just like an onion – go on peeling the layers, go on peeling the layers; a new layer comes, another new layer, another new layer, and then suddenly the whole onion is gone: emptiness in the hands. That is you.

But this emptiness is not negative, so don't misunderstand me. The very word *emptiness* looks like an absence of something. No, it is not. It is a presence of something infinite. It is not absence, it is not negative, it is not like darkness; it is a positive phenomenon. You are a no-self. This positivity has to be remembered because the word *emptiness* may give you a wrong notion about it, you may think it is simply empty. I am not saying there is an emptiness of something, I am not saying that there is absence of something – no. It is empti-ness, it is the very emptiness, it is emptiness itself. Emptiness is being used as a positive term; when it is positive it is totally different.

You have known emptiness only in a negative way. You go into a room, there is no furniture and you say the room is empty, there is nothing. You come out and if I ask you what you saw in the room you will say it is empty – no furniture, no pictures on the walls, nothing – just empty. You went into the room but you saw only the negative part. The room is filled with roominess that you didn't encounter. A room is emptiness, a room means space. Something can be brought in because there is room, there is emptiness. The furniture can be brought in, there is space. You have not seen it that way. Otherwise you would have come and told me that the room is complete; there is nothing, only emptiness exists, the room is ready to receive any-thing – it has space. Then you have looked at the positive emptiness.

Look at the sky. The sky is a positive emptiness when there are no clouds. If you look at the sky as an absence of clouds then you are looking at it from a negative standpoint. If you look at it as the pres-ence of space, the blue emptiness, and out of that blue emptiness everything has arisen, then it cannot be negative. It is the most posi-tive thing in the world, the very ground of being. Nonbeing is the very ground of being. Everything has come out of it and everything by and by moves back into it. You are born out of it and you will die into it.

How can I know you? Knowledge will become a definition and you are indefinable. No, I don't know you. I don't know myself.

I would like to tell you one anecdote. It happened, and I love it, and I have told it so many times, millions of times, but whenever I remember it again it is so new and so fresh.

Bodhidharma went to China – the man who carried Buddha's emptiness in his hands. Bodhidharma carried the essential Buddhism to China for the greatest phenomenon to happen there. Because of Bodhidharma, Lao Tzu's whole standpoint – the Lao Tzuan way of life – and Buddha's realization met, and one of the most beautiful things was born. Nothing like it exists anywhere in the world: that is Zen. Zen is a meeting, a crossing between Buddha and Lao Tzu. Bodhidharma was the midwife who carried the seed to the womb of Lao Tzu.

When he reached China he was a very famous mystic, his name was known all over the East. When he reached China the emperor himself came to receive him on the border. The emperor asked a few questions. He asked, "I have made many Buddhist temples – thousands. What *punya*, what virtue have I gained?"

If he had said the same thing to any other ordinary Buddhist monk, he would have replied, "Emperor, Lord, you have gained infinite virtue – your heaven is absolutely certain, guaranteed." But he asked the wrong person. Bodhidharma said, "Virtue? Nothing! On the contrary, you have accumulated much sin."

The emperor was shocked, he couldn't believe it. He asked, "Why? What are you saying? I have made many temples of Buddha. I have published and distributed Buddha's sayings to millions of people. Every day I feed thousands of Buddhist monks and you say I have accumulated sin? What do you mean?"

Bodhidharma said, "The very idea that you have accumulated virtue is a sin, it is very egoistic. Your hell is certain, Emperor. You will fall to the seventh hell – the first won't do."

The emperor could not believe it. He felt a little anger also. And he said, "I have a question to ask. What is inside me? What is it that I am?" – the same question you have asked: "Do you know who I am?"

Bodhidharma said, "A vast emptiness, a nothingness."

Now the emperor was really angry. In anger he asked Bodhidharma, "Then who are you? Who is standing before me?"

Bodhidharma said, "I don't know sir."

I don't know. How can you know emptiness? You can be it, but you cannot know it. Knowing means you are separate from it, knowing needs distance. How can you know yourself? If you know then you are divided in two, the knower and the known. And of course the known can never be you, only the knower; so whatsoever you know can never be yourself, the knower. And the knower is irreducible, it cannot be made known. How can you put yourself in front of yourself? You cannot, that is impossible. And if you can then it is something else which is in front of you, not you. You are always behind – the knower. Always the knower. Always the knower, never the known.

I don't know myself, and this is self-knowledge. It looks contra-dictory, paradoxical, but this is how it is. Nothing can be done about it, this is the nature of things. That's why a man of self-knowledge will never claim that he knows. Because who will claim? He becomes like an ignorant man. He says, "I know only that I don't know."

Move inward. One day you will come to this emptiness, the hub of the wheel. The hub is empty but it holds the whole wheel in it; the hub is empty but without the hub the wheel will disappear, it will fall into pieces. You have known only the wheel – that is your personality up to now, your *nama-rupa*, your name and form. Your wheel you have known; the deeper you move within you, you will come one day to the hub: that is *anatta*, no-self, emptiness. But remember again it is not negative, it is not emptiness in the sense of being empty of something. It is emptiness itself. It is the most positive thing in exis-tence. It is existence itself. Hindus have called it *sat-chit-anand*: *sat* – it is; *chit* – it is aware; *anand* – it is bliss. Remember, it is not blissful; otherwise it would not be empty. It is bliss, not blissful. You will not be filled with bliss, you will suddenly find you are bliss.

Emptiness has the nature of bliss, has the nature of existence, has the nature of consciousness. Not that consciousness fills it. It is not like a lamp burning in a room so the light is filling the room. You can turn the lamp off and the light goes; you cannot turn off conscious-ness. It is the very nature of that inner emptiness – it is not that it is filling it. You cannot destroy it. How can you destroy emptiness? You can destroy everything in the world; you cannot destroy emptiness. That's why you cannot be murdered, you cannot be killed. There is no possibility, because you are not. The sword can kill the wheel, but the hub? – the hub will remain intact. It cannot be destroyed, it was not there in the first place.

Isness is the nature of the inner emptiness; consciousness is the nature of the inner emptiness, bliss is the nature of the inner emptiness. That's the fear people feel when they move into meditation. When they move into meditation they become afraid, they start trembling. A deep inner trembling arises. A deep anxiety and anguish arises. Why should it be so? You are coming nearer to a blissful state, nearer to an alert, aware consciousness, nearer to existence. Why are you scared of death? You are scared because you don't know how to be empty. You know only how to be filled, you don't know how to be empty. You don't know how to die, how to die to the personality, how to remain in the inner emptiness. You don't know. When you come inward and thoughts start moving away from you, suddenly fear takes possession. Where are you going? You feel like you are disappearing, you feel like you are dying. A sort of non-existence grips you – as if you are standing at an abyss and you are looking down and it is bottomless. And you start trembling and perspiration pours from every pore of your body. Death is encountered.

If you escape from this point you will never be able to meditate. Hence a master is needed. When you start getting afraid he can persuade you not to be afraid, he can help you: "Look at me. I have passed through this and yet I am. I have become empty and yet I am. And I am more than you, more than the whole existence put together." Somebody is needed to whom you can look, into whose eyes you can glimpse the same emptiness that you are coming to within yourself. And yet you can see that he is, and he is totally and absolutely. So don't be afraid. His being gives you courage, his presence gives you courage. A master does nothing in fact. He is a catalytic agent, just his presence is enough. Once you fall into that emptiness you will start laughing and you will say, "There is no death. I was unnecessarily afraid, baselessly afraid." Passing through death you become deathless.

This much I can say to you: you are a no-self. Become a no-self. And no-self is not empty in any negative sense, it is the greatest positivity.

The second question:

Osho,
You said that you encompass all opposites in you, that you do not deny the sinner or the hate in you. In another lecture once you said

you do not deny the Devil in you, you are total. This puzzles me though. All I have ever felt from you are vast, vast reaches of love and compassion and a feeling of absolute goodness. When and where is your Devil and your hate?

When you are both, the Devil is absorbed by the divine because it is a part of it. In fact this is the inner arithmetic. If you live a part life you will be the Devil, because the Devil is nothing but a part claiming to be the whole. A part claiming that it is the whole; this is what devilishness is. When you accept it, it is absorbed by the whole. If you fight with it, then you will be fighting with yourself and you will always remain divided. In division the Devil can exist; it exists in division. It cannot exist when you are whole and total. When you are divided then it exists in the cracks; it gets rooted in the cracks, in between two parts. When you accept everything, the whole of life as it is, without denying, without renouncing, without calling it names – this is bad and that is good – when you accept life as it is, whatsoever it is, whatsoever the case, when you accept it in its totality, the Devil disappears. It is absorbed by existence, it is absorbed by the divine.

The Devil is divine – in the very word also. *Devil* comes from the same root as *divine* – they both come from the Sanskrit root *dev*. Devil is divine, that is the root meaning of the term. Things have gone a little astray, but the Devil is divine. He has to be called back, and by fighting you cannot call him back. By fighting he goes further away, and you will always miss a part. That missing part will not allow you peace. It has to be called home, it has to be absorbed into the whole.

If you accept everything suddenly love flowers, hate disappears. So when I say accept hate, I am not saying be hateful; in fact, I am cutting the very root of being hateful. When I say accept, in that acceptance I am cutting the very root. You will never be hateful again if you accept; if you don't accept you will remain hateful, and your love will lack something. This has to be understood deeply because it is not a metaphysical problem, it is existential. It is a problem that everybody has in him.

You hate somebody. When you hate, what happens inside? What is hate? What do you want to do to the other person? You want to kill him, destroy him. You want to throw him away, as far away as possible. You don't want to see him, you don't want him to be near you.

You would like him to disappear, to no longer exist – that's why you want to kill and destroy. When you love a person what do you want to do to him? You want him to be always alive, never to die, to be near and close, to be available. You would like to protect him, care about him, and you cannot believe that your love is going to be destroyed by anything. You would like your lover or beloved to be immortal.

Look at both the phenomena. They are opposite. But can't you feel? – they are two aspects of the same coin. Love is creative, hate is destructive. But have you observed? – no creation is possible without destruction; no destruction is meaningful unless it is for creation. So you can destroy if you are going to create, then there is no problem. You can demolish a house if you are going to create a better house; nobody will say that you are destructive. You can destroy a society if a better society is possible. You can destroy a morality for a better morality; nobody will say that you are destructive because you are destroying to create, and no creation is possible without destruction. Destruction is absorbed by the creation; then it is beautiful, then it is part of the creative process.

But you destroy. You destroy a society with no idea what you are going to do next, with no creative idea in mind. You simply enjoy destruction. You demolish a house, you destroy a thing, and if somebody asks, "Why are you doing that?" then you say simply, "I like to destroy" – then you are mad, something has gone wrong in you. Destruction has become whole in itself, it is trying to claim that it is the whole. When destruction claims that it is the whole then it is the Devil; when destruction is part of a greater whole, creation, then it is divine.

When you love a person, many, many times you will have to hate him also, but then it is part of love. A father loves his child. Many times he will be angry also and he will hit and beat the child. And a child is never offended by anger, never. A child is offended when you are simply angry without any cause, when you are destructive without any cause. When a child cannot understand why, then he cannot forgive you. If he can understand why – he has broken a clock, now he understands that the father is going to hit him, and he accepts it. In fact, if the father does not hit him he will carry the guilt and that is very destructive. He will continuously be afraid that some day or other it is going to be known that he has broken a precious watch or a clock or something, and guilt will be there and a wound will be there. He wants it to be cleared up, he wants it to be finished, and the only way it can be finished is that the father becomes angry – now everything is in balance. He committed something wrong, father became angry, he is punished. Things are finished. He is clean. Now he can move unburdened.

In the West, because of the psychologists in this century, much absurdity has happened in the relationship between the parents and the children. And one of the absurd things that they have taught is: never be angry with your child, never hit him, never hate him. Because of this teaching, parents have become afraid. This is something new. Children have always been afraid of parents, but now in America parents are afraid of children. Something may go wrong psychologically and then their child may be crazy or go mad or become schizophrenic or split – neurosis, psychosis, something may happen in the future and they will be responsible. So what is happening? A father, if he loves the child, feels the anger – so what will he do? He will suppress the anger. And that a child can never forgive, because when a father suppresses anger the anger becomes cold.

Try to understand this. Whenever anger is cold it is of the Devil; whenever anger is hot it is of God. A hot anger is beautiful, alive; a cold anger is deadly, poisonous.

When a father is really hot, perspiring, red in the face, and hits the child, the child knows that the father loves him, otherwise why bother so much? When the father is cold – sarcastic, not angry – but in subtle ways showing his anger in a cold way: the way he moves, the way he enters the house, the way he looks at the child or doesn't look at the child... This coldness shows that the father doesn't love him, doesn't love him enough to be hotly angry.

And that has created the generation gap in the West, nothing else. Children have moved on their own; parents have remained in a cold, dead emotion, imprisoned. Vast distances have appeared. There is no communication. A father cannot talk to the child because he is afraid that if he talks – really communicates, becomes hot – anger will come. So it is better not to talk, avoid the situation, don't communicate.

The same has happened between wives and husbands in the West, and now it is happening in the East – because in fact the East is disappearing. By the end of the twentieth century, the whole world will be West. There will be no East, it will exist only in the books of history, in museums; it will be a nostalgia. The East is disappearing – it will be there in geography, but in the human consciousness it will have no place.

What has happened in the West? The same – if you love your wife how can you hate her? If you love your wife how can you hit her? If she loves you she loves you twenty-four hours a day, constantly. You are demanding impossible things.

In life everything is a rhythm. Only in death are things absolute and there is no rhythm. In life there is a rhythm – the day comes and then the night. Heraclitus says: "God is summer and winter, day and night, hunger and satiety, life and death." Life is a rhythm, a constantly vibrating phenomenon between two polarities. You cannot love a person twenty-four hours a day; if you try, the love will become dead. You can love a person intensely for a few moments, then you have to move because you have to relax. Otherwise love will become such a fever – and how can you remain in such a feverish state twenty-four hours? Day has to be followed by night, a rest, a relaxation.

Love is excitement. You cannot remain excited forever. You have to love and you have to hate the same person, and nothing is wrong if you love. Remember, that is the point to be remembered: if you love then nothing is wrong. Love sanctifies everything, even hate. Love purifies everything, even hate. Love makes everything holy, even hate. You love your wife and then you hate her, she loves you and she hates you. This makes life a rhythm. It is not a dead monotony. There are changes of moods, changes of seasons. And the change is good, because change is an alive phenomenon; otherwise, if somebody loves you and loves you and loves you, even love will become a boredom. And nobody can love like that, a twenty-four-hour-a-day love can only be pretended.

Try to understand this: if you pretend love then you can pretend twenty-four hours a day, but then it is false. Only a plastic flower will not fade, only a plastic flower will not die. If you are really alive you will die also; that is part of life. If you really love a person you will be angry also, that is part of it. And nothing is wrong in it. It becomes a sin only when it becomes the whole. If it is surrounded by love; the island of hate surrounded by an ocean of love is beautiful. It is beautiful. It gives tension to love, relaxation to love. It gives a rhythm to love, it makes life a harmonious whole. Just think of a world where the sun never sets and you have to be awake twenty-four hours a day – within three weeks you will all go mad. And that is what has happened in love – you all have gone mad, pretending, pretending, false faces, masks, hypocrisy, showing that which is not there. The real trouble is that when you are angry and you don't show it, by and by this mechanism of suppression becomes so deep-rooted that everything becomes false. You will not feel love and you will show it, you will not feel compassion and you will show it – then your life is not authentic, not honest. An honest life is river-like: it changes, it moves. Sometimes it is summer and the river has completely disappeared, only a dry bed is left. And sometimes it is the rainy season and the river is in flood and breaks all the banks, and flows all over, becomes oceanic.

Just try to see: in life there is a rhythm between polarities, and humanity is caught in a trap because we have decided to remain on one pole. You cannot remain there; you will move inside, you will try to pose just on the surface. Then the whole life becomes poisonous. Then everything enters into everything else. In your love hate is hidden, because when there was hate you tried to smile and pose; now it is in your blood and when you love it is mixed in it. Man now is an adulterated phenomenon, impure. And this has happened because of the wrong teachings of your so-called religions and moralists. They have all tried to make you live on one pole. That pole they call God, compassion, love – all that is good, all goodie-goodie. The other pole they call the Devil, all that is bad.

Lao Tzu or I, we are not in favor of this division, this dichotomy, this schizophrenia. We are for both. And then a sudden transformation happens: destruction becomes part of creation – it is – and hate becomes part of love. Love is bigger than hate, creation is bigger than destruction. Life is bigger than death, and death should be a part of it. And if death is part of it, it is beautiful. Remember this, and then by and by you will see that even your hate has taken the color of love; your destruction has taken the shape of construction, creation, creativity; your anger has a compassion in it.

Jesus was angry. Christians have not been able to solve the puzzle up to now because they think, "How can Jesus be angry? He has to be always smiling like a politician. How can he be angry?" He was angry. He was deadly angry. He entered the temple of Jerusalem and he was so angry he attacked, physically attacked, the money changers. He must have been really tremendously angry because he was alone and he disturbed many money changers. And he threw them out, tables and all, he chased them out of the temple alone. When a man is really angry he has the strength of hundreds.

You may also have felt it. When you are angry you can easily throw a big rock, when you are not angry you cannot even move it. Anger is energy, concentrated energy. Anger is a deep concentration of being: one-pointed, the whole existence forgotten, all energies narrowed down to one point.

Jesus must have been beautiful in that moment. Christians hide the fact, they try to avoid the story. Jesus, and angry? – The man who says that if somebody hits you on one side of your face show him the other side, angry? This man angry? It looks contradictory. The man who says that if somebody snatches your coat give him your shirt also – this man angry? It doesn't fit.

But I say to you that only this man can be angry because his anger will be part of compassion; only this man can be really angry because he knows what compassion is. He has known one pole, he knows the other pole also and he can move, he is alive, he is not dead. He is not a fixed thing, he is not a thing; he is an alive movement, alive, throbbing – he can move to the other pole. And he threw those money-changers out of the temple because of compassion. He was angry because of compassion. He was so compassionate, and sometimes I feel that his compassion is deeper than Mahavira's and Buddha's because it is so true and so lively. Mahavira and Buddha look more like wax figures – fixed. Maybe it is because of the descriptions from their disciples, maybe true stories have not been recorded because in India the concept that a man of enlightenment cannot be angry is very old. It was not so in Jerusalem. The Jewish God can also be angry so there is no fear about an enlightened man being angry. No fear. Even the Jewish God can be angry. He behaves in a very human way. The Jewish God behaves in a human way, but Jaina and Buddhist human beings are always expected to behave like a dead God. Maybe that's why disciples edited the lives of Buddha and Mahavira. They have chosen parts and dropped other parts out. That seems to be so; there are grounds for one to say so.

There are two sects of Jainas, two sects of Mahavira's followers: Swetambaras and Digambaras. Digambaras in their life story of Mahavira say that he was never married, that he remained an absolute *brahmrachai*, a celibate, from his very childhood. Swetambaras say that he was married; not only married, he had a daughter. Now what is the matter? Why do Digambaras say that he was not married? They are afraid that marriage is too human a phenomenon. Mahavira falling in love with a woman? No! That doesn't suit their concept of a *tirthankara* – Mahavira not only falling in love with a woman and getting married, but making love to the woman because a daughter was born. They cannot conceive of Mahavira in a posture of intercourse. Impossible! They have simply dropped the whole thing because it is dangerous. Mahavira was never married.

The Swetambaras' story seems to be truer. Why do I say so? Because if it were not the case even Swetambaras wouldn't add it. If it was not already the case that he was married and a daughter was born to him, Swetambaras wouldn't invent it; it is so against the rules, they would not invent it. So the only possibility is that Digambaras dropped the idea. And later on Digambaras dropped the whole idea of Mahavira's life – a life is a life, it is bound to have both the polarities in it. So Digambaras say that the real life story has disappeared, because man in this age is not capable of understanding it. So the original scriptures have disappeared, they are lost – there is no life story of Mahavira. They completely deny his life in this way. So you can make an ideal out of him – he is a wax figure, not a real man then, with no human biography, with no human biology.

Digambaras say that he never perspired. How can Mahavira perspire? It is ordinary human weaklings who perspire. How can Mahavira perspire? He never perspired.

It looks foolish, looks blind, but this is how we fix things and then we try to make our ideals out of them – false ideals – then false personalities are created around them.

Christians could not do it. They were not so clever. They didn't know that later on it was going to be difficult. Jesus' life seems to be more real, more historical, but then there are troubles. For me there is no trouble. For me this is how things should be. Only a Jesus can be really angry, but his anger is because of compassion. You think, "How can he be angry if he has compassion?" And I say he can be angry only because he has compassion. Then compassion covers anger – then it changes the very quality of anger, because it becomes a vital part of the compassion. Once you absorb both, you have a different quality of being. Hate also becomes part of love, anger part of compassion.

Don't try to choose. Rather remain choiceless and create a

harmony, become a harmony. Don't create any conflict within you – whatsoever you are, you are beautiful. You have all the ingredients to create a harmony. If you discard something, later on you will repent because that discarded part will some day be needed. Some day you will miss it and you will see then that it was necessary. It was to be there, and you discarded it. Don't discard anything. Use everything that existence has given to you, make a harmony out of it. Harmony should be the goal.

The third question:

Osho,
You said that just being in the presence of an enlightened master will transform. Before coming to you I felt more or less independent. Since being with you I seem to have become totally dependent on you. You are the light in my life. When I think of you leaving I get into a panic. Is this a natural stage which will pass by itself or is something wrong?

It is a natural stage if you allow it to pass. If you cling to it, then something goes wrong.

There are three steps in the spiritual growth – steps or stages. They can differ with each individual but there are always three. One is independence. That is an egoistic state: you want to be independent of all which is false, which is not possible because you are not independent, you cannot be. You are a part of this vast whole, of this cosmos. How can you be independent? You have to depend on millions, for millions of things. You have to depend on the sun for light, on the sun for life, you have to depend on the air for life, on the oxygen, you have to depend on the trees for food. How can you be independent? You cannot. That is an egoistic effort and is bound to fail.

When independence fails, suddenly dependence arises; you move to the other pole. Because you don't know how to be in the middle and how to create a harmony, you move to the other pole. Then you become dependent. Then you become afraid that if the object of your dependence is lost, what will happen to you? Then there is panic. But this is a second state: independence is false, dependence is also false.

Then there is the third point which has to be achieved, which I call the harmony. That is interdependence – a feeling of interdependence – you depend on the whole, and not only that, the whole depends on you.

I am reminded of a Jewish mystic, a Hasid mystic, Zusya, who used to say to God in every prayer: "I know my Lord, that I depend on you, but you must also know that you depend on me. I know that without you I cannot be, but let me remind you that without me you also cannot be."

How can there be a God there without you? – impossible.

Scientists say that the plants, the trees, the whole vegetation on the earth depends on the sun, without the sun they cannot be. But now they have started suspecting that this idea of one-way traffic must be wrong somewhere, because in life it is always two-way traffic, never one-way traffic. If the plants depend on the sun, somehow the sun must depend on the plants, because it is a mutual give and take. They have started suspecting, and sooner or later they will discover how the sun depends on the plants.

Everything depends on everything else. You feel happy when you look at a flower, a rose – your happiness is created by the rose. Now scientists have proved that when you are happy the rose also feels happy. He depends on you, he waits for you to come and if you don't come he is just like a lover, feels very sad. No, it is a scientific fact, not poetry. Now it has been absolutely proved that when a lover comes to a rosebush the whole bush thrills, celebrates; it depends on you. Now they say that if you love the rosebush it will grow faster, it will produce bigger flowers because somebody is there to care and love and see. And somebody waits. How can the bush betray you? It has to produce bigger flowers. If nobody loves, and the garden is neglected, and nobody bothers, only servants come and water the plants without any care, then for what, for whom should the bush try to bring big flowers? Then small flowers will do; even without flowers there will be no harm. For whom to flower? For whom to bloom? The rosebush depends on you.

Never pass a tree without saying hello in your heart; never pass a tree without looking at it with deep care and concern. It costs nothing. And remember: if you can make a tree happy, the tree will make you happy. You can try the experiment, it is simple – big scientific instruments are not needed for it. It is a simple experiment. Choose a plant, a tree in the garden of your house or in a public garden. Go every day to the tree, talk to it, become friendly.

It is difficult to persuade the tree because human beings have treated trees so badly that they have become afraid of all human beings. The moment you enter, all the trees say: "Human being is coming" – the most dangerous animal on earth. It can harm without any cause. No animal does that. If a cow is hungry she will eat the grass, but man can simply sit and go on pulling it up, for no reason at all. He is not hungry, he is not going to eat it. Why are you pulling it? Why are you destroying it? The inner destructiveness of the mind, the inner destructive mind goes on being destructive. You pass by the tree, you pull a branch off – and then you throw it away. Are you absolutely asleep? If it is needed for food – then too: the whole tradition in all the primitive societies, the old traditional lore in Mexico, in primitive aboriginal tribes in India, in Thailand, in many countries, says: "Go to a tree. If you need something, ask her." If you need a few leaves, five leaves for your worship, ask the tree, take permission, and pull the leaves off as carefully as possible. Don't hurt the tree. Then the tree is always ready to give and there will be no hurt feeling left behind. And thank the tree. "You gave me five leaves when I needed them. Whenever you need something, don't be shy, just tell me."

Go to a tree, talk to the tree, touch the tree, embrace the tree, feel the tree. Just sit by the side of the tree, let the tree feel you, that you are a good man and you are not in a mood to harm. By and by friendship arises and you will start feeling that when you come, the quality of the tree immediately changes. You will feel it. On the bark of the tree you will feel tremendous energy moving when you come. When you touch the tree she is as happy as a child, as a beloved. When you sit by the tree you will feel many things. Soon you will be able to come to the tree if you are sad, and just in the presence of the tree your sadness will disappear. Only then will you be able to understand that you are interdependent – you can make the tree happy and the tree can make you happy. And the whole of life is interdependent. This interdependence I call godliness, Lao Tzu calls Tao – this whole interdependence.

God is not a person somewhere, this whole interdependence is godliness, Tao, dharma. The Vedas call it *rit*, the law. Whatsoever you like to call it, call it, but this interdependence is the whole thing. And if near me you can learn interdependence, you have learned all.

First your independence will drop – that is not very difficult, because independent you feel so burdened, you are always ready to

drop the burden. That is not very difficult. Then you become dependent. That can be more difficult, because when the burden is thrown on
somebody else you feel good, unburdened, weightless. Then the fear
comes: if this man leaves the world, is no longer in the body, then what
will happen? Then you are afraid, then – panic.

Don't cling to it. This is a phase – just as the first was a phase
this is also a phase, this is the reverse aspect of the first phase. Try
to feel more and more interdependence.

I am talking to you here. If you were not here and somebody
else was here, if even a single person was different here, I would not
have talked the same. It would be impossible because I have no
mind to talk. I am simply responding to you. You create the situation, you are here – and I talk. If somebody not present here today
had been present I would not have talked the same. It would have
been impossible, because his presence would have created a different situation. I am not talking in a vacuum, I am talking to you.
And I am not talking from the mind, because when you talk from the
mind you don't bother who is there, you have certain things to say
and you say them.

I had a teacher, he was really a philosopher. And he was such a
crazy man, as philosophers are, that for years nobody would join his
subject. He was eccentric and it was impossible to pass in his subject
because he would either give a hundred percent or he would give
zero. There was no midway with him – either yes or no. He was
absolutely Aristotelian. "Either you are right or you are wrong," he
used to say, "nothing in between." So students were afraid. But I liked
the man. He was really worth watching, and there was only one way
to watch him: to join his subject. So I was the only student.

And this was his way – the first day he told me, "Remember, I
can start by the bell of the university, but I cannot stop. Unless I finish
whatsoever I am saying I cannot stop. So the periods will start with
the bell, but they will never stop with the bell. Sometimes I will talk
only twenty minutes and be finished, sometimes I will talk for two or
three hours. So if you feel very fed up or bored, or if you want to go
to the bathroom or something you can go, but don't disturb me."
And I was the only student! "You can go and you can come, but go
and come in such a way that I am not disturbed; I will continue."

I tried the first day. I was curious to see if he was really going to do it. Did he mean it? He meant it. When I left the room, he continued, when I came back he was still going on.

For two years I was with him. Sometimes I would go for hours, because I have a habit of sleeping. After eleven-thirty it is difficult for me not to sleep, so at eleven-thirty I would go to my hostel room and I would have a sleep of one hour, then I would come back and he was still talking. He was completely mad. He was really a philosopher.

But I am not talking to you that way. I am not a philosopher at all. I am talking to you – it is an interdependence. Whatsoever I say you are responsible for it as much as I am responsible, because you provoke it. You and I, these are just two polarities. Something between us is created, that's what is happening. When I am talking to you it is not that I am talking to you, not that you are listening to me; we are talking to us. We are talking to us – this is interdependence.

You are talking through me, I am listening through you – this is interdependence.

Independence you have dropped, now drop dependence also – become interdependent. And this is just a learning here, let your interdependence spread to the whole existence – feel interdependent everywhere. And you are, that is the reality. Dependence is false, independence is false; only interdependence is true, only godliness is true. Godliness is interdependence.

The fourth question:

Osho,
According to you, women are closer to the whole than men. How come so few women attain enlightenment then?

Not so few. Exactly the same number of women attain to enlightenment as men, but they don't fuss about it as much as men – that's all. They don't advertise it as much as men. They enjoy it. That is how woman, the feminine being, is.

Man enjoys talking about his enlightenment more than enlightenment itself. He is interested in how many people have come to know that he has become enlightened. Women are not worried. They are not worried at all. If it has happened they enjoy it, they nourish it deep inside. It becomes a pregnancy. They live with it; they don't talk about it. That's why you don't know many names. Only a few names are known and those are of women who had some quality of man in them, that's why you know. Otherwise you would not have known them.

In Kashmir there was a woman of the name Lalla. In Kashmir they have a proverb: We know only two names – Allah and Lalla. Lalla was a rare woman, a buddha, but she must not have been very feminine; she must have had a little more of a male mind than a female mind. She lived her whole life naked. She is the only woman in the whole world who did that. Many men have lived naked: Mahavira, Diogenes, all the Jaina *tirthankaras*, and thousands of others, but only one woman. It looks very unfeminine, because the very essence of the feminine mind is to hide, not to show – to hide in the inner cave.

Lalla is known to be an enlightened woman; few other women are known to be enlightened. One woman, Maitreyi, is known in the days of the Upanishads, but she must have been a very male type.

It is said that King Janak had called a great debate among all the learned people of his kingdom to decide the ultimate question: What is reality? It was going to be a great discussion and all the learned people, all the pundits of the country gathered together. And there was going to be a great prize for the winner – one thousand cows, the best of the country, with gold-covered horns, with jewelry around their necks. They were standing there outside the palace – one thousand cows. Whosoever won the debate would take the cows.

Yagnawalkya came, one of the great learned men of those days. And at that time he must not have been enlightened, later on he became an enlightened sage. He came with his disciples – he was a great teacher – and he was so arrogant, as scholars are, that he told his disciples, "Take these cows. I will decide the matter later on, but you first take these cows because it is too hot and the cows are suffering from the heat."

He must have been very arrogant – so certain. Only ignorance is so certain. Wisdom is always hesitating because it is so vast – and how to decide the ultimate nature of reality? Who can decide it? All the other scholars were offended but they couldn't say anything because they knew that they could not defeat this man in argument. In argument he was superb. And he argued, and he defeated all.

But a woman was sitting there; she was the only woman, and

she had not said anything. She was Maitreyi. And then she stood at the end, when the debate was almost finished and he was going to be declared the winner. She said, "Wait. I have to ask a few questions." And she asked simple questions; but in fact simple questions cannot be answered.

She asked, "On what is this earth supported? Who is supporting this earth?"

The old Indian tradition says the earth is being supported by eight elephants, big white elephants. So Yagnawalkya repeated the old tradition, that the earth is supported by eight elephants: "Are you absolutely illiterate, don't you know this much?"

The woman asked, "Then on whom are those elephants supported?"

Now Yagnawalkya suspected trouble. So he said, "On Brahma, on God." And he was thinking that now she would stop.

But she said, "I would like to ask on whom is your God supported, on what?"

Yagnawalkya became angry, and he said, "Woman! Stop! Otherwise your head will fall off. You will be killed!"

This woman later on became enlightened. But she must have been a very male type. She argued and even got Yagnawalkya into trouble and in fact she remained silent but she was not defeated – anyone can see that. In fact Yagnawalkya was defeated. If I had been the judge she would have won and the cows would have had to be given to her, because this is no argument to say that your head will fall off. This is no argument. Anger is no argument, violence is no argument; this way you can keep somebody silent, but you have not won the debate.

This woman became enlightened but she must have been a male type. Otherwise no woman bothers to argue about such things.

Once I asked Mulla Nasruddin, "How are things going between you and your wife? I never see any arguments."

He said, "On the first day we decided one thing and we have been following it, so everything is going very, very well."

I said, "Tell me, because many people come to me for my advice about problems, so I can suggest it to them."

He said, "It is a simple law. We have decided that on ultimate questions, final questions, great problems, my advice will be final. And on small things, petty things, her advice will be final."

So I said, "This is a very good decision. Then what problems do you call petty and what problems do you call great?"

He said, "For example, which movie we should go to see, what type of food we should eat, what type of restaurant we should visit, where we should send our children, to which college or to which university, what type of education should be given to them, what type of clothes should be purchased, what type of house and car – these are all petty things. She decides."

So I asked, "Then what are the great problems?"

He said, "Whether God exists or not. Great problems I decide!"

Women really are never interested in great problems because they know deep down they are foolish. You can decide whether God exists or not, or how many angels can dance on one point of a pin – you can decide.

And Nasruddin told me, "This arrangement has been so good that not a single argument has arisen – I always decide great problems, she always decides small problems. And things are going well."

By and by every husband comes to know that he is free only to decide metaphysical problems – otherworldly. No woman is interested in writing scriptures. They have never written any. But that doesn't mean that women have not become enlightened – the same number have. Life follows a proportion. It should be so, otherwise the balance will be lost. Life completely follows a proportion.

I would like to tell you one thing, maybe it will suggest something to you. To every one hundred girls, one hundred fifteen boys are born. And this has been a problem for biologists. Why does it happen? Always – to a hundred girls a hundred fifteen boys are born, and by the time of the age of marriage fifteen boys have died. So the proportion remains the same, because boys are weaker than girls and more girls survive. So nature has a balance. From the very beginning fifteen boys are extra, spare, because they will die. By the time the marriage season comes, one hundred girls will be there, and if only one hundred boys had been born then only eighty-five or eighty boys would be left, and twenty girls would be left without husbands. That's not a good arrangement.

One hundred fifteen boys are born so that by the time the marriage

age comes the number is the same. This cannot be solved – how nature arranges this, by what method, how this proportion...

And then, in the two world wars another problem arose, because in wars the proportion becomes very disproportionate. After the First World War and after every war more children are born than ever. That too is something. In war many people die; immediately nature has to make arrangements. Some unknown force, some unconscious force goes on working. After the war many children are born, but that too is not difficult to understand because it can be explained in other ways – maybe soldiers come back home very starved for sex and they make love more. That may be the cause of it. If that was the only thing, it could have been explained – but more boys are born than ever, and less girls are born, because in wars men die, women remain. More men die in wars than women, because all the soldiers are men, so the ordinary proportion of a hundred to a hundred fifteen changes. To a hundred girls almost three hundred boys are born.

There is a subtle balance somewhere. In fact, for each man a woman exists; for each woman a man exists – they are part of one whole. Whenever one man becomes enlightened, one woman has to become also. Because one man is freed out of existence, now he will not be coming back; he will no longer enter into a womb, into the world. Somewhere one woman has to be relieved of the bondage. So this is my reading: as many men as women, the same number, have become enlightened, but women are not known because they don't make a fuss about it. They enjoy it.

The last question:

Osho,
You always say wait and see. Wait, I can understand. But how to see?

You need not worry about that. You simply wait and seeing will come to you. No need to worry about it. Waiting gives you insight. When I say "Wait and see," I don't mean that you have to do both. I simply mean wait and you will see. In fact, wait and seeing will come to you.

Waiting creates seeing. Patience creates the possibility. Absolute patience creates the absolute possibility to see. With tense, impatient minds eyes are clouded, filled with smoke – they cannot see. When you silently wait, by and by clouds disappear from the eyes, because they are created by impatience. When you patiently wait they disappear. Vision becomes clear, a clarity is attained. You can see. Wait and see – when I say this I don't mean that you have to do both, I mean wait, and you will see. Seeing will come by itself, on its own accord. Simply wait. You understand me?

If you can wait it means you have dropped the reaching mind, the achieving mind; you have dropped the desiring mind. Only then can you wait. Waiting means now you are here and now, this moment is enough, this moment is all – and suddenly the eyes are clear. No clouds roam in the eyes then – no smoke. The flame burns without smoke. And you see.

Enough for today.

on the danger of overweening success

On the danger of overweening success, Lao Tzu says:

Stretch a bow to the very full,
and you will wish you had stopped in time.
Temper a sword-edge to its very sharpest,
and the edge will not last long.
When gold and jade fill your hall,
you will not be able to keep them safe.
To be proud with wealth and honor
is to sow the seeds of one's own downfall.
Retire when your work is done,
such is heaven's way.

ogic moves to the very extreme; life never. That's how logic misses life. Logic has the tendency to reach to a conclusion, life is never concluding.

Life has no conclusion. It goes on and on and on without any conclusion. It is without any beginning and without any end; it is always in the middle, it is always in the present, it is an on-going process. That's how a logical mind becomes by and by dead; that's how logic becomes its own downfall. Don't conclude. Live without conclusion. That is the only way to live because only then do you live in the middle and the middle is the balance.

Life is a balance between opposites, it never comes to an end. The balance goes on and on, it is eternal. A man of understanding never comes to any conclusions, he cannot. When life itself is non-conclusive how can a wise man be conclusive? If you ask Lao Tzu for any conclusive answer he will laugh. He will say you are foolish. He lives according to life and the most basic note – if you live according to life – is balance. Never move to one opposite, don't cling to one polarity; then you will lose balance.

I have heard...

Once it happened that a great king had to decide something against his heart. Two of his ministers had committed some crime and he loved the ministers very much. Even if they had committed the crime he wanted to forgive them, his love was such for them. But that was against the law of the country, and it wouldn't have been a good precedent. So they had to be punished. And the law of the country said that for such a crime the only punishment was death. So what to do?

It was too difficult, so he found a way out. He said, "They have to be sentenced to death, but I will give them one more chance to live. Between two hills a tightrope will be stretched. If they can walk over it and survive, then I will forgive them."

It was almost impossible. It was impossible because they had never walked on a tightrope, let alone on one between two hills over a big valley – death everywhere. To walk on a tightrope is a great art, one has to learn it, it is a great discipline. They had not even dreamed in their lives that they would become tightrope walkers.

One of the two couldn't sleep. The whole night he prayed to God to help him. He couldn't take his tea in the morning. He came to the place where this phenomenon was to happen; the whole capital had gathered.

The other, knowing well that he didn't know anything about tightrope walking, that nothing could be done and it was almost certain that he was going to die, so why not sleep well? – he slept. In the morning he took his usual tea. He walked leisurely, came to the place. The other was trembling, feverish; but he was quiet and calm knowing well that death was to happen – and when it is certain, why bother? Die silently.

He started walking on the rope, and wonder of wonders – he walked!

Nobody could believe it. Even the tightrope walkers had come to watch – even they could not believe it. It was difficult even for them, the distance was too great and the danger was too much. One step wrong, a little too much leaning toward the left or toward the right, and you are gone; a little unbalance and death is waiting at every step. But the man walked and he walked so leisurely, just as leisurely as if he had gone for a morning walk. He reached the other hill.

The first man was trembling, perspiring. He shouted from his place to the other man, "Please tell me how you walked, so I can also walk!"

The other man shouted back: "Difficult, because I don't know how. I know only one thing – this is the way I have been walking my whole life. I'm not a tightrope walker, but now I know I am, because this is the way I have been living my whole life – balanced, never going to the extreme. Or, if I lean toward the left immediately I balance it by leaning toward the right. I have not done anything else. But this won't help you because this is not something you can learn suddenly. If you live in this way the knack of it comes to you."

Remember the word *knack*. I emphasize it. Religion is a *knack*, it is not a science. Otherwise it could be taught very easily, it could be explained very easily. It could be theorized, there would be no trouble about it.

Even the greatest problem in science can be solved – if not today then tomorrow, but it will be solved through intellect, through intellectual effort. And some day, when it is solved, it is not solved only for the one who has solved it, it is solved for all.

Einstein solved the mystery of relativity. Now there is no need for anybody else to solve it, it is solved for all. You have just to understand it, that's all. You need not go into the vast effort of solving it. It is solved. Science is a public phenomenon: one man solves something, then it is solved for everybody; one man invents something, it is invented for all. It is a mass phenomenon.

In religion thousands of Lao Tzus may have happened, but nothing is solved. You have to know it again and again on your own. It is not science. Science can create scriptures, theories, but religion cannot create scriptures and theories. It is a lived experience. You cannot reduce it to a theory, it is too subtle for that, too delicate for that. Theory is very rough, gross; experience is very subtle. Can any tightrope walker make a theory out of tightrope walking, just by understanding the theory? You can understand the theory perfectly, you can be examined and you can get a hundred percent mark. But do you think that you will be able to walk on that tightrope just because you have understood the theoretical background of it? No, it won't help. It is not a science. And I say to you, it is not even art – because art can be imitated; knack can never be imitated. Art is something you do outside of you: you paint a picture, you make a poem, you dance, you do something which is visible, which can be imitated. Even Picasso can be imitated.

But religion can never be imitated; it is nothing outside, it is something within. You can imitate a Picasso, a Michelangelo, but how can you imitate a Lao Tzu? You feel something is there but it is elusive. You know that he knows something but you cannot pinpoint it, you cannot figure it out. It is a knack.

Then what is a knack? A knack comes when you do many, many things on the path: trial and error, falling and rising, going astray and coming back, thousands of experiments in living and then suddenly one day you have the knack of it. A knack is the essence of many errors, mistakes, of trial and error. Something grows in you, and once you know it you can forget about it, you have it always. You need not remember it. If you need to remember it, it is still not a knack, it is something in the mind. If it is a knack it goes into the blood, into the bones, into the very marrow, into the very being. Then you can forget about it.

A Lao Tzu has not to remember how he has to walk, how he has to be. It is not a discipline. Once you know, you know. You can forget, you can simply drop it out of the mind. But you will follow it, you will follow it without knowing it. A knack is neither science nor art, it is a lived experience. And this is the greatest art or the greatest science – the science of life or the art of life.

You have to walk in life and see how you fall; you have to watch yourself and observe how you go astray. The mind will insist on going to the very extreme. Whenever you feel an imbalance immediately balance it by moving to the opposite.

Mind is either a rightist: it moves toward the right then it never moves to the left; or mind is a leftist, then it moves to the left and never moves to the right. And I have come across a very strange phenomenon, sometimes mind becomes a middlist – remains in the middle but as fanatic about the middle as others are about right and left. But this man is not in the middle because a man who is in the middle is never fanatic. Only extremists are fanatics, they cling to a certain position. The middle is not a position, it is a constant gaining of balance.

Try to understand. This is the most meaningful feeling that Tao can give to you. The middle is not a fixed state, it is a constantly changing movement. So you cannot be in the middle like the man who can be on the left or on the right. You cannot cling to the middle. One who wants to be in the middle will constantly have to lean toward the right and left; sometimes you will see he is a leftist, and sometimes you will see – now, look – he has become a rightist. He has to walk like a tightrope walker. Only between these two extremes: balancing constantly, continuously, is the middle.

The middle is an alive situation, it is not a fixed and dead point that you achieve forever – no. Moment to moment you have to achieve it, again and again and again. Watch a tightrope walker; it is an experience.

In my childhood, whenever I heard about a tightrope walker anywhere, in my village or in the neighboring villages, I would run and watch, because from the very beginning I felt that he knew something which was very, very significant for life.

What is he doing? He is not statically in the middle, otherwise he will fall. He is never for a single moment static. He is dynamic, constantly changing, a flux, but the flux has a balancing center. Sometimes he moves to the left, sometimes to the right; he is very contradictory, he is not consistent. If you ask for consistency he will fall and die. If you say, "Stick to one situation, to one position. If you are a rightist, be a rightist; if you are a leftist, be a leftist; or if you have chosen the middle as your position, then be in the middle. But what are you doing? You are constantly moving" – you will kill him. Any static position kills. To be static is to die, and die uselessly. To be static is to miss life. No, he cannot remain in the middle. To remain in the middle – he cannot remain in the middle – to remain in the middle he has to constantly move and balance. Every moment life is changing, how can you remain fixed? Every moment everything is changing. Nothing is static.

Heraclitus says: "You cannot step in the same river twice." By the time you come to step in the river twice, the river has changed. And not only has the river changed, you have changed. How can you step twice in the river? Neither the river remains the same nor you. Nothing remains the same. Sameness is illusion. Flux is reality. In such a changing world, in such an alive world, vibrating with life, if you cling to a position you are dead, you are seeking suicide.

That's why all those who have reached and concluded are dead. If you have concluded that you are a Hindu you are dead. If you have concluded that you are a Mohammedan you are dead – because sometimes a Hindu needs to lean toward the Mohammedan to gain balance, and sometimes a Mohammedan needs to be a Hindu to gain balance.

Balance is life. If you have decided that you are a Communist you are dead. To remain alive even the Communist needs to lean toward the capitalist and the capitalist to lean toward the Communist. Life is not as clear-cut as thinking. Thinking is very linear, life is maddening.

I have heard one anecdote, not written by a Taoist but the anecdote is Taoist – knowingly or unknowingly, the man has brought Taoism into it. It is a German anecdote.

It happened once...

A small chicken was sitting in the hen house, absolutely Buddha-like, not a single worry in the world. Then suddenly a man appeared. She became afraid, she ran away. When she came back the man had gone but there was some corn just before the hen house. She started brooding, thinking. A scientific curiosity came to her mind. From where had this corn come?

Then again the next day the man appeared. She again ran away, came back. The man had gone, but again the corn was there. Certainly there was some relationship between the man and the corn. But it was too early for a scientific thinker to come to a conclusion. She didn't want to commit to a theory so soon, in such a haste. So she waited – she must have really been a scientist. She waited and waited and waited and every day it happened.

Then by and by the theory became materialized in her small mind that there was a cause-and-effect relationship: whenever the man appeared the corn appeared. Nine hundred and ninety-nine times she watched. Now it was absolutely certain – there was a cause–effect relationship. When the man appeared, the corn appeared. The man was the cause, the corn was the effect.

Nine hundred and ninety-nine times was enough. She concluded now that there was a necessary relationship. And she had waited and experimented, watched and observed enough – now she could say that without exception it happened. So it must be a law. She was very happy and waited for the man. He appeared for the thousandth time.

The chicken went to the man to thank him for his kindness – and had her head wrung.

Life is like that. It has no cause-effect relationship. Even if something appears for nine hundred ninety-nine times don't conclude; the thousandth time may be the exception.

And this is not only a story. Now in scientific circles a philosophy of uncertainty is arising and gaining hold. After Heisenberg, science is not as certain as it used to be before. Now they say everything is uncertain, and certainty is just approximately certain – not absolutely certain. Nine hundred and ninety-nine times, okay – but then comes the exception. Even science is shaken. It has to be shaken because it also deals with life. Life cannot be reduced to a scientific cause-and-effect relationship. Life remains mysterious.

To remain in the middle, if you stick to the middle you will miss. This is the mystery of life. To remain in the middle you have to be constantly moving toward the left and right. Only then can you remain, because the middle is not a fixed point. The middle in fact is nothing outside you. The middle is something inside you: a balance, a music, a harmony.

Lao Tzu says: "Beware of the extreme." Don't go to the extreme, otherwise you will fall. Everything on the extreme changes to its opposite.

If you are in love and twenty-four hours a day you are after your lover, and you move to the extreme as lovers do, everything will be destroyed. You will destroy love yourself, because it is too much. It becomes unbearable.

You cannot love for twenty-four hours a day. Loving for twenty-four hours a day is like a man eating for twenty-four hours a day. Love is food. You should not move to the extreme, otherwise food can become poison. That is how things turn to their opposite. Food nourishes, but eat too much and food becomes poison, it kills. That which was a nourishment becomes a poison and a killer. Love is a nourishment; do it too much, overdo it, and it kills. And only hatred is left. Do anything too much and you will find the opposite of it has happened.

Be after money too much and in the end you will find you are a beggar, empty. You have missed a whole life and the very point of it. You missed all the enrichments that life could have given to you because you were too much after riches. Be after happiness and move to the extreme and you will be the most unhappy man in the world. To be happy one need not go after happiness too much. Sometimes one has to forget about it; sometimes one has even to enjoy unhappiness. To be happy, I am saying sometimes one has to enjoy unhappiness also. That too is part of life – and beautiful. This is how the balance is maintained. If you are laughing twenty-four hours a day, your laughter will become neurotic. It will no longer be a laughter – you will go mad. To keep laughter alive and sane, tears are also needed. You cannot laugh twenty-four hours a day.

Watch children, because they are pure beings and they reflect things absolutely clearly; they are mirrorlike. In the villages, if a child laughs too much mothers say, "Don't laugh too much, otherwise you will weep." There is some wisdom in it. If a child laughs too much he is bound to weep. You can see – he is laughing, he is laughing, he is laughing – and suddenly he has started crying. The laughter came to the extreme and became crying.

You cannot be happy twenty-four hours a day; unhappiness is a relaxation. You cannot be unhappy for twenty-four hours; happiness is a relaxation. It is tightrope walking. And man is foolish because man is too logical.

You live in the world as a *grihastha*, as a householder. Then for twenty-four hours a day you live in the world; not for even one hour in twenty-four are you out of it – in meditation, in prayerfulness, in isolation, alone, enjoying just yourself, not bothering about the world and worldly things – no. Then one day you get fed up with it. It is bound to be so, it is going to happen; if you remain a householder twenty-four hours a day, one day you will get fed up, you have come to the extreme. Then you renounce and run away to the Himalayas.

I have watched: people who run away to the Himalayas are per-fect householders. Perfect, I say. They did too much, they overdid it. And when you overdo, the other extreme is bound to be born. It takes revenge. A man who was too much in the world, just accumulating riches, money, a bank balance, suddenly feels frustrated. He laughed too much, now tears are flowing. He escapes. He renounces, he becomes a sannyasin, goes to the Himalayas, moves to the caves. What has happened to this man? – you think a revolution? It is nothing like that. It is just a natural phenomenon; he was too much in the world, now he has to become just the opposite. And now twenty-four hours a day he will try to be a sannyasin – now again the same foolishness. One day he is bound to come to the marketplace again. Twenty-four hours a day he tried to be a householder – he could not be; now he is doing the same stupid thing again, for twenty-four hours a day he is trying to be a sannyasin.

Life is a rhythm. You breathe in, you breathe out. You cannot only go on breathing in, breathing in, breathing in – you will die. You cannot go on breathing out, breathing out, breathing out – you will die. You have to breathe in and breathe out, and you have to keep a balance. The same amount of breath going in has to come out, then you are healthy. The life of the world is in-breathing and the life of a sannyasin is out-breathing. They both have to be together.

People come to me and they ask, "What type of sannyasins are you creating? We have never heard of this. What type of sannyas is this? People are living in their houses, they are doing their business, they go to the office, work in the factory, they have wives and children. What type of sannyas is this? We have never heard about it." Yes you have never heard about it. But this is the only sannyas that is right, this is the only sannyas that is balanced. This is the only sannyas which has a harmony of in-breathing and out-breathing.

And the greatest possibility of attaining peaks of bliss is possible only when in-breathing and out-breathing are completely balanced. You are not leaning to any side too much – suddenly you are beyond both. Lao Tzu says:

Stretch a bow to the very full,
and you will wish you had stopped in time.

Because the bow will break. Stretch a bow to the full – it could have served you for long if you had been a little alert. Never stretch a bow to the full because fullness is always death. Life doesn't want anything perfect, because with perfection evolution stops. Perfection is death; imperfection is life. Life loves imperfection. Become perfect and you are useless, life will throw you into the rubbish heap, you are no longer needed. Remain imperfect, and you will be alive and life will support you from everywhere. That's why perfection is not the goal for Lao Tzu or for me – but totality.

You can be total without being perfect and you can be perfect without being total. In fact, you can only be perfect if you are not total, because perfection will choose either the right or the left; then you become a perfect rightist, or you become a perfect leftist, or you become a perfect middler. But perfection means you are fixed; perfection means no change moves within you; perfection means now you are frozen, not flowing. And perfection is always partial.

The greatest of men have never been perfect, they have been total. Total means they have everything in them, but they are not just the sum total of everything. They are more than that sum total. They have everything in them, and then a harmony arises which is beyond, beyond everything that they have. They are not just an arithmetical total, they are an artistic total. A poem is more than all the words in it – it has to be, otherwise it would be simply words. A painting is more than all the colors in it – it has to be, otherwise what type of painting is it?

It happened once...

An American wanted to have a portrait painted by Picasso. He knew that Picasso would ask a fantastic price but he could give it, he had enough. So they didn't decide the price first. He asked and Picasso did the portrait. When it was ready Picasso really asked a fantastic price. Even the American could not believe that for such a small portrait, just a small piece of canvas with a few colors on it – ten thousand dollars?

The American said, "It seems a little too much, even for me. What is there in it worth ten thousand dollars?"

Picasso said, "What do you see?"

He said, "I see a piece of canvas and a few colors."

Picasso said, "Okay. Bring ten thousand dollars or whatsoever you want."

He said, "I will give you five thousand dollars."

When he brought five thousand dollars, Picasso gave him not the portrait but a piece of canvas and a few tubes of colors. And he said, "You take it. This is all you wanted."

A portrait is more than a piece of canvas, more than a few

colors – because it is a harmony. And when Picasso paints something it is a great harmony. The price is not for the color and the canvas, the price is for the harmony that he has brought to the colors and the canvas – something that transcends.

When a man is total he has all; left, right, middle and all other positions in between. He has all, the whole range. He is a rainbow. The whole range of colors are in him, but he is more than that range – he is a harmony of them. That harmony is a constantly changing phenomenon; you have to attain it again and again and again. And that is the beauty of it because then it is never old, never boring, never flat, never stale. Each moment it arises out of nothingness, each moment it is fresh like the morning dew. It is ever-fresh.

A Lao Tzu lives in an ever-freshness, an ever-greenness. If he had attained something, attained it forever, guaranteed – then it would become stale. Then dust would gather on it, then the past would gather on it and sooner or later one would be feeling bored with it and one would like to throw it away. Even enlightenment, if you are not gaining it again and again, will become a boring phenomenon – the same. You will feel fed up with it.

Stretch a bow to the very full,
and you will wish you had stopped in time.

Don't *stretch a bow to the very full...* If you are laughing, it is better to smile than to laugh because a smile never brings tears, only laughter. Or if you laugh, keep balance. Don't go to the very extreme. Remain on plain ground, otherwise sooner or later you will be thrown to the other extreme and then you will suffer. When you are happy, keep control; don't be too happy. There is no need. Smile in happiness, don't laugh; keep quiet about it, then happiness can stay for a long time. If you know the knack of it, it can stay forever.

A smile can stay forever – not laughter. So you can find a buddha smiling but not laughing. He knows the art of how to keep balance. Love, be nourished by it, nourish the other by it, feel ecstatic, but don't go mad. Otherwise sooner or later you will finish everything. Sooner or later everything will turn into hatred. Lovers can become enemies very easily; in fact, how can you make an enemy unless first you make him a friend? And the deeper the friendship the deeper will be the enmity if it ever comes. You cannot create an enemy without creating friendship first. Friendship seems to be the first requirement.

If you move in too much, if you come too close, you will create enmity. Never go too close. Always keep a little distance. Kahlil Gibran in his wonderful book *The Prophet* says, "Lovers should be like pillars of a temple, supporting the same roof, but not too close to each other." Like pillars. If they come too close, the whole temple will fall; if they go too far away, then too the whole temple will fall. They cannot come too close; they cannot go too far. They should be like pillars of a temple, supporting the same roof.

This is the art, the knack. If you want your love to be eternal, don't come too close, because if you come too close then the need to go far away arises. If you come too close then you trespass on each other's freedom – and everybody needs a space of his own. Love is beautiful when it co-exists with your space; if it starts trespassing on your space then it becomes poisonous. And lovers always behave foolishly and stupidly. When they are in love they don't listen to anything; they try to come too close and then they destroy their love. Had they been a little wiser, they would not have come too close and then they would have remained close forever.

Bernard Shaw has said somewhere, "By the time a man becomes wise in love, his life has gone." Very old people become wise in love, but then the possibility of love is gone. Bernard Shaw says, "I always wonder why God wastes youth on young people." It should be given to old people, who are wiser, who have lived, known and attained a balance – but God goes on wasting youth on young people.

In everything this should be the golden rule: always keep balance. An imbalanced being cannot exist in life; life does not allow imbalance. The more balanced you are the more life gives to you; the less balanced you are – you become a beggar on your own accord. Life cannot give to you.

Stretch a bow to the very full, and you will wish you had stopped in time. Just a few days ago I was reading a German poet. In his introduction he writes, "Had Hitler known this sentence of Lao Tzu: *Stretch a bow to the very full, and you will wish you had stopped in time...*" Hitler was successful, but he did not know Lao Tzu. People like Hitler never do.

Stretch a bow... Now Indira has stretched the bow too much. Don't succeed too much, otherwise you will fail. You have heard the proverb, that nothing fails like failure; that is not true. I will tell you the right proverb: Nothing fails like success.

If you go on succeeding you are bound to fail. There is a limit to everything. If you go on succeeding, a moment comes suddenly – flop – and everything goes beyond your control. Take everything in measure. If you are succeeding don't be in a hurry and don't move to the very end, because after success nothing is left, only failure.

Always take everything in homeopathic doses. Allopathy is good, but allopathic doses are not good. And be alert: are you moving to the very limit of a thing? If you are moving to the very limit you are moving to the opposite in fact. *Stretch a bow to the very full, and you will wish you had stopped in time.* Because you will break it.

Temper a sword-edge to its very sharpest,
and the edge will not last long.

Only balance lasts, nothing else, and balance is the most difficult thing in existence, in life, because balance needs tremendous wisdom.

It happened...

Lao Tzu's disciple, Chuang Tzu, lived in a town for many years. Then one day, suddenly, he told his disciples, "We are leaving."

They said, "But what has happened that you are leaving? We don't see any point. Why should we go to another town? Everything is good, everything settled, comfortable. In fact, now we have been able to make everything comfortable and you are moving again. What has happened?"

Chuang Tzu said, "Now people have started to know me, my fame is spreading. And when there is fame one should be alert, because soon these same people will defame me. Before they start defaming me I should leave this town."

A moment comes when fame becomes defame, when success becomes failure. Remember always to remain in the middle. A constant alertness is needed, otherwise the tendency of the mind is to think that when you are succeeding why not succeed a little more? The mind says, "When you are succeeding why not try a

little more?" And you see that the road is clear and nobody is bar-
ring the way – why not try a little more? The mind goes on; mind
is obsessive. Whatsoever it gets, it becomes obsessive about it. If
it is success mad, has success mania, then it goes obsessively
after success – until it fails. Unless it fails it will not take a rest. It
goes on and on and on.

Try to understand the nature of the mind: it is obsession. If you
do something the mind goes on doing it twenty-four hours a day, it
won't give you rest. It is like a demon – it will not allow you rest. And
rest is needed.

Do, but don't do too much, otherwise the same energy will
become the undoing.

Temper a sword-edge to its very sharpest,
and the edge will not last long.
When gold and jade fill your hall,
you will not be able to keep them safe.

When everything is too much, it is bound to be taken away.
It happened once...

A follower of Lao Tzu was made a judge. The first case that came
before him in the court was about a thief. The thief had confessed
that he had stolen. The case was clear – the thief had confessed, the
things had been found – but the follower of Lao Tzu took a very, very
strange approach and attitude to the case. He jailed the thief for
six months and he also jailed the man from whom he had stolen
the things.

Of course the rich man could not believe it. What nonsense! His
things had been stolen and he was being sentenced – for what?

The disciple of Lao Tzu said, "Because you have gathered too
much. Now if I go to the very root of the problem you have provoked this man to steal. In the whole village people are poor, almost
starving, and you go on piling up riches. There is a limit to everything. So if I look, who is the real criminal? – then you are the real
criminal. You started the whole thing first. This thief is just a victim.
I know that he couldn't control himself, that is his fault. But you
accumulated too much, and when riches accumulate too much with
one man, the society cannot remain moral. Thieves will bubble up,

robberies will happen, murders will happen. All sorts of immoralities will happen – they are bound to happen."

Nobody listened. The judge was removed from his post. The emperor said, "This is too much. This man is dangerous. Someday he will catch me – because if he goes to even deeper roots, he will find me. This man has to be removed."

But Lao Tzu has to be heard. He touches the very nerve of the whole disease: if you gather too much it will be stolen, it will be unsafe.

Remain in the limits, remain balanced. Too much poverty is bad, too much richness is bad – too much is bad. In fact for Lao Tzu too much is the only sin. Don't do too much, don't overdo, and then life is a flow. And life is moral.

To be proud with wealth and honor
is to sow the seeds of one's own downfall.

It happens every day but you are blind so you cannot see. It happens every day, everywhere. Every day you see your politicians in this country – in every country – they are too egoistic, too filled with their own ego. Then reactions start. Then somebody throws a shoe and somebody throws a stone and then people start to disrespect them.

A balance has to be created. If you feel that your ego is supreme, then somebody is bound to come from somewhere to pull you down to your right size. Somebody else is needed – because you could not remain in control by yourself. And life always creates balance, because imbalance is an ill state of affairs. If in a country politicians are too egoistic and they ask for too much respect, soon disrespect will come in. Soon there will be rebellion, soon there will be revolution, soon everything will be destroyed. All codes of morality, respect, manner will be destroyed.

Politicians should not ask too much respect; they should come a little lower, within the limits. Then nobody, nobody bothers to throw stones at them. Why? There is no question. In the old days rich men never showed their riches, they lived as ordinarily as everybody else. Even kings and emperors used to come to beggars like Buddha and Mahavira to pay their respects. They were always honored. There was a balance. Now the balance is completely lost. No politician bothers to pay respect to anybody. He becomes supreme when he is in power.

He trespasses the limit, then he has to be pulled down by his leg. Then somebody somewhere else arises. That is simply a balance. Always remember life is never unjust. If it looks unjust then you must have done something wrong. Somewhere you must have gone beyond the balance; then life seems to be unjust. Otherwise life is never unjust. And whenever you feel the injustice it is better to look at yourself; you have done something wrong and you have been punished. In fact, people have been thinking for millennia that sins are punished, but I say to you that sins are not punished. Sins are the punishment. When you say sins are punished you have time to wait. Maybe they will be punished in the next life – who bothers? We will see in the next life. You can postpone. But I say to you that sins are the punishment, they are not punished somewhere in the future.

Sins carry their punishment in themselves. Punishment is intrinsic to every sin. It is not a result somewhere in the future. It is not that you sow today and you reap tomorrow – no. There is no time gap. You sin and immediately you are punished, immediately the punishment has started. Here you sin and here immediately the punishment starts – you feel ugly and you feel sad and you feel guilty, and a turmoil and a chaos arise inside and you are unhappy and in hell. Hell is not somewhere in the future, neither is heaven. Each act carries its own heaven or hell.

Remain balanced and you are in heaven; become unbalanced and a hell is created – nobody else is creating it for you.

Lao Tzu has no God, no personal God to punish anybody. It is simply Tao. Tao is just a law, a universal law. If you move according to it you are happy, if you move against it you become unhappy. In fact, unhappiness is a symptom, just as happiness is a symptom – a symptom of how you are moving: according to Tao or against Tao.

When you are moving according to Tao you are happy, blissful, celebrating. Every moment is a joy, a delight. Life seems like poetry. Every moment you see something flowering, growing; every moment you see a thousand things to be grateful for. You are blessed.

Life is a benediction if you follow, move, according to the law. And the law is of balance. If you move against it, if you go contrary to the law, suddenly you lose balance. Happiness disappears; you become unhappy, you become sad, miserable. A hell is created. Hell is just a symptom. Don't try to fight with it. Just try to understand where you have moved against the law, that's all – and then move

back, gain balance. Whenever you are sad don't try to change sadness. Don't try to do anything with it; sadness is symptomatic. It
simply shows that somewhere you have gone against the law. Find
the balance again. Maybe you need a turning. Maybe you need to
lean a little more toward left or right so the balance is gained again.
And this has to be done continuously.

People come to me and they say, "If we meditate and if we succeed will silence and peace remain forever and forever?" They are
asking a stupid question. Then meditation would be a dead thing –
like a stone, not like a flower. And meditation is not like a stone, not
even like a plastic flower. It is a real lotus. It blooms. It changes. With
the sun it opens, in the night it closes. There is a continuous balance,
and you have to find the balance every moment. Meditation is not
something you do once and you are done with. It is something that is
like breathing, like blood circulating. It is not that once the blood has
circulated it is finished, once you breathe there is no more need of it.
No, you have to breathe and you have to go on meditating; every
moment you will need it.

By and by it will become natural, that is right. By and by you will
go less and less against the law. When the knack is found, the very
moment your step is going against the law you will see the hell and
you will move back. You will come back to the path, you will not
go astray.

> *To be proud with wealth and honor*
> *is to sow the seeds of one's own downfall.*
> *Retire when your work is done,*
> *such is heaven's way.*

Retire when your work is done... When you see that a work has
given you balance, that you have attained happiness, don't ask for
more; when you feel good don't ask for more; when you are surrounded by a well-being don't ask for more. Retire, enjoy it. Revel in it.
Dance with it. Don't ask for more. The mind is always asking for more.

The mind says, "Okay, this is good, that I am feeling a certain
well-being, but more is possible. So first I should attain the more."
Then you miss that which was possible; that which had already
become actual, you miss. And if you listen to this mind, which goes
on for more and for more and for more, it will lead you to the end,

to the extreme. And suddenly you fall into hell, and you are miserable, unhappy.

Whatsoever you gain, make it a criterion: if you are feeling good, if you are feeling well, if you are feeling blissful, silent, peaceful, a certain delight around you, life has become a song for this moment – then sing it! Don't ask for more. Chew it, absorb it. Don't ask for more. Retire, that is the meaning of retire. Now stop further efforts – enough! You have gained, now let it be, enjoy it. Live it! And then you will see: a different dimension comes to your being.

There are two dimensions. One is horizontal: more, more, more – that is the horizontal dimension. You move in a line. You are on the point A; you want to be on the point B. When you are on the point B, you want to be on the point C. Soon you will reach to XYZ. And from Z is hell, Z is the door of hell. But you cannot stop, the mind goes on. The mind says, "Look, you are on C, and D is possible. So why waste time on C, go to D. Then E becomes possible, so go to E." No moment to enjoy, no moment to celebrate, no moment to retire and be. Doing, doing – never being, because being means that C is enough, now enjoy it. You have earned the bread for today – now retire. But the mind says, "What about the safe in the bank? It is still half-filled. You have to fill it completely."

In India they call it the vicious circle of the ninety-nine. They have a story:

A poor barber was very happy, tremendously happy, as sometimes only poor people can be. He had nothing to worry about. He was the barber to the royal king; he used to massage him, to trim his hair, to serve him every day.

Even the king was jealous and he always asked him, "What is the secret of your happiness? You are always bubbling. You seem not to be walking on the earth, you are simply moving on the wing. What secret is there?"

The poor barber said, "I don't know. In fact I have never heard the word *secret* before. What do you mean? I am simply happy. I earn my bread and that's all, and then I retire." He must have been a Lao Tzuan.

Then the king asked his vizier, his prime minister – and he was a man of knowledge, a very, very knowledgeable man. He asked him, "You must know the secret of this barber. I am a great king. I am not so happy, but this poor man, having nothing, is so happy."

The prime minister said, "He does not know anything about the vicious circle of ninety-nine."

The king said, "What is this?"

The vizier laughed and said, "You are in it but you don't know it. We will do one thing. Tonight we will throw a bag containing ninety-nine rupee coins into the barber's house, and then see what happens."

They threw a bag containing ninety-nine rupees into the house.

The next day the barber was in hell. He became very sad and worried; in fact, he didn't sleep the whole night. He counted the rupees in the bag again and again – ninety-nine. And he was so excited; how to sleep when you are excited? The heart was throbbing, the blood was circulating; there must have been a high blood pressure, an excitement. And he tossed and turned, and he could not sleep. He would get up again, touch those golden rupees, count again. He had never had the experience of counting rupees and ninety-nine was the trouble – because when you have ninety-nine you want them to be a hundred. So he was planning what to do the next day to get one rupee.

One golden rupee was a difficult thing to get. He was getting only a few paisa, and they were enough in those days. How to get one rupee? – because one rupee, one golden rupee meant almost one month's earning. What to do? He planned many ways – a poor man, not knowing much about money, he got into trouble. He could think of only one thing: that he would fast for one day and eat for one day. This way, by and by, he could accumulate one rupee. And a hundred rupees would be good. Mind has a stupidity: to complete things. Mind is a perfectionist. Ninety-nine? The obsession is created: they must be a hundred.

He was sad. Next day he came – he was not flying in the sky, he was deeply on the earth – not only deeply on the earth, but a great burden, a stone-like thing hanging around his neck.

The king asked, "What is the matter with you? You look so worried."

He said nothing because he didn't want to talk about the bag. But every day the situation grew worse and worse. He could not massage well – he had no energy, fasting.

So the king said, "What are you doing? Now you don't seem to have any energy. And you look so sad and miserable. What has happened?"

So one day he had to tell the king; the king insisted, "Tell me, I can be of help. Just tell me what is the matter."

He said, "I am now a victim of the vicious circle of ninety-nine."

When you have ninety-nine there is a vicious circle – you want them to be a hundred. This is the horizontal line. And don't think that when they are a hundred, things will stop. Things never stop. Mind does not know where to stop. It knows no stopping. That's why it falls. It goes without stopping anywhere, from A to B, from B to C, and goes on and on until at Z it falls into hell.

Then there is another way of life: the vertical – not horizontal. You don't move from A to B, from B to C – no. You don't move in a line, on the same plane, on the same level – no. You move from A to A1 to A2 to A3 in a vertical line, in depth. You move into the depth of the A. Whatsoever is in the moment you move deep into it – not from this moment to the next, but in this very moment you move as deeply as possible. And then even one moment becomes eternity. And your happiness grows, knows no bounds. Your bliss grows, knows no bounds. And there is never an imbalance. You are always balanced. A vertical mind is always balanced because a vertical mind is no more a mind.

The whole effort of meditation is to give you a vertical mind. A vertical mind virtually means no-mind. Then you move from A to A1, A2, A3 in depth, or in height vertically. When B comes, again you move from B1 to B2, B3. You never fall from anywhere because you always go into the depth. This is what retirement is. You have earned the bread today, now retire.

But you don't know how to retire; you go on earning the bread in your dreams also. You lie down and you plan for tomorrow, and nobody knows whether tomorrow is going to come or not. In fact it never comes. It is always today. You are planning for the future, not knowing that death will destroy all future. Remain in the moment – be wise. Live it as totally as possible and then you will know no death. Because a man who is not worried about tomorrow knows no death – he becomes deathless. Because death is tomorrow – life is today.

Death is in the future, life is always in the present – this is the meaning of retire. If you want me to translate this word *retire* I will call it sannyas. You have not to retire at the end of life; retire every day, retire every moment. When you have enjoyed a moment it is retirement, it is through retirement, it is sannyas.

When you come back from the office to your house, leave the office in the office. Don't carry it in your head, otherwise the head will have a headache – bound to have. Such a big thing, the office, you carry in your head. It is heavy. The whole market in your head – it is heavy. Falibhai goes to the stock market. He knows. You can carry the stock market in your head; then it is madness. But he never carries it; he has learned how to retire in it.

Retirement every day, retirement every moment. The very word *retirement* does not look good to us; it gives the feeling of old age, inability. Somewhere beyond sixty-five, when death comes near, then one retires. No, the word *retire* is very beautiful. It is the meaning of sannyas. *Retire* means rest: the work is done, now retire, enjoy it. Don't postpone enjoyment, that is the meaning of the word *retire*. Enjoy here and now.

Retire when your work is done, such is heaven's way. That is Tao. Never go to the extreme, the work is always done within the limits. Remain in the limits, enclosed in the limits. That is the discipline, the discipline of a sannyasin – always remaining in the middle, always remaining within limits, always remaining satisfied, not hankering after more and more and more.

Drop the horizontal line; move into the vertical. Retire, and you will be fulfilled. You will know the greatest fulfillment that life can give you. That is a deep moment of total balance, tranquility. We have called it enlightenment, liberation, *moksha*, nirvana – or you name it.

Enough for today.

there is no meaning

The first question:

Osho,
You have said that every gesture from a master is significant, and
often the answer is given in what is not said rather than what is
said. But often when you look or glance at me, and I feel there is a
message, I do not know how to identify the message without using
my mind. And even when I do use my mind I am not sure.

The mind cannot be used. Once you use the mind you have
missed the point. Silence has to be understood in silence; a
no-word message is to be understood wordlessly. If you try to
understand through words and through mind you will miss it, you
will misunderstand it. Then your own mind has come in. Then you will
interpret it. Then it will not be pure, it will not be the same.

And if you ask, "Then what to do?" you ask a wrong question.
The question of how arises from the mind. There is no question of
how. Be silent. Don't do anything, don't try to interpret it, don't try in
any way to interfere with it – let it spread over your being. You may
not be able to identify it right now because it is vaster than the mind

and all identifications are from the mind. You may not be able to know exactly what it is, but there is no need. You may not be able to decipher, decode the meaning of it, but there is no need. Let the wordless message reach to your wordless center. It is a deep contact, and the contact is the meaning. It is a deep penetration, and the penetration is the meaning.

You pass by a rosebush and you look at a roseflower. What is the meaning? If you start thinking about the roseflower, the mind enters and the roseflower is lost. Then the mind creates a wall of words, thoughts, concepts and then you cannot even see the roseflower there.

Don't try to find the meaning. Meaning and a constant obsession with meaning is a disease of the mind. What is the meaning of a rose? There is no meaning. It flowers without any meaning. It needs no meaning to justify itself, it is justified in its being. Just let it be, and be with it. Let the rose penetrate you, let the rose spread its fragrance around you and within you and suddenly something stirs within your being – something has arisen. The rose has done something in you. Even then you may not be able to know what the rose has done, but you will feel happier, blissful; you will feel there has been a contact with the unknown. You will feel that you have been given an opportunity to look into the unknown. You will feel that the rose has become a window and a vast sky has opened – there has been a crack in the wall of your mind, and a ray of light penetrated. Don't bother about the meaning.

When I am looking at you, simply look at me. When I am giving you my being, give your being to me. Be available, let it be a contact. It is not a communication, it is a communion. I am not communicating a certain message which can be deciphered, decoded – no. I am giving myself to you in that gesture. It is bigger than any meaning that can be given to it and you are also bigger. If the contact happens, you will feel that boundaries have dissolved. For a moment you were not there. For a moment you were possessed by me – and not only by me but, through me, by the whole. So whenever I look at you, whenever I want to penetrate into your eyes, whenever I knock at your door, at your heart, open the doors.

Don't try to find the meaning. In finding the meaning you will miss the meaning, because the contact is the meaning, a deep inner embrace is the meaning.

The second question:

Osho,
My mind is in such a state of confusion that it is impossible to
remain in the middle. Wouldn't it be better to follow the mind in all
its extremes so that I can experience the whole absurdity of it?

The first part of the question: "My mind is in such a state of confusion that it is impossible to remain in the middle."

I am not saying that you should remain in the middle. If you try
to remain in the middle you will never be in the middle. The middle
is a balance, you cannot try to be there. You will have to lean to the
left, you will have to lean to the right. Don't cling to any position. Be
free. And between leaning to the left and leaning to the right, somewhere a subtle point arises in you. It is not outside of you. If you go
to look outside there is left and right, there is no middle.

It is just like time. Space and time are together. Try to understand. If you look at the clock there is past and there is future, there
is no present. Your clock never says what the present is – it cannot
say, because the moment it has said it, it is already the past. So the
hands of the clock move from the past to the future; there is no
present in your clock – cannot be. Present is not part of time. You
have learned in your schools and your universities that the present is
part of time; that is absurd. Present is not part of time. You have
heard it repeated so many times that time is divided into three
tenses: past, present and future; that it has become a conditioning in
your mind. No. Time has only two divisions: past and future.

Then where is the present? The present is in you. If you look out,
you will find past and future; if you look in, you will find the present
and always the present. There is no past and no future – there cannot
be. Move inward and you move into the eternity of the present; move
outward and either you move into the past or you move into the future.

The same is true about space – in space there is either left
or right. If you lean toward the left it is outside, if you lean toward the
right it is also outside. But if you gain a balance between the two,
suddenly you are in. The middle point is within you, it is not a part of
space outside. In fact, the present and the middle are together.
Whenever you are in the present you are in the middle, whenever
you are in the middle you are in the present. The middle is not a

position outside you. It is an inner phenomenon just like the present. So when I say or Lao Tzu says, "Be balanced," we are not saying make balance a static phenomenon in your life. It cannot be static, you will have to continuously maintain it, moving to the left and the right. In that movement sometimes you will pass the innermost point of your being and suddenly you will be in the middle. And suddenly you will find an implosion, not an explosion. Implosion. Something inside implodes; suddenly you are no longer the same. Whenever you pass the position of the middle inside, you are no longer the same – you become intensely alive, you become intensely innocent, you become intensely pure and holy. In that moment there exists no darkness for you, no sin, no guilt. You are divine, you are godliness whenever you can find that balance. But you cannot find it once and for all – no. Life is always a constant balancing, a continuity, a continuum. You cannot make it a commodity that you purchased once and now it is always there in your house. No. If you are not aware you will miss it again and again.

This is the first part of your question: the middle is not a fixed point outside. You can reach it from either point, or try to gain a balance moment to moment between the opposites – hate in love, anger in compassion.

Go on balancing between the opposites. By and by you will come to feel the knack of it. Somewhere between hate and love it happens. I say "somewhere" – the point cannot be figured out; it is such an alive phenomenon that you cannot pinpoint it. It is just like butterflies flying in a garden, if you catch a butterfly and pin it down it is dead. You can pin it down but it is no longer a butterfly, the life has left it.

Just like a butterfly is the inner balance, you cannot pin it down. That's why it is indefinable, elusive. Lao Tzu says: "The Tao that can be said is no more Tao." The truth that can be uttered has already become untrue. Indian scriptures say "that" cannot be known by scriptures. *Nayam atma pravachanen labhya.* You cannot understand "that" by any verbal communication. "That" is elusive because it is so alive. By the time you reach it the butterfly has gone. Just go and see. Move in the garden: you come nearer and nearer and the butterfly is getting ready to take off. When you are nearly at the point of catching it, it has left the flower, it is already on another tree. You cannot pin it down. If you can, it is dead.

I was reading just yesterday one of the very perceptive poets of the West, Wallace Stevens. In one of his maxims he says Aristotle is a skeleton. I liked it. Logic is a skeleton. Logic is always of the dead, of death. It does not belong to life. Anything fixed is always dead. That's why I say marriage is a butterfly pinned down; love is an alive phenomenon.

You can define marriage, you cannot define love. Even a court can decide what marriage is or is not, but nobody can decide what love is. Marriage is legal; love transcends all legality – something of the unknown penetrates into love, into the phenomenon of love.

Inner balance cannot be pinned down, you will have to find the knack of it. And you can find it – because if I can find it, why not you? If Lao Tzu can find it, why not you? If one man finds the inner balance, the inner tranquility, the inner still small voice, the inner knack that passes all understanding, then every human being becomes capable of it. In Lao Tzu is your future, your possibility; you can also do it.

You say: "My mind is in such a state of confusion that it is impossible to remain in the middle." Don't try to remain in the middle, forget about the middle. Just try to be balanced. Move into the opposites but always remain alert so that someday you can find the balance between the two. And you are doing it – only awareness is needed. Just a moment before you were happy, then in another moment you are unhappy. You have moved to the opposite. You must have passed through the middle. How can you move to the opposite without passing through the middle? Maybe you passed it for only a fragment of a second, but that is not the point; you passed it. If you had been a little alert you would have known where the middle was. Just now you are so silent, then a single minute passes and your whole mind starts chattering. You must have passed the middle somewhere.

When a man dies he is alive just a moment before, then he is dead. If he is alert he will find the middle which is beyond death and life, which is deathless. But he is not alert. You have died many times; millions of times, in fact, you have passed the middle but you were not alert. And every day you pass the middle many times, thousands of times: compassion and anger; a man feeling so good and suddenly so bad, a man feeling so saintly in the morning. Look at people praying near the Ganges or in the temple, look at their faces, so beautiful. The ugliest faces become beautiful when there is prayerfulness. And then look at them in the market, even the most beautiful face looks ugly. They must have passed it somewhere – from the temple to the market there must have been a middle point – but they were not aware.

So what is to be done? Don't try to be in the middle. I'm not saying try a little anger and a little compassion together – no. I'm not saying try to be in the middle – you will go mad. I am saying move from one opposite to another, but move so alertly that you can find the middle point inside you. The moment you find the middle point, for the first time you become the master of your life. Up to now you have been just a slave. For the first time you become awake; up to now you have been fast asleep.

And the second part of the question: "Would not it be better to follow the mind in all its extremes so that I can experience the whole absurdity of it?" Nobody has ever been able to experience the whole absurdity of the mind. It is infinite. You will not be able to experience the whole of it; it is very creative, it goes on creating new absurdities. You have been here in this existence so long and yet you have not been able to experience the whole absurdity of it. You are not on this planet Earth for the first time, you have been here before. I can see your ancient faces hidden behind your fresh skin. You are ancient ones.

There was a teacher in Buddha's time in India; his name was Prakuddha Katyayana. He was a rare teacher. He always addressed his disciples as ancient ones. Even if a child came to see Prakuddha Katyayana he would say, "How are you, ancient one?" – because everyone is so old, older than the Earth. The Earth is not very old, just in fact very young, adolescent. But you are older than the Earth, you have been on other planets. You are older than the sun. You have been here since existence has been here, otherwise is not possible – you cannot suddenly bubble up. How can you happen so suddenly? You have been here all the way.

One of the most important American psychologists, William James, was writing a book which became a very important mile-stone in the history of psychology and religion. The name of the book is Varieties of Religious Experience. He traveled all around the world to collect material for the book. Many books have been written since then on religion, but no book has yet reached that peak. William James worked hard on it. He also came to India, he had to – if you are writing a book on religion then India becomes a must.

He came to India and he went to see a sage in the Himalayas. He does not give the name; in fact sages have no names, so there is no need. He went to see the sage and he asked a question. He had been reading an Indian scripture in which it is said that the Earth is supported on eight white elephants.

He was puzzled – he was a logician – so he asked the sage, "This looks absurd. On what are those eight elephants standing? How are they supported?"

The sage said, "On another eight white and bigger elephants."

William James said, "But that doesn't solve the problem. On what are those bigger white elephants standing?"

The sage laughed and he said, "Elephants on elephants, elephants on elephants, all the way down. You can go on asking," said the sage, "and I will go on answering the same thing – to the very bottom."

So William James thought that once more the question could be asked: "And on what is that bottom being supported?" The sage said, "Of course, eight bigger elephants."

It goes on and on – of course it has to be so. If you move backward you will find yourself again and again and again. Otherwise how could you be here? You are supported by your past life, that's why you are here. And your past life is supported by another past life, that's why you were in your past life. And this goes on and on and you cannot ask, "How did I come for the first time?" You never came for the first time because even before that you were. Even before the first time you were supported by a past life: elephants on elephants, elephants on elephants. Hindus are really beautiful. They create absurd stories, but those stories have deep meanings and significances. You are here only because the whole past – not your past, the whole past of existence – is supporting you. You are the whole past and yet you have not been able to exhaust all the absurdities. Do you think it will ever be possible to exhaust all the absurdities of the mind? No, nobody has ever been able to. If you become aware, even one day is enough. If you remain unaware, even millions of lives are not enough. If you become aware, even a single moment is enough to see the absurdity of the mind. And if you go on sleeping and snoring then you can go on sleeping and snoring. That's how you have been in the past, you can be the same in the future.

No, by sleeping you will never exhaust the absurdities of the mind. Don't hope; that is hopeless. That cannot be done. It is impossible.

Become alert. It is time, in fact it is already getting late. Become alert, and suddenly you can see – because absurdities cannot be exhausted by experiencing, they can only be exhausted by experiencing with awareness. By experience alone you will not be able to exhaust them.

You love one woman but the relationship becomes stale and everything goes wrong. Then you start thinking of another woman. The mind says, "This woman is not right for you, but there exists a right woman. Try to find her. You got hooked with the wrong woman, that's why the problem has arisen." The problem has not arisen because of this woman – remember. If you are alert you will see the problem has arisen because of desire, not because of this woman. But the mind says, "Leave this woman, divorce, move to another." And with another the same thing happens – the mind again says, "Find someone else." And you go on and on and on. And the mind will always hope that somebody will turn up someday and everything will be right, and you will be in heaven.

It has not happened, it is not going to happen. Otherwise there would be no need of religion, no need of Yoga, no need of Tao. By and by everybody would have come to the right life – but it never happens. But hope goes on winning over experience, and to the very end you go on hoping that someday, somehow, everything will be good.

Hope is the basis of all absurdities and the existence is such that with ignorance and a sleeping mind there is no hope. Become alert.

It happened...

Alexander was coming toward India. He met Diogenes on the way. Diogenes was a rare being – if Diogenes had met Lao Tzu, they would have both sat and laughed and laughed and laughed. They are of the same quality.

Alexander was passing. He heard that Diogenes was just nearby so he went to see him. Even Alexander was impressed by the man, even Alexander felt puny before him. Diogenes was a naked fakir, he had nothing, but his being was such – so magnetic, so powerful – that Alexander was impressed, very impressed. In fact it is said that he was never impressed again by any other man.

He asked the secret of it, "How have you become so powerful, not having anything? And I am a world conqueror, I have almost won the whole world. Just a little more is left; soon I will finish. And you – a naked man, having nothing – what is the secret of your happiness?"

Diogenes is reported to have said, "I renounced hope. That is the secret. And I tell you, you also renounce hope; otherwise you will always suffer."

Alexander said, "I will come to you to learn the secret, but not now. I am on the way – half the world, more than half the world I have won, but there is a remaining part. I have to become a world conqueror, then I will come."

Diogenes said, "Nobody has ever been a world conqueror. Something or other always remains to be done. The dream is never complete and the desire is never fulfilled. If you really understand me, and if you really see that I am happy without bothering about winning the whole world, then you can also be happy without it."

Logically, intellectually, Alexander understood it. But he said, "I will come later. This is not the right time for me."

When he was leaving Diogenes, Diogenes said, "Remember, you will die before you have conquered the world; everybody has died and you cannot be an exception."

And it happened. Alexander never reached back home. Returning from India, he died on the way. He must have remembered Diogenes, that naked fakir, in his last moments.

And then there has been another story; I cannot vouch for it. There is a story that on the same day Diogenes also died. And they met on the way to the other world, passing the river that flows between this world and that. They met on the river. Diogenes started laughing loudly, and he said, "Look, do you remember, you fool? You died, and you died in the middle, and the victory was not complete."

Just to save his face, Alexander also tried to laugh but he could not. Just to save his face he said, "Yes, this is strange, the meeting of an emperor and a naked beggar in this river. It may not have happened before, it may not happen again."

Diogenes laughed even more uproariously and he said, "You are right, but you don't understand who is the emperor and who is the slave. And who is the emperor and who is the beggar – that you don't know exactly. There you are wrong. Otherwise you are right, it is the meeting of an emperor and a beggar, but I am the emperor and you are the beggar. You were begging for the whole world – you are the biggest beggar ever. And I lived like an emperor, but look what has happened to your empire."

Now even Alexander was naked – because everything has to be

left on this shore – and he was feeling very shy and awkward, embarrassed. But Diogenes was not embarrassed. He said, "Knowing this well, that someday one has to become naked, I threw away those clothes myself. Now look how embarrassed you are feeling before God. I will stand laughing, and you will feel guilty and embarrassed and everything. Everything is wrong around you."

There is no possibility of exhausting the absurdities. Even Alexanders never exhaust them. If you want to exhaust them the only way is to become aware. The more aware you are the more absurdities look like absurdities. When they look like absurdities, when you see them as absurd, you simply stop. You don't do them anymore. There is no need to renounce anything in the world – one has just to be aware and things which are useless, meaningless, drop by themselves, on their own accord.

The third question:

Osho,
Every religion degenerates into a moralistic institution. You commend Lao Tzu because no religion could grow from his way. How can those who love you avoid such an institutional degeneration of your inspiration?

If you start avoiding, you have already started creating it. Don't bother about it. If it is going to happen it is going to happen; if it is not going to happen it is not going to happen. You don't bother about it, because if you start wondering how to avoid it you have already taken for granted that it is going to be there. You have already become self-conscious about it – and that will help to create it.

Buddha tried hard to see that his religion would remain an alive phenomenon and not a dead institution. He tried hard – but he failed. The harder he tried, the more people tried to create an institution around him.

Krishnamurti is trying hard – and he will fail, because this is the law. Why are you trying so hard? You must be afraid deep down that it is going to happen. And if even Krishnamurti thinks that it is going to happen, it is going to happen. I have talked to you many times about the law of reverse effect. It is a very deep psychological law: do something and just the reverse happens. That's the whole teaching of Lao Tzu. He said: "Talk about order and there will be disorder." Try to make people moral and there will be immorality. Try to make people be good and they will be bad.

You all know that this happens. Try to make your child be saintly and you will create the first revolt in him against you. He will go against you; he will do exactly what you wanted him not to do.

It never happened with Lao Tzu because he was never worried about it. If it happens it is okay – what can you do?

When I am gone, I am gone. Whatsoever happens is none of my business. So don't be worried about it. If it happens it had to happen. If it doesn't happen, good; if it happens, that too is good. Who are we to take the responsibility for the future? Who are we to decide for the future? No, it cannot be done. Simply drop the whole idea. Don't be worried. Drop the idea completely and don't be worried; don't try to create it and don't try to avoid it. While I am here be with me, celebrate with me, delight in me. Let me help you, allow me, that's all. When I am gone and you are gone, whatever happens – how can we decide it and why should we worry about it? While we are here we should use the opportunity, the door that has opened, the path that has become visible for you – tread on it, walk on it. Whether people create an institution out of it or not is for them to decide. And nothing can be done about it right now.

Never create any worry for the future because your very worry will create the reverse effect. Have you watched? – if you travel in a train, just have a look around. You can judge who is traveling without a ticket because he is constantly worried about the ticket checker – the law of reverse effect. He looks afraid, he looks worried. Whenever somebody enters the compartment he looks startled. You can simply see who has come without a ticket; he is creating his own difficulty around him.

And sometimes it happens that you have purchased a ticket, and it has fallen out of your pocket but you are not aware of it. You don't know that you don't have a ticket. Then you walk and you sit as if you have a ticket. Nobody can judge, nobody can catch you; even the ticket checker will not come to you. He knows that you must have a ticket. People are always surprised that when they have tickets nobody comes to check, and when they don't have a ticket suddenly the ticket checker comes, because he has become aware of this small law – that you can judge who is the culprit. There is no difficulty about it. He cannot be natural, he creates his own unnatural vibrations around him. Immediately the ticket checker goes to him.

Don't bother. You are here, the phenomenon is alive right now; vibrating, talking to you, penetrating you, helping you. Just delight in it. And if you delight in it, and if you yourself become a lighted phenomenon inside, others will delight in you.

An alive religion is alive because people are still enlightened in it, people are still aware in it. If you become aware with me you can help others to be aware with you – it is a chain reaction. Once awareness disappears, the chain disappears. A gap comes, an interval where nobody is alert, nobody is awakened – then religion is dead. Then it becomes a sect: Hindu, Mohammedan, Jaina. Then it becomes a church, then rituals, then just dead gestures.

But nothing can be done about it. Rather, only one thing can be done about it and that is that you don't bother, because you can waste your time thinking about it. Just live within me and allow me to live within you. Soon through your lighted candle other candles can be lighted. Create chains and they will move on their own.

And never think of the morrow. Future is not a concern at all. Only the present is.

The fourth question:

Osho,
You say I am an emptiness. Since being here I am beginning to
feel my own center. How does the center exist in emptiness?

It exists. I cannot explain to you how or why, it is a simple fact. Just as science says H_2O is water: two parts hydrogen, one part oxygen – two atoms of hydrogen, one atom of oxygen – and the combination is water. You cannot ask why. Why not three parts hydrogen, one part oxygen? Why not four parts oxygen, one part hydrogen? Why H_2O, why not otherwise? Science will shrug its shoulders, it will say: "We don't know. It is how it is."

Yes, your inner being is an emptiness and yet a center exists. Have you seen a cyclone? In summer days in India there are cyclones, whirlwinds. Go and look when the whirlwind has gone: it has disturbed every particle of dust around, but just in the center there is no disturbance. Even to a whirlwind a center exists, even to a cyclone a center exists, even to emptiness a center exists. One comes upon it, it is a fact of existence – no how to it.

A small boy was walking with D. H. Lawrence in a garden, and he suddenly asked, "Why are trees green?"
D. H. Lawrence said, "Trees are green because they are green."

Nothing more can be said about it. All explanations are useless because you can say, "Because of this, because of that" – but that too again brings the same question: why? It is absurd that a center exists to emptiness – it is illogical, it is irrational. But life is irrational. One has to accept life, life is in no way to be forced to accept your logic or reason.

It happens every day in science. When for the first time Einstein said "Everything is relative, even time is relative," the whole old world of science was disturbed. People started asking why, how? Einstein said one very absurd thing, and that is: "If a traveler goes into infinite space on a journey in a vehicle which moves faster than light," – light moves at one hundred and eighty-six thousand miles per second – "if the vehicle moves faster than light or even equal to light, and if your son goes on a journey into space and comes back after twenty-five years, he will still be of the same age." If he had gone at twenty-five years of age, he will remain twenty-five years of age. His friends will have become fifty years old here on the Earth but he will remain the same age. It is absurd. People started asking, "What is the logic?" Einstein said, "I cannot say what the logic is, but it is so."

At such a tremendous speed you cannot age. It is just like at a hundred degrees the water evaporates, that's all. At such a tremendous speed you cannot age; you will remain the same. And even more absurd – if the speed can be doubled you will come back younger than when you left. If you had gone at twenty years of age and you come back after ten years, you will be ten years of age. You will move backward in time – because, Einstein said, aging depends on speed, on the speed of the Earth. The Earth is moving at a particular speed; on that speed depends your aging. Impossible to believe! Contradictory to all logic!

Then physicists penetrated into matter and suddenly one day they found there is no matter. So they had to say that matter consists

of emptiness; they had to say that matter is nothing but dense emptiness. This looks illogical. How can emptiness be dense? How can this
pillar be created out of dense emptiness? But now physics says it is
so. And nature and existence do not follow our logic. They have their
own ways and we cannot force our logic on them, our logic has to
follow their ways.

The same is true about inner space. Of course, logic says: how
can emptiness have a center? Logically it cannot. When for the first
time I came to that center the same question arose in me also: how
can emptiness have a center?

To have a center something is needed – and it is there, but it
doesn't listen to our logic. Accept it, and don't create any logical
problem in your mind, because that is not going to help. Life is illogical. You are here. Have you any logic to say why you are here? If
you were not here, could you ask why you are not here? Things
simply are. Nothing can be claimed, nothing can be posed, nothing
can be projected, nothing can be asked. When you grow into this
awareness: that things simply are – then a deep acceptance happens. Then even if they are illogical you accept. You don't fight, you
float. You don't even swim, you simply are in a let-go.

And by and by more and more mysteries are revealed. That's
why religion says that life is a mystery, not a problem. A problem can
be solved; a mystery can never be solved. The more you solve it the
more mysterious it becomes. The more you know it the more you
feel has to be known. The more you come nearer the more you feel
you are far away.

The Upanishads say God is both far and near. Why? Because the
nearer you go the farther away you feel he is. You almost touch him
– and you feel far away. You almost penetrate him, you are almost in
his heart, but still the mystery is not dissolved. On the contrary, the
mystery has become more mysterious. And that is the beauty of it.
Just think of a world where all mysteries are solved – how boring it
would be. Just think of a world which is absolutely logical, rational,
mathematical – how boring and monotonous it would be. Then there
would be no possibility of poetry, there would be no possibility of
romance, there would be no possibility of love, and there would be
no possibility at all for any meditation.

Meditation is to enter into the mystery; love is to knock at
the same door in a different way. Prayerfulness is also to allow the

mystery, and not to struggle against it with the mind.

Everything is beautiful because everything is mysterious, and you cannot get to the bottom of it. Analyze if you want to analyze, but every analysis will create more problems, more mysteries; the answer, the final answer, cannot be found. And it is good that it cannot be found. If it is found then what? Then the very meaning and significance is lost.

I am not a philosopher, not in the least; I am just a poet at the most. I look at life and accept its facticity. If it makes two plus two four, okay. If it makes two plus two five, okay. If it makes two plus two three, okay. I have said yes to it. And this is what to be religious means to me – to say yes, it is so.

The fifth question:

Osho,
Is Carlos Castaneda's guru, Don Juan, an enlightened master?

If there were someone like Don Juan he would be enlightened, he would be like a Buddha or a Lao Tzu – but there is nobody like Don Juan. Carlos Castaneda's books are ninety-nine percent fiction; beautiful, artful, but fiction. As there are scientific fictions, there are spiritual fictions also. There are third-rate spiritual fictions and first-rate ones: if you want third-rate, then read Lobsang Rampa; if you want first-rate, then read Carlos Castaneda. He is a great master of fiction.

But I say ninety-nine percent fiction. One percent of truth is there, hidden here and there; you will have to find it. It is good even to read it as fiction. Don't bother about Rampa's fiction, because it is rubbish created by a mediocre mind – and of course created for mediocre minds. But Carlos Castaneda is worth reading. When I say fiction I don't mean don't read him, I mean read him more carefully, because one percent of truth is there. You will have to read it very carefully, but don't swallow it completely because it is ninety-nine percent fiction. It can help your growth, it can create a desire to grow. That's why I say it is beautiful. But it can hinder growth also if you take it at its surface value.

This man Carlos is really crafty, very clever. Rarely it happens, such cleverness – because it is very easy to create scientific fiction, not much imagination is needed, but to create spiritual fiction is very, very difficult; one needs a great artistic and imaginary mind. Because how can you even imagine things you don't know? That's why I say one percent of truth is there. On that one percent of truth he has been able to create a big edifice. On that one percent of truth he has been able to project much imagination. On that one iota of truth he has made the whole house, a beautiful palace – a fairy tale. But that one percent of truth is there, otherwise it would have been impossible.

So, one percent of Don Juan must be there somewhere or other. He must have met somebody; maybe his name was Don Juan, maybe not, that is not material, that doesn't matter. Carlos has come across a being superior to himself, he has come across a being who knows some secrets. Maybe he has not realized them, maybe he has stolen them, maybe he has just borrowed them from someone else. But he has met somebody who has somehow got some facts of spiritual life and Carlos has been able to create imagination around it. And the imagination becomes possible if you use drugs as a help – very easy, because drugs are nothing but an aid to imagination.

This man has come across some being who knows something, and then through drugs, LSD and others, he has projected that small truth into imaginary worlds. Then his whole fiction is created. It is a drug trip, but a good experiment in itself. And when I say all these things I am not condemning Carlos. In fact I have come to love the man. It is a rare flight of imagination, and if it is a hundred percent fiction then Carlos himself is a rare being. If he has not come across anybody at all then he must have that one percent of reality in himself. Because otherwise it is impossible – you can only build a house on a foundation, even an imaginary house needs at least a foundation in reality. You can make a house of cards but at least the ground, the solid ground is needed. That much is true.

So read, because you will have to read. Every age has its own fictions, romances; one has to pass through them. You will have to read. You cannot escape Carlos Castaneda. But remember that only one percent is true – and you have to find it.

If you have been reading Gurdjieff's books, particularly *All and Everything*, then you can become artful about how to find the true, how to sort out chaff from wheat. If you have not read *All and Everything*, it is a good beginning. First you should read *All and Everything* by George Gurdjieff and then you can read Carlos

Castaneda's books. It is a very difficult training to read Gurdjieff; in fact no more than a few dozen people exist in the world who have read his book *All and Everything* completely. It is difficult. It is a one-thousand-page book and Gurdjieff is a master of hiding things. He goes on saying irrelevant things, useless things, spinning tales within tales – hundreds of pages and then one line of truth, but it is worth seeking, it is a diamond. A hundred pages of rubbish, but then comes a diamond – it is worth it.

If you can find the diamonds in Gurdjieff it will be a great training for you. And then you can find in Carlos Castaneda what is true and what is not true. Otherwise you can become a victim of a fiction. And I think many Americans particularly are roaming in Mexico in search of Don Juan. Foolish!

The sixth question:

Osho,
Like Tilopa and Bodhidharma, do you think you will have to leave India to find a suitable successor?

You fools! Can't you see I have already left India? I am no longer here in India.

And the last question. Chinmaya has been asking this question continuously for many days, and I have been avoiding it. But now it is time. He has been asking:

Osho,
Are all enlightened masters bald?

And now I cannot avoid it any more, because in the effort to become bald he has shaved his head.

There exists no relationship, so don't try to be bald. Bald people are very clever, they create rumors about themselves. One rumor they have created all around the world is that they are potentially more sexual than anybody else. Of course bald people are not so sexually attractive; they have to create rumors around themselves. All over the world in all countries the rumor exists that bald people are more sexual, more potential sexually than anybody else. This is a trick.

But now to create another rumor that bald people are the only ones who become enlightened will be too much!

Enough for today.

CHAPTER 7

on the utility of not-being

Writing on the utility of not-being, Lao Tzu says:

Thirty spokes unite around the nave;
from their not-being, loss of their individuality,
arises the utility of the wheel.
Mold clay into a vessel;
from its not-being, in the vessel's hollow,
arises the utility of the vessel.
Cut out doors and windows in the house (wall);
from their not-being, empty space,
arises the utility of the house.
Therefore, by the existence of things we profit.
And by the non-existence of things we are served.

The deepest core of being is nonbeing. The foundation of *isness* is nothingness. And when I say nothingness I don't mean nothing-ness. I only mean no-thingness.

Form exists on the base of the formless. The form comes out of the formless just as waves come out of the sea, and then the form drops, dissolves into the formless again. The name arises out of the nameless, falls back, returns to the original source, becomes nameless again. Life arises out of death and moves to death again. The very basic thing to remember is that these opposites are not opposites, they are complementary. Death is not against life, nonexistence is not against existence, nonbeing is not against being. They are two polarities of the same phenomenon, which transcends all understanding.

Sometimes it expresses itself as being and sometimes as nonbeing, but it is the same that expresses in both. This has to be understood as deeply as possible because your whole *sadhana*, the whole effort toward ultimate understanding, will depend on it. Unless you are ready to become nonbeing you will never become a real authentic being. It looks like a paradox.

Jesus says to his disciples: "Unless you lose yourself you will not gain yourself." If you cling to yourself you will be destroyed, if you don't cling you will be saved. He is saying that if you move into nonbeing, only then is the being saved.

In India there exists a very old and very beautiful parable in the Upanishads:

A great sage, Uddalaka, was asked by his son, Shvetketu, "Father, who am I? What is it that exists in me? I try and try, I meditate and meditate, but I cannot find it."

Shvetketu was a small child but he raised a very, very difficult question. Had somebody else asked the question, Uddalaka could have answered easily, but how to help a child to understand? And he was asking the greatest problem that exists.

Uddalaka had to create a device. He said, "Go there, yonder, where you see the *nigrot* tree and bring a fruit from it."

The child ran; he brought a small fruit from the *nigrot* tree.

The father said, "Now cut it. What do you see inside it?"

The child said, "Millions of small seeds."

The father said, "Now choose one seed and cut that seed. Now what do you see in it?"

The child said, "Nothingness."

The father said, "Out of that nothingness arises this big tree. In the seed just at the center exists nothingness. You cut it – there is nothing, and out of that nothingness arises the being of this big tree. And the same is true with you, Shvetketu." And one of the greatest sayings ever uttered by any human being was born: *Tattvamasi,*

Shvetketu – "That art thou, thou art that, Shvetketu."

You are also that nothingness which exists just at the heart of the seed. Unless you find this nonbeing within you, you will not attain to authentic truth. Then you can move in theories, then you can philosophize, but you will not realize.

The boy meditated on his nothingness and he became very silent. He contemplated, he enjoyed this nothingness, he felt it very deeply. But then again a question arose. After a few days he came to his father again, and he said, "I can feel, but things are still not very clear, they are vague, as if a mist surrounds everything. I can see that out of nothingness everything is born, but how does nothingness mix with thingness? How does *isness* mix with nothingness? How does being mix with nonbeing? They are paradoxical."

The father was again in difficulty. Whenever children raise questions it is very difficult to answer them. Almost ninety-nine percent of the answers that grownups give to children are false – just face-saving devices. You deceive. But Uddalaka didn't want to deceive this child. And his curiosity was not only a curiosity, it was deep inquiry. He was really concerned. His body may have been that of a child, but his soul was ancient. He must have struggled in the past, tried hard to penetrate into the mystery. He was not just curious – he was authentically concerned. It was not just a vagrant question in the mind, it was very deep-rooted.

The father said, "Go and bring a cup of water."

The boy fetched a cup of water.

Then the father said, "Now go and bring a little sugar."

He brought the sugar, and the father said, "Mix them both."

The sugar dissolved into the water, and the father said, "Now, can you separate the sugar from the water?"

The boy said, "Now it is impossible. I cannot even see where the sugar has gone."

The father said, "Try."

The boy looked into it but he couldn't see any sugar; it had dissolved, it had become water.

Then the father said, "You taste it."

The boy tasted, it was sweet. And the father said, "Look, just like this. You may not be able to decide what is being and what is nonbeing; they are melting into each other just like water and sugar. You can taste and you can know that this water contains sugar. You may not be able to separate them right now – in fact nobody can ever separate them because they are not separate."

Water and sugar can be separated – that was just a device to make the child understand – but nonbeing and being cannot be separated, life and death cannot be separated. It is impossible. They are not separate, how can you separate them? They always exist together. In fact to say that they exist together is not to say it rightly, because the very word *together* carries the concept of twoness. They are not two, they are one. They only appear two.

From where have you come? Have you ever pondered over this very basic problem? From where have you come? Nothingness. Where are you moving, where are you going? Nothingness. From nothingness to nothingness, and just in between two nothingnesses arises being. The river of being flows between two banks of nothingnesses. Being is beautiful, but nonbeing is also beautiful. Life is good, but death is also good, because life cannot exist without death. Ordinarily you think that death is against life, that it destroys. No, you are wrong. Without death life cannot exist for a single moment. It supports it. It is the very base. Because you can die, that's why you can live. Life and death are not two things but two wings – two wings of the same phenomenon.

Science has always thought that religion talks in paradoxes, is irrational, illogical. But just within the past few years in science, particularly in physics, a phenomenon has arisen which can be very helpful to understand this meeting of being and nonbeing. The phenomenon is called the black hole. Science has come somehow to feel that in space there exist a few spaces which are holes, black holes – nonbeings. In the beginning it was difficult to conceive of it. But now by and by the concept is becoming clearer and clearer, because science also feels that everything exists with its opposite. How can existence exist without nonexistence? Life exists with death, love exists with hate, compassion with anger – how can existence just exist without nonexistence being there, somehow involved in it? It has to be there.

They searched, and now a man has got a Nobel Prize for the discovery of the black holes. The black holes are nonexistential holes in space where nothing exists, not even space. And they are very dangerous phenomena because if something goes into a black hole it simply disappears, because the black hole turns everything into nonexistence.

The discovery of the black hole has solved many mysteries. Just a few years ago it happened in America:

An airplane belonging to the army was flying in the sky. There was communication with the plane, then suddenly the communication stopped. Another plane was sent to search for the first plane: what had happened? Exactly after the same time gap, after half an hour, the second plane went out of communication.

Now it was dangerous. So three more planes were sent together in the same direction to find the last two. Exactly after half an hour those three planes were also lost, communication was broken. And never has anything been heard about those five planes, what happened to them. They have not left a single trace behind. If they had fallen then they would have been found. They could not go on flying forever and ever – what happened? Now it is suspected that they suddenly came across a black hole; they simply entered the black hole and disappeared.

A black hole means the power of nonexistence, the power of non-being. If you are caught in it, everything simply disappears, not a trace is left behind because matter becomes un-matter – you un-materialize.

You have heard the word *materialization*; you have heard about miracles, that there have been people who can materialize things out of nothing. But you have not heard the word *unmaterialization*, that things can simply go into un-matter, simply disappear.

It has happened many times. Once a ship carrying seven hundred people simply disappeared – such a big ship! When it passed the last port everything was okay; it never reached the next port. And the distance was not very far, it was very short. If the ship had sunk, with seven hundred people on board someone must have survived. And if nobody survived, then the skeleton of the ship would have been found. But nothing has ever been found. It simply disappeared. It must have come across a floating black hole.

That is happening every day, but when things happen every day you become oblivious of them. Suddenly a man dies. What has happened? He has entered the black hole. Just a minute before he was okay – breathing, talking, alive, conscious – and just a second afterward nothing is left, just a deteriorating body. What has happened? Something has gone into nonexistence. Death is the black hole.

Scientists say that stars are also born and die. They live millions of years, but that is not the question. They are born – from where do they come? Right now many stars are being born. Just as many children are being born in maternity wards, many stars are being born. They are coming out of nothingness. No matter existed before; it was a vast space, then suddenly a nebula comes into being, smoke arises out of nothingness. The smoke starts gathering, condensing, starts becoming more and more solid. It takes millions of years. Just as it takes nine months for a child to be born, it takes millions of years for nothingness to become condensed and become a star. Then for millions of years the star remains alive, then it dies. Then again it disperses, by and by becomes less and less solid, becomes vapor, smoke. For millions of years it remains on its deathbed and then one day the star has disappeared. The place where the star once was now will be a black hole; it has become nonexistential. Now, if you come across this black hole you will be simply absorbed. When the black hole absorbs a whole star – such a vast phenomenon!

Our sun is a mediocre star. It is thousands of times bigger than the earth. If our sun, thousands of times bigger than the earth, dies – it will die one day. Scientists say that it seems it can be alive nearabout four billion years more. It is already old, ill, has to be hospitalized, but there exists no hospital for stars. It is dying. Four billion years it will take, then one day it will be no more. First the light will disappear, then the matter will disappear, and then it will become a black hole. The space where once the sun was and now is no more will be a tremendous whirlpool of nothingness. If the earth is caught into it – finished. In a single moment it will crush you; nothingness to nothingness.

And there are bigger stars, our star is a mediocre one. Millions of big suns exist in existence, many of them have died already. In space travel, to go to the moon is nothing. But once we get out of the solar system, then there will be trouble because then your spaceship can come across any hole and you cannot know beforehand. Your ship can be simply absorbed and nothing will be heard of it ever again. These black holes are the other part of existence: they are nonexistence. And it has to be so, because existence has to be balanced by nonexistence.

Lao Tzu believes tremendously in nonexistence. He is the first to bring the utility of nonexistence to its ultimate glory. Of course he didn't know about black holes, otherwise he would have talked about them. He was a simple man, living in a village, living the simple life of a peasant – raw, simple, not very cultivated and civilized. He was against civilization, he was for nature. He has only simple similes: the wheel. He says the nave of the wheel, the hub of the wheel is empty, but the whole wheel depends on it.

Why is it called the nave of the wheel? – because it is just like the nave that exists in man. Just near your navel, the Japanese say there exists a point called hara. The hara is the black hole in your body. Japan has discovered, following Lao Tzu's idea, that somewhere in the body death must have a home. Death doesn't come from the outside, it is not an accident as people think. People say death is coming. No, death is not coming, death is growing within you; it is not that somewhere on life's path you suddenly meet death. If it were so, then methods could have been devised to avoid death, to deceive it or not to go to that point where death waits for you, to bypass it or to send somebody else instead of you. There would be such a possibility if death were an outward phenomenon, happening to you from the outside. But death is carried within you like a seed. It comes into existence when you come into existence, in fact it existed even before you. You have come out of it.

Death must have a point within your body somewhere. So the Japanese searched the body to find out where the black hole exists. It is just below the navel. Two inches below the navel exists the point of death. It is a very subtle point. You must have heard the word hara-kiri; the word comes from hara. Hara means the black hole inside the body, and hara-kiri means suicide, to use that black hole.

The Japanese have become very efficient in killing themselves; nobody can kill themselves as easily as the Japanese, because they have found the exact point of death. With a small knife, they simply penetrate the hara; not even a single drop of blood comes out. The suicide is bloodless, and no pain at all is felt, no suffering – life just disappears. They have touched directly the black hole in the body, the point of death. If you cut your throat you will die, but there will be much suffering – because from the throat to the hara there is much distance; that distance death will have to travel. So if somebody's head is cut off, the body remains alive for a few minutes; it goes on trembling and throbbing because you have not penetrated the hara directly. The Japanese can kill themselves so easily and so silently that when you see a man who has done hara-kiri, who has committed suicide, you will not see any sign of death on his face; his face will look as alive as ever. He has simply disappeared into the black hole with no struggle.

That hara in the body is nonbeing. It is absence, it is a nothingness. And the whole of Taoist practice is to be alert to the hara. They have created a different type of breathing for it; they call it belly breathing. You cannot find a more silent man than a Taoist who has been doing belly breathing and has become attuned to it.

You breathe from the chest. All over the world chest breathing, which is a shallow breathing, exists. Maybe it is because of the fear of death that you don't breathe from the belly, because when you breathe from the belly the breath goes deep down to the hara. Then you touch death. Afraid of death, you practice shallow breathing. Remember, whenever you are afraid your breathing will become shallow. Whenever fear takes you, you will not be able to breathe deeply – immediately the breathing becomes shallow. Every fear is basically a fear of death; you may not be consciously aware of it, but your body knows where death is: don't go that way. Your body is wise, wiser than your mind – has to be, because mind is very much a newcomer. Body has existed longer than mind, has passed through millions of lives, mindless lives, and has accumulated much wisdom. Whenever you are afraid you stop breathing or you breathe very shallow, afraid to come nearer to death.

Deep breathing absorbs death into life, deep breathing creates a bridge between life and death; the fear disappears. If you can breathe deep down through the belly, then fear will disappear completely. That's why the Japanese can commit suicide more easily than anybody else in the world. It looks like a game. They can commit suicide for such simple things that nobody can understand what the need was, because they know life and death are not separate, they are one. Death is also life – the other aspect of the same coin. It is rest.

If you breathe deeply you will feel rest flowing all over your body; a relaxation, a non-tense state of affairs. Have you ever watched a small child breathing? He breathes from the belly. You can watch and you will see. That's how Lao Tzu wanted everybody to breathe. That is the Taoist Yoga: just like a child, the belly goes up and down and the chest remains absolutely unaffected, as if the chest has nothing to do with breathing – and it has nothing to do with breathing.

But there are many problems: the fear of death – you cannot breathe deeply, the hara is there. And, just near the hara is the life-point, which you call the sex center – that too is a fear. If you breathe deeply, then sex arises. So people who have become afraid of sex cannot breathe deeply. If you breathe deeply immediately you will feel that suppressed sex has become alive again, it starts flowing into your veins and into your blood. And of course it is as it should be: the center of life should be just near the center of death. The hara, the center of death and sex, the center of life are just so near, so close that they almost touch each other – two aspects of the same coin. That's also why in sex people are afraid, because death starts throbbing with sex. A real sexual experience is also an experience of death: you die. That's why people are so afraid of sex, so afraid of women; I have not come across many people who are not afraid of women. The fear: woman has given you birth, she must be carrying your death also.

Look at the Hindus' conception of Kali, the Mother Kali. She is both life and death, the giver and taker. A beautiful woman, but black, black like death. A beautiful woman, but very dangerous – so dangerous that she is dancing on the body of her own husband, almost killing him. Shiva is lying there and she is dancing on his body almost crushing him. And she wears a garland of skulls and in one of her hands she has a cut head, freshly cut with blood dripping from it. In the West they cannot understand why a mother should be so dangerous, why a beautiful woman should be depicted in such a dangerous and terrible and horrible way. Hindus know better. They have penetrated the mystery of life better than anybody else. They know that sex and death are so close, so close that they are almost one. And when the sex center starts throbbing and spreading its waves over your body, the death center also starts throbbing. That's why orgasm has become just a word. You don't achieve orgasm in sex – you cannot. Unless you accept death you cannot achieve orgasm. Because *orgasm* means losing all control, *orgasm* means losing all mind, *orgasm* means the whole body throbs in ecstasy, every fiber and every cell of it. The whole body celebrates in an unknown bliss and the mind is no longer the controller and the manipulator.

Man can achieve only a local orgasm, which is nothing but ejacu-lation, not an orgasm at all. Because if orgasm takes over then you are no longer there; you are possessed by both life and death. And fear takes over. For thousands of years women have not achieved orgasm. Even now in India, I don't see that even two percent of women achieve orgasm. Only in the past few years has man become aware that women can also achieve orgasm. It has been a suppressed thing, because if the woman achieves orgasm she will go so mad that she will become Kali. She will be so mad with ecstasy that she may start dancing on your chest and she will be no longer in herself. She will be something else – a natural force, a whirlwind, a storm. She will laugh and cry and nobody knows what will happen; the whole neighborhood will know that a woman has achieved orgasm.

And sex is such a private affair – we have made it such a hidden and secretive thing, in darkness. The partners don't even see each other, and the woman has been trained to remain absolutely passive, non-moving, because of the fear. Because once she knows the beauty of going completely mad, then she will be uncontrollable. It will be impossible for any man to satisfy any woman because a woman can achieve multiple orgasms and a man can achieve only one. A woman can achieve within minutes at least six orgasms – six to sixty. It will be impossible for any man to satisfy a woman, and she will go so mad because she is so natural, it is better to suppress her.

Sex has been suppressed as part of death. Only two things have been suppressed in the world, sex and death. And it has been my observation that whenever a culture suppresses sex it does not suppress death so much, because there is no need – the suppression of sex alone will do. Whenever a culture suppresses death it does not bother to suppress sex, there is no need – the suppression of death alone will do. If you suppress one, both are suppressed because both are together. And both have to be freed; then you live tremendously, but you always live on the verge of death. You become a being, but you are always looking into the nonbeing. And that is the beauty of it, and the horror also. In fact, all natural beautiful things are also terrible.

Existence is not only beautiful, existence is also terrible. It is not only a mystery, it is not only *mysterium*, it is also *tremendum*; it is not only life, it is also death. And once you suppress your own being or your nonbeing you drop the bridges; then you cannot reach the existence. Be like existence, only then is the bridge there; then you are connected and joined with it.

In the West, after Freud, they have allowed sex a little freedom, but now they have become more suppressive of death. In the West nobody talks about death – as if it doesn't happen. Even professionals exist who work on the dead body so that it appears alive – painted, colored. A woman dies; her face is painted, lipstick is used, beautiful clothes, a beautiful coffin, and she is carried as if she has gone into deep sleep, not death. This is the fear of death: you don't want to look into the face of it.

Cemeteries are built outside of the town and you put beautiful marble stones on them; you decorate them. You decorate death so that you can avoid it, so that there is no need to encounter it – and death is the very source of life.

Use life, use death also: that is the message. Use being, use non-being also. Don't be afraid of anything because nothing that is yours can be taken away; nothing that you have can be taken away. That which you don't have, you don't have; it has already been taken away, you cannot carry it for long. And if you carry it you simply carry a burden.

Try to understand Lao Tzu's sayings. On the utility of not-being he says:

Thirty spokes unite around the nave;
from their not-being, loss of their individuality,
arises the utility of the wheel.

A wheel moves because in the nave, in the center, there is emptiness. If there is no emptiness in the center, the wheel cannot move. It moves on emptiness.

Mold clay into a vessel;
from its not-being, in the vessel's hollow,
arises the utility of the vessel.
Cut out doors and windows in the house (wall);
from their not-being, empty space,
arises the utility of the house.
Therefore, by the existence of things we profit.
And by the nonexistence of things we are served.

This is how one can become total and whole, and to be whole is holy for Lao Tzu. There is no other holiness. It is not a cultivation of religious ritual and it is not even a cultivation of morality. It has nothing to do with character. Holiness means a life that is whole; a life that has not denied anything, a life that knows no denial, a life that has not said no to anything, a life that accepts, accepts the opposites, a life that doesn't choose. A life that is choiceless is holy. *Holy* comes from the same root as *whole*. If you are whole you are holy, and if you are whole it means you are at the same time life and death also. You don't hide the fact of death and you don't try to hide your inner hollowness, emptiness. You don't try to fill it with rubbish. You enjoy the purity of emptiness also. Nothing is as pure as emptiness, nothing can be – because whenever there is something, impurity enters. Only emptiness can be absolutely pure.

But we are so afraid of emptiness. People come to me and say it is so difficult to be alone because one starts feeling one's emptiness. Then you seek friends, then you seek lovers, and the whole effort from the very beginning is doomed – because a man who is afraid of his emptiness cannot really love. He is afraid. Deep down there is fear. How can he love? When he moves and pretends that he is in love with somebody he is just trying to escape from himself, his own emptiness. He is trying to forget that somewhere inside there is emptiness and nothingness. He is trying to fill that emptiness with somebody's presence – and the other is also doing the same.

So almost ninety-nine percent of the love affairs on this earth are false. Sooner or later you come to realize that they have been deceptive. Lovers come to realize that they have been deceived, fooled. But they think that the other has fooled them, they never think that they have also done the same thing to the other. And they don't understand the misery of human beings and their stupidity. If they understood their own stupidity, what they are doing, they would be able to feel compassion for all. When you cannot be alone, silent, it means you are afraid of your loneliness, you want to fill it with somebody. You pretend. The other is also doing the same with you, he cannot be alone. Two persons who cannot be alone are trying to be together; now this is going to be a miserable phenomenon, a hell.

If you cannot love yourself in your loneliness, how can the other love you? How can you expect anybody to love you if you cannot love yourself? If you are so fed up with your loneliness, sooner or later the other will also be fed up with your loneliness. You cannot fill it, it is something that cannot be filled. It is something that exists as part of your being – you cannot fill it, it has to remain empty. It will remain empty. All efforts fail to fill it.

So the first thing is to get in tune with this emptiness, to allow it, to live it. Don't suppress and don't escape. Feel it, enjoy it – and by and by you will understand the beauty of it. Once you understand the beauty of your loneliness it becomes aloneness. Then it is no longer empty, then it is no longer nothingness. Then it is a purity – it is so pure that it is formless.

Always remember the difference between aloneness and loneliness. Loneliness is like a wound. Loneliness means you are missing the other. Loneliness means you are thinking of the other constantly, you are hankering for the other constantly. The other is in your fantasy, in your mind, in your dreams. The other is not real, is imaginary, but the other is there and because it is not real you feel lonely.

When you start feeling your aloneness, the other has dropped from your mind completely. It no longer shadows your dreams, it no longer touches your purity. You are happy with yourself, you are ecstatic with yourself, you are enjoying yourself. Now for the first time you are in tune with your being and with your nonbeing. You are whole.

Now you can be in love. Now love can flow. But now love will be a sharing, not an escape. Now you can go and share your being – and your nonbeing also. Now you can share your wholeness. Now you can allow anybody who is open to join your openness, now you can become partners in the eternal journey. This love will not be possessive, because you are ready to be alone anytime. In fact you are happy being alone, you are happy being together – you don't choose. Both are good. Whatsoever the case you feel happy. Your happiness cannot be destroyed now; the other can enjoy it and share it, but cannot destroy it.

You can share and you can distribute it and you can give it to the whole world; you have so much of it that you can bless the whole world with it. And it goes on growing; the more you give the more you find it is there. Now you are not a miser; now your being is not constipated, you are not closed, not afraid. You can give, you can share, because you know your nonbeing also. Now you are not afraid of being a nonbeing. Now you know definitely that it is part of your being and the beauty of your being; it is your inner space where you can move, the inner shrine, the real temple.

The temple exists in you. If you search your body it exists near the navel. That's why Hindus became navel gazers. People laugh in the West; whenever somebody meditates they say, "Have you become a navel gazer?" Hindus know in the body – the point of death that the Japanese call the hara, Hindus call the temple of the body. They close their eyes and they bring their consciousness to the temple of the body. Your body is a temple because it carries you. And from that temple you enter deeper, and then you find your nonbeing – that is a greater temple of being. The body becomes the door and when you reach your inner shrine, surrounded by nonbeing, on the throne is the divine. That is the center of nonbeing.

Just the other day somebody was asking how it was possible for the inner emptiness to have a center. Yes. It has only the center and no circumference – center everywhere and circumference nowhere. This is illogical, because logic itself is illogical and irrelevant to life. Life has its own logic, and the basis of life's logic is that opposites are not opposites, they are complementaries.

Emptiness has a center. You see a wheel – in the center there is emptiness, the hub. The wheel is matter, the hub is non-matter. But when you move in, just the reverse is the case: in the hub is the being, and the wheel is of nonbeing. Nonbeing is just the aura of your being, the light of your being, the space of your being, the territory of your being. And it is beautiful because it is absolutely empty; it is pure because it is absolutely empty – don't be afraid of it. In the beginning it looks like death; if you allow it, it becomes resurrection. After every inner death there is resurrection.

That is the meaning of the story of resurrection in Jesus' life – not that he was physically resurrected, but that he passed through death, the cross, and he came to the innermost life. You have to pass the emptiness – that is the cross. Everybody has to pass it. Nobody else can carry that cross for you, you have to carry your own cross. And unless you do, unless you pass the emptiness, you will not reach the innermost center. At that innermost center you are no longer an individual, you have become godliness.

Hindus say, "*Aham brahmasmi*"; Hindus say, "I am the God himself." This saying comes from those who have reached the innermost point, who have passed the nonbeing part and who have come to the shrine where godliness is and you are not. But you are trying to escape from it, you don't know how to use it. If you are empty and you have nothing to do you start doing something, anything. You put on the radio or the TV, you study the newspaper, you read a novel, you go to a hotel or you go to the club – you do many things. You can do anything whatsoever, but you cannot just do nothing. People have the idea that if you can't do something relevant, then do something irrelevant, but don't sit idle.

Sit empty. Just sitting empty one comes to the greatest encounter of life – one encounters one's own death. If you can pass that, if you can pass that dancing, happy, enjoying it, if you can be nourished even by emptiness, then nothing can destroy you – you have attained to the eternal, the non-destructible, the deathless.

That's why my insistence is always on a dancing meditation. It is not only an outward dance. The outward is nothing but a training for the inner. You dance outwardly, you go on dancing outwardly – by and by an inner dance arises and then you can dance inwardly and move toward the innermost center, the very core of being. Remember – death can be crossed only by dance, death can be won over only by a deep laughter. One can carry one's cross only happily, blissfully, ecstatically. Sad, serious, it will become such a burden. Your own emptiness will become such a burden that you will want to escape from it, you will come out and move into the world.

Learn how to dance outwardly, just as a training, as a discipline, so that the inner dance becomes possible. It is a mood, a climate – dance is a climate, it has nothing to do with any activity of dancing. It is a climate, an inner bubbling of bliss, an inner throbbing of bliss. Only on that boat can the part which is very, very difficult for you to cross be crossed. Otherwise one escapes. The moment you face your inner emptiness you escape, you become scared to death. That's why so many people never think about themselves. They think of the whole world, they worry for the whole world, but they never think about themselves, because that point seems to be touching a wound inside. They are afraid.

Don't be afraid. The existence of things is good; you can profit by it, but it is not enough. Unless you learn now to be served by emptiness also, you have not learned the art, the total art. If you know only how to live, you know only half the art; if you know also how to die, then you know the whole art – and the whole art will make you whole.

Remember, until you die you cannot be reborn. As you are you have to pass through death. And you are clinging too much to life.

That won't help – death will come. But death comes in two ways. One way, the ordinary way it comes is you are clinging to life and it comes as the enemy; you fight with it, you resist it, you do everything that you can do to avoid it. But how can you avoid it? The day you were born death became certain; every birth carries the seed of death. In fact, in life nothing else is certain but that. Everything is at the most probable, but death is certain. It will happen. You can avoid it, you can postpone it a little, but that doesn't change the situation. It will happen. One way to face death is as the enemy, which is the way ninety-nine percent of people face it – and miss it. Because of their enmity they cannot use it, they cannot be profited by it, they cannot be served by death.

There is another way: to accept death as a friend, to accept it as an innermost part of your being, to enjoy it, to welcome it, to be ready for it and when it comes to embrace it. Suddenly the quality of death changes. It is no longer death, it becomes a door. It no longer destroys you; on the contrary, you are served by it. It leads you to the deathless.

Die – you will have to die. But die gracefully. I am not saying die like a stoic, I am not saying die like a very controlled man. No, I'm saying die gracefully, beautifully, as if a friend is coming, knocks at your door, and you are happy. You embrace the friend and invite him in, you have been waiting for him so long.

If you can love death you become deathless; if you can understand nonbeing then your being becomes the very ground of beinghood, the very ground of existence. If you can love nonbeing then nothing can destroy you, you have transcended time and space. Then you have become one with the total, and this is what holiness is – to become whole is to be holy.

Enough for today.

witnessing

The first question:

Osho,
You have said much lately about inner silence and emptiness.
After two years as your disciple, much of the time, particularly
during the meditations, my mind seems more than ever to be out
of control and working like a computer gone mad. I try to be a
witness to the whole absurdity, but the monster goes on and on!

Let the monster go on and on and don't you be worried. The
very worry is the problem, not the monster.

The whole world is going on and on: rivers go on flowing,
clouds go on moving in the sky, birds go on chattering in the trees.
Why are you so against only the mind? Let it also go on and on – be
unconcerned.

Witnessing is not an effort. When you are unconcerned the witness
arises. Be indifferent to the mind; in the climate of indifference the
witness arises. The very idea that you have to stop it is wrong, that you
have to still it is wrong, that you have to do something about this constant ongoing process is wrong. You are not required to do anything.

If you do anything it won't help – it will help the trouble, not you. That's why when you meditate you feel the mind going more mad; when you don't meditate it is not so mad. When you are meditating you are too concerned with the mind, trying your hardest to make it still. Who are you? And why should you be worried about the mind? What is wrong with it? Allow the thoughts, let them move like clouds.

When you are indifferent, suddenly you are watching. With nothing left to do, what will you do? You can only watch, you can only witness – and in witnessing mind stops. Not that you can stop it. Nobody has ever been able to stop the mind, because the stopper is also part of the mind. The idea of meditation is part of the mind too – the idea that if you become silent you will attain to the ultimate is also of the mind. So don't be stupid. The mind cannot silence the mind. Who is asking this question, you or the mind?

You are not aware of yourself at all; it's the mind playing tricks. The only thing that can be done and which is possible, is to be indifferent and let the mind go. When you are indifferent suddenly a distance arises between you and the mind. You still listen to it because it is knocking continuously at your doors, but now you are indifferent. Now, inside, you are not worried whether it goes on or stops, you don't choose. You say to the mind, "If you want to go, you go on; if you want to stop, you can stop. It is none of my concern." This unconcern is needed. In this climate of unconcern and indifference the witness arises. Suddenly you see that the mind never belonged to you; it is a computer, it is a mechanism. You are absolutely separate from it.

Drop all efforts to still it and just remain passive, looking at what-soever is going on. Don't give direction to the mind; don't say, "Be like this." Don't be a guide to the mind and don't be a controller. The whole existence is going on, nothing disturbs you – why only this mind, a small computer, a small mechanism? Enjoy it if you can. If you cannot, then be indifferent. And then suddenly one day you find that something which was fast asleep within you is awakening. A new energy is coming up in you, a distance from the mind. Then by and by the mind goes on – faraway, faraway, faraway. Then still it goes on chattering but you know that somewhere far away, near a star it is chattering; you cannot even make sense out of it, what it is saying. And this distance goes on and on and on, and one day suddenly you cannot find where the mind has gone.

This silence is qualitatively different from a silence that you can practice. The real silence comes spontaneously, it is not something to be practiced. If you practice it you can create a false silence. The mind is so tricky, it can give you a false notion of silence – and that too will belong to the mind. So don't try hard to still it. Rather stand aside, by the side of the road, and let the traffic pass. Just watch it, just look at it with eyes of unconcern, indifference, and the thing that you have been desiring will happen – but not through desire because desire will not allow you to be indifferent. Buddha has used a word *upeksha*; the word means absolute indifference. And he says that you can never become meditative unless you have attained to *upeksha*, to indifference. That is the very soil. In that soil the seeds of meditation sprout – and there is no other way.

The second question:

Osho,
For thousands of years enlightened masters have been helping
their disciples to use words less and silence more. Lao Tzu talked
the least. But you seem to be the person who has talked more than
anyone else on the earth! Why is it so?

They tried and they failed with you. So I thought: let me try the other way round.

The third question:

Osho,
It is said that all the knowledge of heaven and earth is contained in
the sixty-four hexagrams of the I Ching. Is this so? If so, how to
utilize it?

All the knowledge of heaven and earth is contained in everything, not only in the sixty-four hexagrams of the I Ching. Even in a small pebble on the path all the knowledge of heaven and earth is contained; in a small blade of grass all the knowledge of heaven and earth is contained; in everything because every part of existence carries the whole in it. Even a drop of sea is the whole sea – the whole knowledge, the whole being of the sea is contained in the drop. It is sea. It may not be the sea, but it is sea.

You also contain the whole. So no need to go to the I Ching and the hexagrams; rather go inward, because finally the I Ching cannot say anything to you, finally you will be the interpreter. If you read tarot cards or the I Ching or use other methods, who will interpret? You will be the interpreter. So finally everything depends on you.

Unless you are awakened no I Ching is going to help. And if you are awakened everything is a hexagram and everything is the I Ching. So don't waste your time with other things: become awakened. When you are awakened you will see the whole universe written everywhere. In each blade of grass you will find the signature of the divine. And if you can understand a blade of grass you have understood all, root and all.

So don't deceive yourself. People deceive themselves in millions of ways. They waste their time in millions of ways, hoping that somehow they can enter the temple from some back door. There exists none. There is no back door to the temple, only the front door. You will find many back doors but they will not lead you to the inner shrine. You will be caught by some charlatan or somebody else.

Back doors don't exist in existence because existence does not believe in hiding. Look! Everything is so open, the secret is so open. Nothing is hidden, everything is open, you just need eyes to see it, awareness to read it, ability to enjoy it. Everywhere everything is an open secret, nothing whatsoever is hidden from the very beginning. Existence is open, only you are closed. And a closed mind is working with the I Ching – what will you attain out of it? Your own reflections, you will see yourself in it, your own unconscious will be reflected in it.

These methods are just mirrors. They reflect your own unconscious – nothing much. They never give you anything new, they simply reflect you. But you don't know yourself, that's why you think something new has been gained, some new knowledge has been gained through them.

I have heard...

The Russian premier Khrushchev had gone to Paris and went to see a modern exhibition of paintings. He was an uncultured man, and not in any way aesthetic – he had no sense of beauty. He was in fact, vulgar. But he was invited and he had to go.

Great paintings were shown in the exhibition. He looked at one painting and he said, "I don't understand. This looks ugly."

The man who was showing him around, a great critic of art, said, "This is Picasso and it is one of the most beautiful things that has happened in this century, but it needs understanding. It is not so ordinary that anybody can understand it. You have to raise your level of aesthetic feeling, sensitivity; only then will you be able to see what it is."

They moved on. Khrushchev didn't feel good, he had never imagined – in fact, in Russia it would have never happened. No critic, no artist would have been so courageous to say that he lacked understanding.

Then at the next painting he stood for a few minutes, looked deeply, and said, "I think this too is Picasso."

The critic said, "Sorry sir, this is just a mirror. You are looking at yourself in it."

He was an ugly man – it may have looked like Picasso to him, a painting of Picasso's, a distortion.

In the I Ching you will find a mirror. If Buddha reads the I Ching it is going to be totally different because the mirror will show Buddha. If Lao Tzu reads the I Ching, it will show Lao Tzu. If you read it, of course you will see yourself. You can only see your face.

So don't be bothered. Become a buddha, then it will be worth looking in the mirror. But no buddha bothers to look in the mirror. This is the puzzle. No buddha bothers to look in the mirror because deep down he knows his own being so well, so intensely, that there is no need for a mirror to know it. You need a mirror – but then the mirror simply shows you. And you go on befooling yourself. Whatsoever you want to read you will read, and you will throw the responsibility on the I Ching.

Once Mulla Nasruddin didn't go to the office. In the evening he came to see me and he was very happy, because he had slept in bed the whole day – not a care in the world.

I asked, "Nasruddin, why have you taken a holiday today?"

He said, "Couldn't help it. I tossed a coin in the morning to see whether to go to the office or not – if it came down heads I had to go, if it came down tails I could enjoy a holiday."

So I asked, "It came down tails and you enjoyed a holiday?"

He said, "Yes, but I had to toss it ten times, then it came to tails."

This is what is happening. I Ching, tarot cards, whatsoever – this is what is happening. Whatsoever you want to do, do it, but why throw responsibility on the poor I Ching? Just be responsible and do it. These are tricks.

Yes, I say everything is contained in everything. Even in the I Ching the whole universe is contained. Nothing is possible otherwise. This is how existence is. In each part the total is contained, the whole is contained. Anywhere you move, you move into the whole, but how you will read it depends on your understanding.

So I'm not concerned with I Chings, I am concerned with you and your understanding. Try to grow into it. Don't waste your time with anything else. Life is really short and much has to be done. Don't fool around.

The fourth question:

Osho,
Do growth and spirituality have any meaning in Tao?

None whatsoever, because Tao is whatsoever is the case right now. Tao is the present. Growth brings future in. The very idea of growth brings the future in and then everything is distorted. Not that you don't grow in Tao, in fact you only grow in Tao, but the idea of growth is completely foreign to the world of Tao. They don't talk of growth. They only talk of how to be, not how to grow.

And if you know how to be, that is the only way to grow. If you know how to be in this moment you are on the path of growth. You need not think about it, it comes by itself on its own accord, just as a river finds its way to the sea without consulting any guidebook, without asking anybody on the path where the ocean is. It finds the way. Not trying to find it, still it finds it. It goes on moving, moment to moment living its life; finally it reaches the ocean. This moment lived well and totally, the next moment will come out of this moment – from where else can it come? It will grow out of it on its own, you need not worry about it. You live this moment in totality and the next moment is born out of this. If you have lived totally then the possibility for the next moment is born with it – it can also be lived totally.

If you know how to live totally, you will also live the next moment totally. You will become more and more total every

moment and growth will happen on its own. But if you are too concerned about growth, you miss this moment – and that is the only
time one can grow in.

So Lao Tzu doesn't talk about growth because he knows that the
very talk about growth will become postponement. Then one thinks,
"I will grow tomorrow. Today is not the time for me. Many other
things have to be done, growth can wait a little. There is no hurry."
And then you go on postponing and you go on living this moment in
a fragmentary, partial way. And the next moment will come out of it,
and with each moment you will become more and more partial, frag-
mented, divided, split. Then who will grow and how does one grow?

One has to become that which one is already. One has to attain
that which one is born with. You have to become that which is your
very being, the very ground of being – so right now is the work.
This passing moment has to be used so intensely, absorbed so
intensely, then it becomes growth. Growth is not an ideal in Tao, it is
a by-product.

And about spirituality Tao does not concern itself at all – if you ask
Lao Tzu he will laugh. If you talk about spirituality he may slap your
face, he may throw you out and say to you, "Go somewhere else.
Don't bring such stupid things to me." Why? Because the moment you
say spiritual you have divided life into the material and the spiritual –
and he is for the total, the whole. The moment you say spiritual you
have condemned something in the material, in the body, in the world.
The very word *spiritual* carries a condemnation in it, a division.

You can see people who think they are spiritual; in their eyes you
can see condemnation. Don't go very near to them, they are poisonous; in their very breath there is danger and infection. Escape
from them! Whenever you see a spiritual man coming toward you,
run as fast as you can because he is ill. He is deeply neurotic, he is a
schizophrenic because he has divided life into two, and life is an
undivided whole; it cannot be divided.

Life is not soul, life is not body, life is both. You are not body and
soul, you are bodysoul. That "and" is dangerous, drop it. I have seen
people who have dropped the "and" but still when they think of
bodysoul they cannot make it one word, they place a small hyphen
instead of the "and" between the two. Even that hyphen is dangerous,
drop that also. Make *bodysoul* one word. It is one. Make *mattermind*
one; make this world and that world one. Let your godliness be here,

down in the matter, and let your matter rise high and enter into your godliness. Then how can you talk about spirituality?

In India this disease is very old, this disease of spirituality. People come to me, spiritual people. Not knowing me rightly, sometimes they come to me by accident. They talk about their spirituality and in the same breath they talk about others' materialism. It is a cliché in India that the West is materialist and the East is spiritual. This is non-sense. This is just a very bigoted, schizophrenic mind. It arises out of the division between the body and soul – then everything will be divided, then your whole life will always carry a division. Even the body is divided into two: the higher body is something higher, and below the navel the lower body is really lower – lower as a valuation. Body and soul are divided, then the body is also divided: the lower part is somehow dirty, the higher part is holy, sacred. In fact where has your body a division inside it? Can you demarcate a place from where the body becomes lower? The blood circulates all over the body, the same blood. The whole body is one network, how can you divide it? And to people who divide, tell them, "Cut off your lower body and live with the higher. Then we will see." They will die immediately.

That's what happens to spiritual people, they are dead people. This has been my observation: that even materialists are more alive than your spiritual people, because materialists deep down feel that someday they will try to become spiritualists also. They don't condemn. Rather, on the contrary, they feel a self-condemnation inside them, a guilt that they are not going to the temple, they are going to the prostitute. They are not going to prayer; they are going to a singing party, a dancing party. They know that they are doing something wrong, they feel humiliated. So there is a possibility for them because the ego feels hurt. But the spiritual person is an egoistic person. In fact, the concept of God has been created by the greatest egoists in the world – to condemn others and to appreciate themselves.

God is total, but the God of the so-called spiritual people is not total. Their God is just an abstraction, a thought, a pure thought with no life in it.

Lao Tzu is not spiritual in that sense, and he won't allow any spirituality into his vicinity. He is simply for the whole; he is simply for no division.

I am also for no division. When I initiate you into sannyas I am not initiating you into spirituality, I am initiating you into a life of the whole. I am trying to make you holy, not spiritual. And remember by holy I always mean the whole in which you will live an integrated life – an organically integrated life of body, soul, world, God, market and meditation. An integrated life where no division exists – a flowing energy, not compartmentalized.

I don't want any airtight compartments in your being. Your being should be liquid. You should be courageous, so courageous that even the sinner can exist side by side with the saint in you, and the saint is not afraid and the sinner doesn't feel condemned. When your sinner and saint come closer and closer and one day become one, you have become holy. Then you have not denied anything, you are not a no-sayer, you have said yes to the whole of life as it is, with no conditions attached. You have said yes to the whole life – this to me is what a religious man is, not spirituality.

The same is true with Lao Tzu. He does not bother about growth, growth will take its own course – just live the moment. He does not bother about spirituality; just live totally and spirituality will take care of itself. It will come, it is a flowering not a discipline.

When one is total, life flowers. And that flowering is spirituality. Spirituality is not an attitude, it is not a discipline. It is an outcome of a life lived totally, joyfully, delightfully; of a life of no complaint; of a life lived courageously, intensely. Then this flowering happens.

The fifth question:

Osho,
You spoke of balance, the meeting point, the blending of opposites – but it seems to be an invisible timeless point. Then how can it be known by me who is time?

You are both time and timelessness, otherwise balance could not be attained. But you have known only part of your being, that part is time. If you know your whole being you know the timeless part also. For the whole there exists no time. Time is a relative concept, it exists only for people who are not whole. This has to be understood – it is a delicate point and very complicated. Time is one of the most abstruse problems.

Saint Augustine says, "I know what time is when nobody asks me, but when somebody asks I don't know." Everybody knows what time is if nobody asks; if somebody insists that you define, explain what time is, then you are at a loss. You have been using it, every moment you have been talking about it and you have a subtle feeling about it, what it is. But when you want to be articulate about it you are at a loss.

Time is one of the most abstruse problems. Try to understand. Time is relative – the first thing to be understood – it is nothing absolute. For the whole universe there is no time because it cannot move from one point to another; both the points are in it. It contains all – the past, the present, the future. If it doesn't contain the future already, how can the future ever exist? The whole cannot move in time because it contains time also. Time is part of its existence. That's why we say about the whole that it lives in eternity: eternity means timelessness, there is no time in it. Past, future, present – all are implied in it.

Time exists for us because we live as parts. Space exists for us because we live as parts. They are relative phenomena. For the whole, space doesn't exist because it is contained in the whole. It cannot go anywhere else because there is no anywhere else. The whole of space is in the whole. Where can it go? It exists here now, it always exists here now; otherwise has never been the case.

You are both. If you live a divided life, if you live a partial life, if you live half asleep, almost sleep; then you live in time. If you live a fully awakened life, suddenly you live in eternity, timelessness. You have become the whole; now no time exists for you.

A German mystic, Eckehart, was on his deathbed.

A disciple – a curious, inquiring man, a student of philosophy – asked him, "Master, I know that you are dying, but I would like one question to be answered before you leave the body, otherwise it will haunt me my whole life."

Eckehart opened his eyes and said, "What is your question?"

The man said, "When you die, where will you go?"

Eckehart said, "There is no need to go anywhere." And he closed his eyes and died.

"There is no need to go anywhere," he said. I don't think that the man's inquiry was satisfied but a beautiful answer was given. It needs very deep understanding. Eckehart said, "There is no need to go anywhere." It means: I am everywhere now. Where is the need to go anywhere?

Buddha was asked the same question again and again, "When a buddha dies where does he go?" Buddha always laughed and kept quiet.

At the last moment again the question was raised and Buddha said, "Bring a small candle."

The candle was brought and Buddha said, "Light the candle."

The candle was lit and then Buddha said, "Bring it near to me."

The candle was brought nearer and nearer and then suddenly he blew it out and said, "I ask you where this candle light has gone; where has the flame gone?" The disciples were at a loss.

In Sanskrit the cessation of a flame is called nirvana. So Buddha said, "Just like this, when a buddha dies, he disappears. He becomes one with the whole. So it is irrelevant where he goes, because where can the whole go? Where has this flame gone? It has become one with the whole. Now it no longer exists as an individual flame, the individuality is dropped."

That's why the word *nirvana* became most important in Buddhist terminology. It means cessation of a flame, total cessation of a flame. It remains because whatsoever is remains, but you cannot find it. Where will you find a flame which is no more? Individuality is lost, form is lost. Where will you find it? But can you say it is no more? It is, because how can a thing which was be no more? It disappeared, of course; became one with the formless, of course; became one with the whole, of course – but it is. Now it exists as the whole.

You have both possibilities. You can live in time, then you live as mind. Mind is time because mind divides life into past, present, future. Mind is the dividing factor. It is a great analyst, the great dissector. It dissects everything. You can live life through the mind, then you live in time. But you can live life directly, you can live life immediately, without mind. You can put the mind aside, then you live life timelessly, eternally. Then there is no past, then there is no future, then there is only present and present and present. It is always there.

Past is that present which you cannot see, and future is that present which you cannot see yet. Past is that present which has passed beyond you, beyond your perception; future is that present which has not yet come within the boundaries of your perception.

Just think of a small example. You are waiting under a tall tree for someone. You can look at the road, but there is a limitation. You can look one furlong to one side, one furlong to the other side, and then the road disappears. Another man is sitting in the tree, at the top of the tree. He can see further. He can see one mile in one direction, one mile in another direction.

You are waiting for a friend. The friend appears – not for you, but for the man who is sitting at the top of the tree. The moment the friend appears on the road he has become present to the man at the top of the tree, but to you he is still future – he has not yet appeared on the road. Unless he comes within your boundary of perception he will not be present. He is future. Past, future and present are relative; it depends on your height and where you are.

That's why Jainas insist that Mahavira knows all the three tenses of time – because of his height. He can see end to end, nothing is hidden from him. So whatsoever you think is past is still present for him, and whatsoever you think is future is present for him.

Then the friend appears – you talk to him and he moves on. After one furlong he disappears for you, he has become past. But for the man on the top of the tree he is still part of the present. It depends how wide the compass of your understanding is. If your compass is total, then there is no time. Then you can see end to end. Then everything of the past is also present – right now. Then everything that is going to happen in the future is also present – right now. Then there is no past, no future; only present exists. Only one moment of present exists – that moment is eternity.

You have both possibilities. You can exist through the mind, then you are limited. It is just as if you are looking from a window toward the sky – then the frame of the window becomes the frame of the sky. The frame of the mind becomes the frame of your world. Then you jump out of the window; you come out under the whole sky. Now there is no frame.

In French painting a new cult is arising, the cult of paintings without frames. It is a beautiful phenomenon, because all frames are false. In life everything exists without a frame, but when you paint a picture you put a frame to it. That frame is the most false thing. And the irony is that sometimes people purchase such beautiful and decorative frames that even the picture is not as costly as the frame. The

frame is more costly and precious – and the frame is false. Life exists
without a frame. Have you seen life anywhere with a frame? But you
take a picture; immediately a frame comes into existence. The frame
is false. All frames are from the mind; mind gives a frame to everything which is frameless, formless.

You can be both, it depends on you. In deep meditation the mind
is no longer involved. It goes on functioning in the beginning but by
and by, when you don't listen to it, it stops its chattering. Seeing that
nobody bothers, seeing that nobody pays any attention, it stops.

The mind is just like a child. Have you seen a child do this? If he
falls down, first he looks for his mother to see if she is around somewhere. If she is, then he cries. If she is not, what is the point? Then he
simply gets up, starts playing again because there is no point –
nobody is paying any attention. Nobody will bother unless the mother
is there. And sometimes it happens that after half an hour the
mother appears and he starts crying. Now it is absurd, but in a way
logical. Because what is the point in crying when the mother is not
there? Even if you are hurt it is pointless. When the mother comes now
the hurt is no more, but it is meaningful to cry and weep for the hurt
which is no more because the mother is expected to pay attention.

The mind is like a child. If you pay attention it cries. If you pay
attention it creates problems. If you pay attention it goes on and on,
there is no end to it. If you don't pay attention, suddenly the child
realizes the mother is no longer there, the child by and by realizes the
mother is gone, and then he stops. When the mind stops you are
immediate, then you face reality directly. Then there is no mediator
in between, nobody to color it. Then the perception is clear, pure –
and you are in eternity.

The sixth question:

Osho,
Can the ego commit suicide?

No, because it is not. To commit suicide it is needed to be there.
Let me put it in another way: can a shadow commit suicide? A
shadow cannot commit suicide because a shadow doesn't exist. If
you commit suicide, if you cut off your head, then the shadow will be
without a head. It simply follows you. The ego is just a shadow, it

cannot commit suicide. If you cut off your head, the ego commits suicide – not that it commits, it happens.

Try to understand that the ego is not substantial; the ego is just like a shadow. The body moves – a shadow is created, a physical shadow; the mind moves – a mental shadow is created. That mental shadow is the ego. When the mind stops there is no ego, when the mind is not functioning there is no ego. When the mind is functioning the ego is there; if the mind functions too much the ego is there too much. That's why you will see that people who work with the head too much are more egoistical than anybody else. Brahmins, scholars, professors, pundits, the so-called intelligentsia; they have the subtlest egos. Intellectuals, writers, poets, philosophers; they have the subtlest egos. They are nothing but egos, too much head.

People who work with the hands, who are technically called "hands," are humble people. Go and visit a small village of peasants, workers, laborers, who work with their hands. They are humble people.

There is a story about Confucius. The story is as old as Lao Tzu...

Confucius was traveling, passing through a village, and he saw an old man, a very old man, pulling water from a well and watering his field. It was hard work and the sun was burning hot. Thinking that this man seemed not to have heard that now there were mechanical devices which could pull the water – you could use horses or bulls instead of man to pull the water out more easily – Confucius went to him and said, "Have you not heard that now devices exist? The water can be pulled out very easily from the well and the work that you do in twelve hours can be done in half an hour. Horses can do it. Why are you unnecessarily straining so much? You are an old man." He must have been ninety years of age.

The man said, "It is always good to work with the hands because whenever cunning devices are used a cunning mind arises. In fact only a cunning mind uses cunning devices. Don't try to corrupt me. I'm an old man, let me die as innocent as I was born. It is good to work with the hands. One remains humble."

Confucius came back to his disciples. The disciples asked, "What were you talking about with that old man?"

Confucius said, "It seems he is a disciple of Lao Tzu. He hit me hard, and his argument seems to be correct."

When you work with the hands no shadow of the head arises, a person remains humble, innocent, natural. When you start using cunning devices, the head comes in. People who work with heads technically are called "heads" – a head clerk, a headmaster – they are called heads. Don't be a head. Even to be a clerk is too bad, and to be a head clerk – finished. To be a master is enough of a hell, but to be a headmaster! Try to be hands. And hands are condemned because they are not cunning, not competitive enough; they seem to be primitive. Try to work more with hands and you will find that the shadow arises less and less.

The ego cannot commit suicide because it is not. If you commit suicide that is what I call *samadhi*, that is what I call the final meditation. If you commit suicide – that means if you disappear, you become a nobody – no shadow falls.

In the old days it was rumored that whenever a man becomes a buddha no shadow falls from his body. This must have been symbolic. It is very meaningful. It doesn't mean that when Buddha walks on the path no shadow falls – the shadow falls, but inside no shadow falls. He moves, he walks, he does things, but the doer does not arise. That is how the shadow doesn't fall. If needed he even thinks, but the thinker does not arise; that's how the shadow does not fall. He lives, but he is not a manipulator, the controller. He flows, his life is a spontaneity. He does not even swim, he simply floats with the river. He does not push the river, he simply leaves himself in a let-go. He is a let-being-be. He floats. He leaves it to the river to do everything – then the shadow doesn't fall, the ego disappears.

Don't fight with the ego directly. If you do that you will fail because nobody can fight directly with the shadow. If you have to do something with the shadow you will have to do something with your being. Something is wrong, a wrong conception. You are a nonbeing inside – realize more and more the inner hollowness, the emptiness, and suddenly one day you will find the ego has left you. In fact you will find it has never been there, you had a misconception, you were in an illusion. It was a mirage. It was not there, it only appeared to be there; it was not a reality, it was a dream – in fact, a nightmare.

The seventh question:

Osho,

Can a man who lives the states of anger and compassion also live
the states of love and hate?

Yes. When a man is total, he is total – unconditionally. But his
hate has a different quality, his hate is even more loving than your
love and his anger is even more compassionate than your compassion. Because he lives totally everything takes on a new quality.
Whatsoever he does, it is different. You cannot judge him from your
side because you don't know what totality means. You know hate,
you know love. Sometimes you have loved, you had a glimpse of it;
sometimes you have hated, you had a glimpse of it – but you have
never been total. If you are total your love is different: your love has
the intensity of hate. Have you ever observed the fact that your love
never has the intensity of hate? When you hate a person you really
hate. When you love, you love so-so. When you love you never put
yourself into it completely. But when you hate, you hate really
intensely – have you watched the fact that your compassion is impotent, maybe just a facade, a mask, but your anger is real?

All that is wrong seems to be real and all that is beautiful seems
to be false. When a man is total his love is as intense as his hate. And
when a man of totality hates, his hate also carries total love in it – he
can hate only because he loves, and he can be angry only because
he has compassion.

No, it is difficult. It will create a deep confusion in you because
right now you cannot understand it, right now your understanding is
not ripe for it. You will have to try it.

Drop lukewarmness. It needs courage. The greatest courage is
needed to live a life of totality because then one never knows what
is going to happen. And you are always afraid. You love a person;
you are afraid to be angry with him or her because you don't know
really whether you love or not. You don't know really if love will be
able to withstand anger. Will it be possible that love will survive
anger? So you have to suppress anger because you are afraid. You
are not really certain that your love is there. You have a certain
feeling – maybe it is, maybe it is not – a vague feeling. You live in a
mist, always surrounded by smoke; nothing is ever clear, your perception is always clouded. So you are afraid: this much anger may
dissolve the whole relationship, may destroy the whole relationship.
No! Suppress anger! Then you suppress anger; anger becomes part

of you – then when you love, in your love the anger also comes in.

Watch two lovers making love. You will see that there is violence. The love act is not graceful. Look at the face of the man making love – it seems as if he is going to murder the woman. Maybe that's why women always close their eyes while you make love to them: it is better not to see what this man is going to be or going to do. The whole thing seems to be nasty. Distortion comes to the face – grace should come, but distortion comes to the face. Faces which look ordinarily beautiful become ugly, as if one is passing through some agony, as if it is not an ecstasy but an agony. Look at the woman's face: the face becomes distorted, all her makeup gone. The face no longer seems to be beautiful. And she seems to be in some sort of pain – suppressing it.

Even while making love, people are afraid that if they move really totally there is a danger point. Their whole mind goes on showing the red light: "Stop! Don't go further!" All that they have suppressed can come up any time. It is there knocking at their doors: "Allow us!"

So they cannot relax in love either, because relaxation can only be unconditional. There is no conditional relaxation. If you relax, you relax for love, you relax for anger, you relax for hate. It is just like when you open the door you open it for the enemy as much as you open it for the friend. If you leave the door open in the night there is every possibility the friend may come – the enemy also. So you close the door. But the closed door is closed for both, for the friend and for the enemy.

You have never been able to be angry, really authentically angry. You cannot love authentically. When you are total you do everything authentically whatsoever the consequences, never thinking of the consequences. This is my mathematics about life: if you live totally, whatsoever the consequences, it is always good. Whatsoever – it is always good. And if you live a fragmentary life, whatsoever the consequence, it is always bad.

You can see from your lives that you have been living a very gentlemanly life, a lukewarm phenomenon, neither cold nor hot. What has happened? Nothing, almost nothing. You have been wasting yourself. Don't waste any more. Be true. There are dangerous dangers in being true, otherwise everybody would become authentic. There are dangers, otherwise why would so many people be so inauthentic? Cowards, afraid, trying to manipulate somehow a little comfortable life. If you want to live comfortably, then it is better to be a coward.

But a comfortable life is nothing but a comfortable death. A real life burns from both ends. It is a flame – surrounded always by danger, surrounded always by death. When death surrounds you, danger surrounds you. Only in that context does life come to its peak.

The last question:

Osho,
A bird came to die at your feet some days ago. Can we also, when our time arrives, come and die at your feet?

There will be no need to come, I will be there. If you really love me and trust me I will be there. But don't wait for death. If I am with you in life, only then can I be with you in death.

Life is the criterion. Death is the culmination. Whatsoever is in life culminates into a peak in death, it comes to a crescendo. If you feel me in your life, near your heart, then you will find me absolutely present in your death. There will be no need for you to come, I will come.

But don't wait for death. It should first happen in life. All that you want to happen in death you should allow to happen in life, because life is the preparation for death. And death is never against life, it is simply the completion. All that has been in life comes to a peak in death.

Enough for today.

on the wise ones of old

On the wise ones of old, Lao Tzu says:

The wise ones of old had subtle wisdom
and depth of understanding,
so profound that they could not be understood.
And because they could not be understood,
perforce must they be so described:
cautious, like crossing a wintry stream,
irresolute, like one fearing danger all around,
grave, like one acting as guest,
self-effacing, like ice beginning to melt,
genuine, like a piece of undressed wood,
open-minded, like a valley,
and mixing freely, like murky water.

Who can find repose in a muddy world?
By lying still, it becomes clear.
Who can maintain his calm for long?
By activity, it comes back to life.
He who embraces this Tao

guards against being over-full.
Because he guards against being over-full,
he is beyond wearing out and renewal.

S ocrates was dying.
      A disciple asked, "Why are you not afraid of death?"
      Death was certain, within minutes he would die. The poison to
kill him was being prepared. But Socrates said, "How can I be afraid
of something which is unknown? I will have to see. When I die, only
then can I see. Two possibilities are there. One is that I will die completely, no trace of me will be left. So there will be nobody left to
know it, nobody to suffer it. So there is no question about my being
worried about it if this first alternative is going to happen. And the
second possibility is that I may continue; only the body will die, but
the soul will remain. Then too I don't see any point in being worried.
If I am to continue, then death is irrelevant. And only these two possibilities exist. I cannot say anything right now about what will
happen. I don't know. I don't know yet."

Socrates was a wise man, not a man of knowledge. A man of
knowledge would have given a certain answer. Men of knowledge have
certain answers, absolute certainty – that is part of their stupidity. In
fact, only stupid minds can be certain. Life is such a vast mystery,
unfathomable, unknowable; if you are wise you cannot be certain.
Wisdom is cautious. Wisdom hesitates. Wisdom is never certain.
That's why wisdom can never be confined to a theory. All theories are
less than life, all theories are narrow, and life cannot enter into them.
Life is so vast, so tremendously vast and infinite. A wise man only
knows one thing: that he does not know. A man of knowledge knows a
thousand and one things and knows that he knows – and therein lies
the foolishness of the man of knowledge. He goes on accumulating
facts unlived by himself: theories, words, philosophies – untouched by
his own being. He goes on accumulating them in his memory. He
becomes a vast reservoir of knowledge, he becomes an *Encyclopaedia
Britannica*, but a dead thing.
The more his memory becomes filled with knowledge the less
he lives in his being. The more he moves into the head, becomes a
part, a fragment, the less he is joined to the vast being and the universe and existence. He becomes in a way nonexistential. He is no

longer a part of this existence, alive, radiant, vibrating. He is a frozen phenomenon; he no longer flows with life. He is like an iceberg, frozen and stuck somewhere – stuck in the head.

Consciousness, when it becomes knowledge becomes frozen; when consciousness becomes wisdom it becomes a flow. A wise man lives, lives totally, but knows only one thing – that he doesn't know. To learn from a wise man is very difficult. To learn from a man of knowledge is very easy. He can give you all that he knows, he can transfer it very easily, language is enough of a vehicle. All that he has gathered, he has gathered through the mind, through language; it can be communicated easily.

A man of knowledge becomes a teacher. He can teach you, and he can teach beautifully, things which he has not known at all. Maybe that's why he is not as hesitant as a man who knows. Because when a man knows, he also knows the opposite polarity of life. When a man really understands and knows, he also knows that everything is joined with its opposite, everything is meeting and melting into its opposite. Nothing can be said definitely because the moment you say anything definitely you have stopped its flow, you have made it a frozen fact. It is no longer part of the river, it is an iceberg. Now you can accumulate it in the storehouse of the mind.

A man who is wise is not a teacher, he can be a master but not a teacher. What is the difference between the two? A teacher is ready to teach; a master is never ready to teach. A teacher is aggressive, active; a master is non-aggressive, inactive. A teacher will go and follow you and force you, so that you can carry his knowledge on your shoulders. A master waits. You have to snatch from him, you have to partake of him. He will not follow you, he will not force you. He will not even knock at your doors, he will simply wait. You can partake of his being. You can enter his inner emptiness, the inner palace of his being, his inner kingdom, but that is up to you. You will have to do all the work. The master is only a presence. If you are attracted, you fall into the presence.

A teacher calls, a teacher tries, a teacher makes every effort so that you can understand. A master simply is there – open of course, not closed, absolutely open for you to come in. But he doesn't make even a gesture, because that gesture may be aggressive, that gesture may force you to come in without your own will. And then it will be bad, then you have been put on a wrong path.

A master is a silent presence. You can learn from him, but he will not teach. With a teacher you will be a student. There exists a relationship, a two-way relationship. With the master you can be only a disciple, it is one-way – you have to learn. If you don't learn, you don't learn; if you learn, you learn. A master is so happy with his own being he does not bother. If you learn he blesses you; if you don't learn he also blesses you – he is a blessing, a benediction.

There are no examinations near a master because examinations are not possible for life. It is foolish to think in terms of examinations. That's why universities go on producing stupid people. There is a reason for it, because intelligence cannot be examined. There can be no criterion to judge it. At the most you can judge the memory, at the most you can judge the capacity to remember, but not the capacity to know. A master has no examinations. You come in, you learn, you partake. He is an opening unto the vast and the infinite.

A man of knowledge becomes a teacher and millions of people are attracted toward him, because when you learn something your ego feels strengthened. Very few rare souls are attracted toward a master because in fact with a master you will have to unlearn, with a master you will have to die. Your ego will be shattered completely – because only then can you enter the temple, the innermost shrine of the master's being.

A master is a wise man but his understanding is so profound that you cannot understand it. You can only live it. A master knows, but he knows in such depth where opposites meet; where life and death become synonymous, where existence and nonexistence don't mean opposites, where all rivers fall into the ocean – in that depth a master exists.

It is difficult to understand him because understanding will be superficial and all understanding will be more or less misunderstanding. With a master don't try to understand him. How can you understand him? How can you understand an infinite phenomenon? You can live it, you can dissolve into it, you can allow it to dissolve into you, that's possible. It is like love: you cannot understand love, mysterious are its ways. You cannot understand it, you cannot pin down what it is. Thousands of definitions exist but love has not been defined yet and it will never be defined. Whenever you define, immediately you feel something is missing. And that something will always miss, because that something is the depth. A definition cannot carry depth, it can only be on the surface.

A wise man lives in the depth. A man of knowledge lives on the circumference. A wise man lives at the center. There is only one way to reach a wise man – you will have to come to your own center. Center to center there is communion with a wise man. Head to head, mind to mind, there is communion with a teacher, the man of knowledge.

The wise man has by and by disappeared from the world. In the West you don't find philosophers, you find only professors of philosophy. This is something absurd. A professor of philosophy is not a philosopher, a professor of philosophy is just a teacher; a man of knowledge, but not a wise man. Not like Socrates, not like Lao Tzu, not like Buddha; they are not professors, they are not professing anything, they are not teaching anything to anybody. They are just there: like the sun is there, you open your eyes and the darkness disappears; like the flower by the side of the path, you just be with it for a few seconds and the fragrance fills you to your very depth; like a river flowing, you come to it thirsty and your thirst is quenched. They are not professors, they are living people. They are more alive than anybody else, and then they become more and more mysterious.

A few more things before we enter these sutras of Lao Tzu. In the East the past has always been revered; we remember the past with deep respect. In the West respect for the past has completely disappeared; rather, on the contrary, a certain respect for the future has come into being. Parallel to it, old people are not respected in the West – if the past is not respected how can you respect old people? You just tolerate them anyhow; even parents are only tolerated. When they are old, deep down a desire arises in you: if they were dead it would be better – because what is the use of them now? The West thinks in terms of use; of course a young man is more useful than an old man.

If you think of utility, a young man is more useful than an old man. An old man has lost his energy, his body is crippled, he is ill, he is going to die any day. He is not useful, he is just a burden. All respect for old people has disappeared. It is a corollary: when you don't respect the past you cannot respect your father, your grandfather, and you don't remember even the name of your great-grandfather. It is as if he never existed. You start thinking and feeling more for your children – they are the future. And they will think of their children, remember. They will not think about you. So don't suffer and don't feel the pain and the hurt of it. In the West the future has become significant; in the East it has always been the past.

There are many things to be understood. Why in the West has the future become more significant? The West is dominated by men of knowledge: professors, scientists, novelists, theologians, political demagogues. The West is dominated by men of knowledge and of course, there is a possibility for a young man to know more than the old man, because he is always standing on the shoulders of the old man – he can look a little farther away.

Your father was studying in the university thirty or forty years ago. In these forty years everything has changed. Whatsoever your father knows is almost out of date. The copyright on the books that he was reading at university is no longer there. Nobody bothers about those books, you can find them only in secondhand bookstalls. They are useless. Whatsoever he has accumulated in forty years is useless, because in forty years an explosion of knowledge has happened. And it is going on and on and on. Your children will know more than you – in fact, already they know more.

I was reading a small anecdote...

Two small children went to a zoo with their old grandmother. The old grandmother was explaining what was what to them. Then they came to a bird, the stork, and the old woman said, "This is the bird which brings children from heaven, which brought you, which always brings children."

These two small children started giggling, and they whispered into each other's ears, "Should we tell this old thing the truth?"

But one of them said, "Why disturb her? Let her remain in her belief."

Mulla Nasruddin called his boy because now the time was ripe and things about life had to be told to him. So he told him, "Come with me to my room, I would like to discuss a few facts about life with you. Now you are mature and a few things have to be told to you." Mulla was feeling a little nervous – as every father feels when facts of life have to be told to children. As old, out-dated minds do, he was feeling a little nervous.

When they went into the room and he closed the door the boy said, "Don't be nervous. Now, what do you want to know? I can tell you, don't be so nervous."

Children can now tell you many more things – and children feel that you are somehow a little ignorant, illiterate. Every child in the West feels that the parents are illiterate. The respect has disappeared. If men of knowledge dominate the society this is going to be so, because knowledge grows every day, changes every day, accumulates more and more. Of course children are more up to date than their parents. It has to be so. They know the latest.

In the East the man of wisdom has been the center of life, not the man of knowledge. Knowledge grows, changes, moves – wisdom is eternal, it is always the same. Whenever you attain it, it is always the same. It is like the sky which remains eternally the same. Seasons come and go: now it is winter, now it is summer, now it is raining, now the rains have disappeared. Trees come and die, generations come and go and the drama of life goes on moving, but the sky remains as it is, eternally the same, eternally new, ever fresh and always old. Wisdom is like the sky.

Of course knowledge can be taught in the universities, colleges, schools. Wisdom can never be taught. Nowhere can it be taught. Wisdom has to be imbibed through life, there is no other way. So only an old man can be a wise man. In wisdom the young man can never defeat the old man, but in knowledge he can always defeat him.

How can you defeat the old man in wisdom? Wisdom comes through experience; knowledge comes not through experience but through learning. You can cram it in, and if you are a little intelligent, more intelligent than the average, you can know more than your teacher. You can know more than your father, there is no problem about it. Just a little effort on your part is needed. But wisdom – there is no way. It comes by and by through life. If you live and if you live totally, if you live and you live with awareness, only then, drop by drop, does wisdom come into being. It is such a subtle phenomenon. There is no direct way to reach it. Only old people can be wise. That's why whenever there is somebody who is wise and young, in the East we know that he is old, he is ancient.

There is a beautiful story about Lao Tzu that he was born old; when he was born he was eighty-four years of age – he had remained in his mother's womb for eighty-four years. Absurd, unbelievable, but a beautiful story – says something, says something very significant. It says that from his very childhood he was like an old man, so wise he could not be a child. It says something. It is symbolic. It says that when he was a child he had as much wisdom as ordinarily a man of eighty-four would have. He must have been tremendously alert.

If you are very, very alert then a single experience can give you much. If you are not alert you will go on repeating the same experience and nothing will be gained.

A wise man falls in love only once, then he knows everything about it. He penetrates the whole mystery, he lives the whole mystery of it, he moves into its world, but so totally that not even a corner is left unlived. Then he comes out of it. Then there is no question of falling in love again – he has lived and he has known. He has become wise through experience. A foolish man will repeat the same thing again and again and again, and will never be able to learn anything from it.

Awareness and a courage to live have to be there, so it will happen only rarely that a child or a young man will be wise. Ordinarily a man will become wise when he is old: when he has lived all the seasons of life, when he is seasoned, when he has known all the climates, all the moods. When he has known the river of life in summer, when it is just a dry bed and nothing is left except a thirst, a hunger, a dry bed, a burning desire, and nothing else. And he has known the river of life in flood when it becomes vast, dangerously vast and it pretends to be an ocean.

He has known all the moods, he has moved in all the ways that life allows. He has lived as a sinner, he has lived as a saint, he is enriched by all experiences. When all the hairs of the head are white, a beauty comes to the face which can come only to an old man, never to a young man. Young men can be beautiful as far as physique is concerned – shape, proportion, strength – yes, young men can be very beautiful. But as far as the soul is concerned, which evolves, grows only through much experience; only an old man can be beautiful.

Rarely it happens, because rarely are people aware; rarely do people live through life with meditation. Otherwise no young man can compete with the beauty of an old man. The beauty of an old man has a grace to it, a depth; a young man's beauty is shallow, on the surface, just skin deep. An old man's beauty has a depth in it – you go in and in and in and you never come to the bottom of it.

An old man is like a snowcapped peak of the Himalayas. Silent. The storm has passed. All that was needed to know he has known, nothing more is left to know. The ego has been dropped on the way somewhere because it was a burden, and with the ego and that burden you cannot reach to such a peak. When one moves toward the peak one has to leave everything by and by, by and by; the final peak is when you have to leave yourself also. You reach the peak as a nonbeing because even being becomes a burden in the final stages of life.

The East respects the old. And if you respect the old you respect the past. And the East has a nostalgia for the past.

Now this sutra:

The wise ones of old had subtle wisdom
and depth of understanding...

The wise ones of old... In the East it is always the old, the ancient who are wise. There is a humbleness about oneself and the present. How can you be more wise than your father? How can you be more wise than your grandfather, great-grandfather? No, you can know more. You can know more than Buddha – you may already know more than Buddha – but you cannot be more wise. In fact, in wisdom, "more" doesn't exist. One is wise or not, there is no more to it, no less to it. In knowledge more and less exist. Knowledge is relative, wisdom is absolute. You cannot be more wise, and in fact if you are wise you will feel very, very humble.

Lao Tzu feels so humble about himself and about his own age that he always talks about the wise ones of old. And if you go to the wise ones of old you will find them talking about the wise ones of older days again.

If you try to understand Eastern scriptures they always say that whatsoever they are saying is not new, it was told to them, they have heard it. That's why Hindus have two names for their scriptures, *shruti* and *smriti*. *Shruti* means: we have heard it, we have heard those who knew. *Smriti* means: we have stored it from those who know.

There is no claim on anyone's part that they have known, because the very claim "I have known" is the claim of ignorance, the "I" is the condensed ignorance. They go back and back and back. In the Upanishads, if you go back, they will say: "I learned from my teacher. My teacher learned from his teacher, he learned from his teacher..." And they go on and on, and in the beginning: Brahma, the creator of the world, learned from the cosmic existence itself, from *brahman*.

He learned from *brahman*; *brahman* is the invisible divinity and

Brahma is the visible divinity. The visible divinity learned it from the invisible divinity, and from Brahma starts the Ganges. And then teacher and teacher and teacher, a long procession – and "I have just heard it."

This is a beautiful phenomenon. It simply says that no man is an island, and there is interdependence. The whole past is involved in you – this is the meaning of it. You are not alone here, you have not suddenly bubbled up. The whole past is carried by you – your consciousness is in a chain, related with the whole past. From the very beginning up to now, everything that has happened, has happened to you and you are the carrier of the whole past. In this way, in time a relationship, the feeling of a relationship, arises.

There can be two types of interdependence. One is spatial: you are related to this tree, this tree is related to today's sun, the sun is related to bigger stars, everything related in space. This is one type of interdependence. There is another type of interdependence which moves in time: the whole past is involved in you. You have come as an outcome of the whole past, and the whole future will come out of you. You are the fruit of the whole past and you will become the seed of the whole future. Then both time and space are interdependent, in both dimensions you are interrelated.

The wise ones of old had subtle wisdom and depth of understanding... What is subtle wisdom? They knew directly, they knew immediately. They knew the truth face to face, it was not borrowed knowledge. And when wisdom is direct, only then is it wisdom. Otherwise it is nothing but a mask to ignorance, you go on hiding your ignorance by your knowledge. And why call wisdom subtle? Why not just call it wisdom? What is the point of calling it subtle?

There is a point. Wisdom is direct but subtle. It is direct in the sense that one faces life immediately, but it is subtle in the sense that in life you never attain anything directly. You have to move in indirect ways.

Try to understand. In the first place, wisdom is direct in the sense that it is not borrowed. It is not that you are simply borrowing somebody else's know-how and accumulating it in the mind. No, you yourself have come to encounter it. In this sense it is direct, more direct than knowledge. But still it is subtle, subtle because it has its own indirect way. What is that indirect way?

If you want to be happy you cannot move directly like an arrow toward the target of happiness. If you do you will miss. For example, somebody says to you, "When I go swimming in the river, it is so beautiful and I feel so happy and relaxed just floating on the water under the sun. I forget every worry, I forget every tension and I am so relaxed the world doesn't exist. I feel so happy, such a deep bliss comes to me through it." And your greed arises, and you say, "Then I will also try." Then you go, but you go very directly. Your mind is not in swimming, your mind is not with the river, your mind is not with the sun, your mind is not with the wind. Your mind is like an arrow moving directly toward the target of happiness – you will miss it.

Because life is very shy, it hides from people who are aggressive. It reveals itself only to those who persuade it in a very subtle and indirect way. Life has to be persuaded and seduced. Life is a woman. Don't be aggressive about it. You cannot rape it. And if you try to rape it you will be empty-handed, you will not gain anything out of it. You can rape it. That is what almost all people are doing – trying to rape life. Because to fall in love seems to be risky, to rape seems to be less risky – there is no commitment in it. But without commitment you cannot learn anything. Unless you are involved you will not be transformed.

You go to the river, but your mind is continuously thinking and hankering for happiness. You don't look at the river. You are not sensitive, you are just greedy. You move into the river, but you simply feel tired and not relaxed. You swim, but you are constantly asking, "Where is that happiness you were talking about? I see the sun, I see the river, I see the winds moving, but where is that happiness you were talking about?"

This is a direct attack. Nobody can attain happiness that way. You have to forget yourself in the swimming and forget that you are here to attain happiness. Forget yourself and forget your greed and forget the goals – and when the goal is forgotten the target is attained. I may appear paradoxical, but I cannot be anything else; I'm helpless, because this is how life is. Forget the target and the arrow hits it; look at the target, look at it too much – and the arrow misses. You cannot attain. You will come home and you will say, "It is useless, I tried."

Somebody meditates and feels ecstatic and you feel infected. Whenever he comes around you, you feel he has something that you don't have. And you ask, "What is happening?" He says he is meditating and it is such a blissful phenomenon – you come and try. You go and try but you fail, because you are always direct. You don't understand that life is feminine, it is really a woman. You will have to persuade it, you will have to play many games with it, indirect, subtle. Don't go and ask the woman directly, "Would you like to come to bed with me?" She will call a policeman.

Be a little more poetic. Write beautiful love letters to life. That's what meditation is all about – writing love letters to life, sending loaded messages, but very indirect. As life leans more and more toward you, you take more and more courage. But move very cautiously, you can miss it. A little aggression and you will miss it. Love, happiness, meditation, truth, or you name it, whatsoever is beautiful can be attained only in a subtle way. That's why Lao Tzu says: *The wise ones of old had subtle wisdom and depth of understanding...*

What is depth of understanding? Depth of understanding is when you can stand in others' shoes, when you can see from others' eyes, when you can feel from others' hands, when you can stand in the other's being, at the other's center, and look through him – how he feels, what he feels, what he says.

A man of knowledge is always blind, argumentative; he is always right and the other is always wrong. He is always discussing; his discussions become disgusting. He is always arrogant and always on the defensive. He cannot understand anybody. Whatsoever you say he will deny – he will say no because in "no" he knows there is power. Remember this: a man who has not learned the power of saying yes is not yet wise. He goes on saying no because whenever he says no he feels powerful. Have you felt it? Just say no and you feel powerful. Say yes and you feel surrendered. Yes becomes difficult, so you go on contradicting whosoever is saying anything. You are always right.

How can this be possible? This whole world – so many consciousnesses, so many ways of looking at life – all wrong, only you are right? This seems to be a very, very arrogant and violent outlook. A man of understanding understands that somehow everybody has to be right in some sense or other.

It happened...

A Sufi mystic was made a *kazi*; he was made a justice, a judge. He was a wise man, a man of understanding – what Lao Tzu calls of "deep" understanding.

The first case was brought before him. The first party argued. He listened intently, and then he said, "Right, absolutely right."

The clerk of the court was worried because he had not yet heard the other party, and how can a judge say this without listening to the other party? So he leaned toward the judge and whispered in his ear, "I think you are not aware of the ways of the court. You should not say this because it is a judgment, the case is finished. But you have not heard the other party! How can you say to one party that they are right?"

The judge said, "You are right. Let me hear the other party."

He heard the other party, listened intently and then said, "Right, absolutely right."

Now the clerk thought that this man was mad. How could both be right together? He leaned over again and said, "What are you doing? Are you drunk or are you mad? How can both be right?"

The judge said, "Of course, you are right. How can both be right?"

This is a man of deep understanding, for whom everybody is right, because he can penetrate to the very depth of your being and can see your viewpoint also. He is not enclosed in his own viewpoint, in his own philosophy, in his own doctrine. He has none, in fact. He is an open phenomenon. He can come into you and look through you and can see why, why you are insisting; he can feel why you feel you are right.

But then this type of man will be a mystery. Either you will call him mad or you will call him a sage who is beyond the world, but it is none of his affair to interfere with your life.

This is what happened to Mahavira. He created a logic; such a logic never existed before. He created a logic which is called *syatvad*, the logic of perhaps. Whatsoever you say he would say, "Perhaps you are right." If somebody came and said, "I believe in God," he would say, "Perhaps God is." Always perhaps. How can you be absolutely wrong? With a life force, a godliness in you, how can you be absolutely wrong? Something must be right. Maybe we cannot understand it, maybe we cannot feel it, but something must be right in you. If godliness exists in everybody, then everybody has a right to be right somehow.

Mahavira penetrates deeply. The man is sitting there, another comes and says, "I don't believe in God, God does not exist." And

Mahavira says, "Perhaps you are also right. There is a sense in which God exists and there is a sense in which God doesn't exist." He created a new logic, a new dimension to logic.

There are only two logics: one is that of Aristotle and the other is that of Mahavira. Aristotle says, "A can only be A and A can never be B." And Mahavira says, "A is A and can also be B, can also be C, can also be D – up to Z." Just so many angles, so many angles of seeing a thing – he says that there are seven standpoints. But it is difficult to understand Mahavira, that's why his following could not grow much. It was impossible. Even those who follow him, follow him because they are accidentally born in his fold; otherwise it is impossible. I have not come across a single Jaina who can really follow Mahavira.

I was talking to a Jaina *muni*, one of the great *acharyas* of Jaina *munis*, and I asked him, "What do you think about syatvad?"

He said, "It is absolutely true."

I said, "Then you are not a *syatvad*. You should say 'perhaps.' Even about Mahavira you should say, 'Perhaps he is right.'"

But no Jaina can say that perhaps Mahavira is absolutely right – there they miss. They say that Jainism is absolutely right, and the whole point of Jainism is that nothing is absolutely right.

Just the other day it happened…

Mulla Nasruddin's wife went to see Sona – you know Sona, the tarot card reader? – and she came back very much disturbed.

The future disturbs. Anything about the future disturbs. It is good not to know about the future because once you know anything about the future it starts changing your present, and disturbance arises.

She was very worried. Mulla Nasruddin asked her, "What is the matter?"

She said, "I have been to a tarot card reader, a very good woman, and she has said a few things and I am very worried."

Mulla Nasruddin said, "Don't be worried. Nothing is certain in life so no prediction can be made. I tell you that only fools are certain."

The wife said, "Are you really certain about that?"

He said, "Absolutely certain!"

Only fools are certain. If a man is absolutely certain about it then he becomes an absolute fool. No Jaina has the courage to say, "Perhaps Mahavira is right. Perhaps those who deny Mahavira are also right." No Jaina has the courage – that's why I say no Jaina has the understanding of Mahavira. It is difficult.

The wise ones of old had subtle wisdom
and depth of understanding,
so profound that they could not be understood.

The more profoundly you move inside yourself, the more incomprehensible you become to others, because they live on the surface. If you live on the surface, everything is okay – they understand you. The surface they know. But if you start moving downward, deeper into your profundity, then a moment comes when you become incomprehensible. You have gone beyond them; they cannot understand you.

Just two, three days ago a sannyasin came to me, and he said, "I cannot come to your lectures any more, because I feel bored." I said, "Don't come! Don't come!" He was thinking he was saying something about my lectures when he said he felt bored. He was saying something about himself, that it goes beyond his understanding, that he cannot move into such profundities, that it is beyond him. Then he felt bored.

A man can feel bored in two ways. Either something is constantly repeated, only a single note repeated continuously, a monotonous tone – then you can feel bored. That is the way a lullaby is created. The mother goes on repeating a certain line, and the child feels bored and goes to sleep. That's what people who suffer from insomnia should do with themselves. That's how a mantra helps; Maharishi Mahesh Yogi's TM helps people who have lost the capacity to sleep. For them TM is perfect, because it creates boredom. You repeat a mantra inside: go on repeating, repeating – the mind feels bored because there is nothing new to know, there is no excitement, the same word again and again and again and again. You fall into sleep.

Or you feel bored when something is beyond you. You feel bored when something is so profound that it is incomprehensible to you. ...*so profound that they could not be understood.* You can understand only to the extent that you are aware. You cannot understand more than your awareness; your understanding is bound to remain confined to your alertness. If you want to understand wise men, you will have to grow into awareness. The more your awareness, the more you can penetrate them. When you are perfectly aware, only then is a Lao Tzu totally open to you. Not that he was closed, he was always open – but you could not enter him. You were not yet capable of it.

And because they could not be understood,
perforce must they be so described...

Because you cannot understand the really wise men you are puzzled about them. Contradictory things, rumors are spread about them, around and around. Somebody says Gurdjieff is a God and somebody says that he is a Satan, and both rumors are true – because a man who has profundity is both together. *...perforce must they be so described...* So people describe them in these ways.

...cautious...

A wise man will look very cautious to you. He is not cautious, he is only alert. There is a difference, a vast difference. When a man is cautious he is afraid. For example, in a dark night, you have lost your way in a forest; you move cautiously. At every step there is danger, death. In that cautiousness a certain alertness comes to you – you may have felt it. Whenever there is danger a certain alertness comes to you, whenever there is danger you become a little more alert – not exactly alert, simply cautious. But to be cautious one has to be a little alert. It comes automatically; that alertness is an automatic shadow of cautiousness. But we don't know what alertness is, so when we see a wise man, a buddha walking, we think he is very cautious. That is our understanding about his awareness.

...cautious, like crossing a wintry stream...

He seems always to be cautious.

...irresolute, like one fearing danger all around...

No, a wise man is not irresolute, but he is not certain like fools. He carries no ready-made solutions about life, that's why he looks irresolute. He does not live with conclusions. He lives open, open to whatsoever is going to happen. He has no conclusions in his mind. He does not force his conclusions on life, he remains alert and helps life to reach its own conclusion. He cooperates, he does not impose – there is a difference.

We live with a conclusion. For example, you have come to hear me. Somebody told you about me. He was a friend and he talked about me. He appreciated me; he impressed you. You have come to hear me with a conclusion: I am a good man. Now you will listen through this conclusion and your conclusion will be strengthened. You will go back home and say that he was right, the friend was right. Then somebody else has come the same morning. He has met my enemy, who told him many things about me. He convinced him that I am a wrong man, but his curiosity was awakened – one wants to go to see even such a wrong man. He has also come this morning to listen to me with a conclusion, and he will go with his conclusion strengthened.

Only those who have come to me without any conclusion, open, mirrorlike, will see my real face. Otherwise your conclusion will become my face, you will impose it on my face.

A wise man is not irresolute, but he appears irresolute because he lives without conclusion, he moves moment to moment. He never carries any conclusion from the past. Whatsoever life brings, he encounters it with a fresh consciousness, not with a consciousness which is burdened by conclusions. Then everything is dead. You look through the conclusion – it means you look through the past, it means you look through your experience, through your mind. You never come directly in contact with life. There is a buffer between you and life, your conclusion functions as a buffer. You are afraid to touch life.

...*cautious, like crossing a wintry stream...* And he is not cautious, he is aware.

...*irresolute, like one fearing danger all around...* No, he is not irresolute, he is without conclusions.

...*grave, like one acting as a guest...*

No, he is not grave but he appears so because he is not shallow. He does not laugh, his laughter is not that of a shallow man. At the most he smiles – even that is too much. In fact he need not even smile because his whole being is filled with so much beauty, with so much beatitude, with so much happiness, that he need not.

You will be surprised that the people who laugh most are really sad inside; by laughing they hide the sadness, by laughter they try to befool themselves that they are happy. People who laugh loudly almost always have deep wounds within them. They don't want to go into those wounds.

Somebody asked Friedrich Nietzsche why he laughed so much. Nietzsche is reported to have said – and he was really a very true, honest man, so honest that he became mad. In this mad world, if you are really honest you will be in difficulty. He said, "I go on laughing because I am afraid that if I don't laugh I will start crying, I will start weeping. And that would be embarrassing. I hide my tears in my laughter."

You see a wise man as grave – it is your interpretation. He's not grave. He's not shallow, that's right. Watch a shallow river, it makes much noise. A deep river moves as if it doesn't move, no noise – not because it is not moving. It is moving, but it is so deep that the noise doesn't reach you. A wise man laughs in the deepest core of his being. It doesn't reach his lips. To know his laughter you will have to become like him.

...self-effacing, like ice beginning to melt...

You think that a wise man is humble, self-effacing, like ice beginning to melt; you think wisdom is humility – no. A wise man is simply egoless, that's all. I will not say that a wise man is humble, because humbleness is also a sort of egoism. To be humble means to be a very polished ego. To be humble means a very cultured egoism. If there is no ego how can you be humble? If you cannot be arrogant you cannot be humble. They both go together, they are both aspects of the same phenomenon. Go and look at humble men, servants of people, this and that, and look into their eyes. They pretend they are humble, they even believe they are humble but you can see their subtle egos shining in their eyes.

It happened...

A man came to see Socrates. The man was a fakir, a very humble man. He was so humble that he would not use new clothes.

He was so humble that if new clothes were given to him he would first make them rotten, dirty, then he would use them. He came to see Socrates and there were many holes in his dress. Socrates looked into him and said, "Do you think you are humble? Through your holes I can see your ego."

Ego can pretend to be humble. Self-effacing men are not really humble, self-effacing men are simply very tricky and cunning. No, it appears to people who cannot move into the profundities of the wise man that he is self-effacing. He does not know the self, how can he be self-effacing? He simply lives without any ego, without any arrogance and without any humility.

...genuine, like a piece of undressed wood...

It seems to you that a wise man is raw, undressed wood because his culture is very, very deep, his subtlety is very, very profound. Only on the surface can you touch him; that roughness is just on the surface. About Gurdjieff it is said that he was so rough that people would escape from him. It was difficult to stand him, but those who could stand him for a few weeks would come to know his deep compassion.

In nature you can observe one thing: wherever you see something very soft you will always find it covered with something hard. A seed is covered by a nut, covered by a hard shell. The seed is very soft – has to be, because a life is going to bubble up, sprout – but it is covered with a hard shell. That is natural.

In man you will find just the opposite phenomenon: on the outside soft, the shell soft and the seed hard, inside very hard. This is a perversion. In nature it is natural to be hard on the outside because if you are not hard on the outside you cannot be soft on the inside. The inner softness has to be covered by a hardness. It protects. But in man you will find just the opposite. This is what hypocrisy means: soft outside, soft like butter, and inside, the more you know the man the harder he is – a perversion. This should not be so. This is what your gentleman is, your cultured man is, your so-called civilized man is – the moral man, the religious man: so soft on the outside and hard inside. This should be impossible; it is possible only because only man can pretend, nobody else can pretend.

A man of wisdom is again part of nature; all perversions have disappeared. He will be rough on the outside and soft inside. You will have to be patient with a man of wisdom – you will want to escape from him, because many times you will feel he is so hard he will kill you. Or you came to get some consolation and he goes on shocking you. You came to get some love, you were seeking some love, and he never looks at you, never pays much attention to you. You came for compassion and he is so hard. You would like to escape. But a man of wisdom is always that way because he is natural, and nature has this way, this is the arrangement: inside soft, outside hard.

Look at the bark of the tree, it is so hard on the outside. Move inside and you will find softer and softer layers. Just at the center is life, absolutely soft. It has to be protected.

...like a piece of undressed wood,
open-minded, like a valley,
and mixing freely, like murky water.

A wise man will look open-minded to you; in fact he is without mind, not open-minded. You can be open-minded and closed-minded; a wise man is a no-mind. But no-mind appears to you as open-minded, at the most. It is so profound you cannot understand. At the most you can understand that this man is very open, his mind is not closed, but you don't know that he has no mind to close. He is not open-minded, he is simply a no-mind. It is not that the doors of his house are open. In fact there exists no house. He is just under the open sky, he has no house and no doors. He is not open, rather he is openness.

But if we try to understand a wise man from the outside, these things will happen to us. Anything that is written about Buddha goes wrong, anything written about Lao Tzu goes wrong, anything written about Mahavira or Jesus goes wrong because the people who write, write through their understanding. And a man like Jesus or Lao Tzu is so profound that there is every possibility that whatsoever you understand about him will be a misunderstanding. So be a little alert and hesitant. Love him, but don't try to understand him. Then one day you may understand him. Be close, near, intimate, but don't try to understand. Then one day there is a possibility that the mystery may be unveiled to you.

If you try to understand you will miss. And those who try to understand and write books and theses will become the professors of the doctrine. They create the religions in the world – those who have misunderstood in the very beginning. They create religions.

...*open-minded, like a valley*... No, because a valley is surrounded by hills. It looks open but it is closed. He is open like the sky, not closed by anything. A valley will disappear if the mountains around it disappear; so mountains are part of the valley. A mind which is open: his openness will disappear if the mind disappears; his openness is just a part of the mind. A wise man is open like a sky. He is sheer openness.

...*and mixing freely, like murky water.* And it will appear to you that a wise man goes on mixing freely like murky water. Jesus stayed in a house with a prostitute because she invited him; stayed with people who were known to be criminals because they invited him. Of course he must have looked like murky water, not pure water like a brahmin, a puritan who says, "Don't touch me because I am pure."

It is reported that Shankara, the greatest Hindu philosopher ever, was awakened by an untouchable. The untouchable became his guru. Up to that time he was a great teacher, a man of knowledge; he had written great treatises on the Upanishads, Brahma Sutras, Bhagavadgita, and he had been propounding a certain philosophy: vedanta, *advait vedant* – reality is non-dual, one.

Then one day it happened that he was coming out of the Ganges in the early morning; he had taken his bath and he was on the steps going back to his hut when a sudra, an untouchable, touched him.

He became angry and he said, "You have destroyed my bath. I will have to go again and purify myself."

The sudra said, "Wait just a single minute. I would like to ask you – if there is only one, if the whole existence is one, how can I and you exist? How can you become impure by my touch? Who has touched you? Who has touched whom?"

As if from a deep sleep, the sleep of the man of knowledge – and it is one of the greatest sleeps, it is almost a coma – Shankara was awakened.

And the man asked again, "What do you think? Has my body touched you or has my soul touched you? Has my body touched your body? Or has my body touched your soul? Do you think bodies are different – your body, the body of a brahmin, pure, and my body, the body of a sudra, impure? Do you think the five elements out of which bodies are constituted are different for brahmins and sudras, the untouchables? Do you think that if my body has touched you, it has touched your soul and made it impure? Or if my soul has touched you, can you say that the soul can also be an untouchable, a sudra?"

A conversion – his whole life turned upside-down. Shankara never went again to take his bath.

He paid his respect to the sudra and said, "You are my guru and you awakened me out of my sleep. I was only talking about that which is one, but I had not known it."

If a real wise man exists he will look to you like murky water mixing freely, because for him there is nobody pure and nobody impure. A man of wisdom never thinks that he is pure and you are impure.

It is reported of Lieh Tzu, a great follower of Lao Tzu, that he had many disciples in his ashram. A certain disciple was found stealing again and again and he was creating a nuisance, but he was always forgiven by the master. But there came a point where it became too much and all five hundred disciples went to Lieh Tzu and said, "Now it is enough. There is a limit to everything. You have forgiven this man so many times, but he seems to be incurable. Now it is time enough, throw him out!"

Lieh Tzu said, "Wait, brothers. You are all good people, moral, of good character. Anywhere you go you will be accepted by other people, respected, loved, served. And even without me you are so moral you will reach the truth. But where will this brother go? He has nobody other than Lieh Tzu because nobody will accept him. So all those who think that you cannot live with this brother, you go. But I have to be with him, because where will he go? Who will accept him? If Lieh Tzu rejects him, then he is rejected, then nobody can accept him."

This is how a man of wisdom is. He will look as if he is mixing freely like murky water. But he mixes freely because for him purity and impurity, good and bad; all divisions have disappeared. For him only one oceanic consciousness exists, that's why he mixes freely. Jesus staying at the house of a prostitute or staying at the house of a nun – it is the same for Jesus; he goes to sleep. It is the same for him because the prostitute is a form of the same and the nun is also a form of the same. And nobody is pure and nobody is impure – all duality gone, transcended. A man of wisdom lives in oneness, that's why he mixes freely. There is no barrier for him.

Who can find repose in a muddy world?
By lying still, it becomes clear.

Lao Tzu says: *Who can find repose in a muddy world?* The world is muddy. How will you find repose in it? How will you find peace in it? By lying still. Don't do anything, don't try to purify it, otherwise you will muddle it more. Just lie down on the bank, wait. By lying still it becomes clear on its own accord. Don't be worried about transforming the world; don't be worried about changing others. Who are you? And who has sent you on this mission to change others? Everybody is directly related to the divine. Why are you there to interfere? Just sit silently.

Who can maintain his calm for long?

Calmness comes, silence comes, but who can maintain it for long?

By activity it comes back to life.

By activity you can maintain it. If you try to maintain it by continuous inactivity it will be impossible; one has to move into opposites to remain always transcendental. In the day you work, in the night you sleep. If you continuously work for twenty-four hours a day it will be death; if you continuously sleep for twenty-four hours a day, that will also be death.

In the day work hard – and in working hard you are gaining the capacity to sleep. In the night sleep completely – in sleeping completely you are regaining, refreshing, rejuvenating your energies to work hard. Move into a rhythm. Lean to the right, lean to the left and always keep the balance. Repose can be maintained, calm can be maintained, only by not remaining inactive forever and ever. That mistake has been made in India; sannyasins remaining continuously inactive cannot remain silent. Be a householder and be a sannyasin together; be in the world and be out of it also, together. Remember always that life is a togetherness of opposites – a deep harmony.

He who embraces this Tao
guards against being over-full.

Whosoever comes to know that Tao is balance, religion is balance, God is balance ...*guards against being over-full.* Don't move too much to one side, otherwise the balance will be lost, and imbalance is the only sin for Lao Tzu. To be balanced is to be virtuous, to be imbalanced is to be in sin.

Because he guards against being over-full,
he is beyond wearing out and renewal.

He is always fresh and young; he is never weary, he is never tired. The balance gives him eternal life. Balance is vitality. Balance is life.

Enough for today.

wisdom and understanding

The first question:

Osho,
Do wisdom and understanding increase gradually or do they come as explosions?

Understanding never comes, neither as a sudden phenomenon nor as a gradual one, because it is always there. You have it right now. It is not going to happen somewhere in the future. You are carrying it within you, just as a seed carries the tree, a woman carries a child. You are carrying it right now. Now it depends on you: if your intensity is total you will achieve it suddenly; if your intensity is not total you will achieve it by and by, in steps. But understanding never comes to you – you are understanding. Enlightenment is not something that happens to you – you are enlightenment.

Remember this; then it is a choice, your choice. If you desire it totally, in that fire of total desire all that covers that understanding burns; suddenly the light is there. But it is up to you. It is not part of the nature of enlightenment to happen gradually or to happen suddenly.

Don't throw off the responsibility, that's how people create philosophies and schools. In Japan two schools of Zen exist: one believes in sudden enlightenment, another believes in gradual enlightenment – as if these are the qualities of enlightenment, as if they belong to enlightenment. They don't belong to enlightenment. Enlightenment is always there, it is for you to choose. If your desire is total not even a single moment is lost. But if your desire is not total it means that you yourself are not willing it to happen right now. You want to postpone it, you want it tomorrow, some other day. Then you go on playing tricks.

If you are really sincere there is no time gap, it can happen this very moment. Not even a single moment is to be lost, because it is already the case. One has just to look within. But if you don't want it right now then you can wait for millennia.

I would like to tell you an old story. It happened in Ceylon:

There was a great Buddhist master who taught his disciples for almost eighty years. When he was a hundred and twenty he said one day, "Now, I am going to die after seven days." So thousands of his disciples gathered for his last *darshan*, to see him for the last time.

The old man, before closing his eyes and dissolving inward, asked them, "Does somebody want to accompany me? If somebody wants nirvana, enlightenment right now, then he should simply raise his hand and that will do."

People knew that he was a man of his word, and he was not joking. He had never joked in his whole life, he was a serious man. He meant what he said. They started looking at each other – thousands of people and not a single hand was raised.

One man stood up and he said, "Please don't misunderstand me. I don't want to accompany you right now because there are many things to be done. I have many things to fulfill, many things to pass through, many karmas to be accounted for. As yet I am not ready for it, but someday I would like to be enlightened. Can you give some key hints? – because you will no longer be here."

And the master had been giving key hints his whole life, for eighty years. Still they wanted something to be said about it so that they could postpone and plan and think about the future. And the old master was ready. If somebody had been ready he was ready to take him with him. But nobody was ready.

People are cunning because the mind is cunning. And the

greatest cunningness of the mind is that it always throws responsibility onto something else. If enlightenment is gradual then what can you do? Nothing can be done; it is gradual, it will take a long time. If enlightenment is sudden then why has it not happened to you? You will ask, "Then why has it not happened to me if it is sudden? No, it cannot be sudden. But if it is sudden and there is no need to do something for it to happen, then what can be done? I will wait – whenever it happens it happens."

You simply want to escape from the responsibility of your own choice. Sartre has said one thing that is really beautiful. He said, "Man is free to choose but man is not free not to choose." You can choose either way but don't be befooled – you have no freedom not to choose, because even when you think you are not choosing you are choosing the opposite.

A man came to me and he said, "I am not yet ready for sannyas. I am ready seventy percent, eighty percent, but twenty percent I am not ready, so how can I take sannyas? I'm not total."

So I said, "Okay. But still you are choosing, and now you are choosing a minor part of your mind – the twenty percent which says, 'Don't take.' Now you are choosing the twenty percent against the eighty percent."

So don't think that you are not choosing. That's not possible. You have to choose whatsoever you do; even if you don't choose you will be choosing. Choice is there. One is free to choose, but one is not free not to choose. If the mind says it is gradual, it is a choice; if the mind says it is sudden, that too is a choice. When you say it is sudden it means that you would like to drop every effort, so you choose sudden enlightenment. Then there is no need to do anything – when it happens it happens, nothing can be done because it is a sudden thing. Just like lightning in the sky, whenever it happens it happens, you cannot make preparations for it. It is not like electricity in the house that you put on and off, it does not depend on you. It is a sudden phenomenon, when it happens it happens. You have to wait for it. If you are thinking about reading a telegram when the electricity happens in the sky, then you have to wait. When it happens you can read it. What can you do?

People who want to escape from effort will choose sudden

enlightenment. People who want to escape from the great, total responsibility of it, that it can happen right now, will choose the philosophy of gradualness.

I don't say anything about enlightenment; I'm saying something about you. It is for you to feel your desire. Total desire – enlightenment is sudden; partial desire – enlightenment is gradual. It has nothing to do with the nature of enlightenment. Remember this.

The second question:

Osho,
Do Taoists agree with the happening of sudden enlightenment or the gradual one?

They don't bother. Lao Tzu does not bother, because he says just to be ordinary is to be enlightened. It is not something special that one has to achieve, it is not an achievement, it is not something that one has to reach. It is you – in your absolute ordinariness it flowers. To be extraordinary is the disease of the ego.

The ego always wants to be extraordinary, someone special, unique, incomparable – that is the hankering desire of the ego. If you can become a Rockefeller, good. If you can become a Hitler, good. If you cannot become a Rockefeller or a Hitler, then renounce the world and think of becoming a Buddha. But become someone, someone special, a historic phenomenon.

Lao Tzu is not bothered about enlightenment and all that nonsense. He says just be ordinary. Eat when you feel hungry, drink when you feel thirsty and go to sleep when sleep comes. Just be as natural as the whole existence, and suddenly there is everything in all its glory. Nothing is needed.

To be ordinary is the most extraordinary state of being because the ego dissolves. The ego is subtle. You get rid of it in one direction, it comes from another. You push it out from one door, go inside the room and it is sitting on the throne – it has entered from another door. Before you even come in, it is already there.

I had a friend who had a small cat, a very beautiful cat. He asked me what name he should give to the cat. I called the cat "Ego" because the ego is very cunning and a cat of course is cunning. There is nothing like a cat for cunningness. So he named his cat "Ego."

By and by he got fed up. He was a lonely man, a bachelor with no wife, no children, and he always wanted to be alone but the cat was a continuous disturbance. He would be sleeping and she would jump on his chest. And she would come in with blood marks on her paws and destroy a whole chair seat or his clothes, because she was continuously hunting mice. So she was a trouble to him, and for a bachelor who had never cared for anybody, she was too much of a wife. He asked me what to do. This Ego had become a trouble. So I told him, "Ego is always a trouble. Go and throw it out."

He said, "But she knows all the ways of the town. She will come back."

I told him, "Go to the forest."

So he went to the forest so that the cat could not find the way home. He went in and in – and then lost the way! Then there was only one thing to do: he let the cat go, followed her, and came back home. That was the only way, there was nobody else to ask. The cat came back as certain as an arrow, not even hesitating for a single moment which way to follow.

So I told him, "Your cat has the perfect quality of the ego. You cannot throw it out easily. Wherever you go to throw it, when you come home, it is already there. Or sometimes you may get lost and then you will have to follow it, because only it knows the way."

The ego is very wise – wise in its cunningness. Lao Tzu does not give the ego any foothold, any ground to stand on, so he does not talk about enlightenment. So if you meet Lao Tzu don't ask him, "Do you believe in sudden enlightenment or in gradual enlightenment?" He will not answer you. He will laugh at you: "What foolishness!" There is no need for any enlightenment. That word doesn't occur for Lao Tzu, it is not part of his vocabulary.

He is very simple. He says just be ordinary. Why this hankering to be extraordinary, to be someone? And if you cannot be someone in the world then become enlightened at least. But why? Why can't you be satisfied and content with yourself as you are? If you ask me, to be content with oneself as one is, is enlightenment. It is nothing special, as yogis have made it sound: kundalini rising, light showing, inner experiences, angels and God and this and that. This is all nonsense if you understand it. Enlightenment is nothing of this sort.

All these things – kundalini and the light and God and angels and heaven and hell – are part of the magician's bag. You want them – he immediately produces, supplies them. You create the demand and the magician supplies the things to you. You want something special, he gives it to you. He exploits you. He lives on your absurd desires.

Lao Tzu is absolutely simple. He has no bag. He says why not just be? What is wrong? What is wrong in that which you are? Why make an effort? And who will make the effort? You will make the effort. Your effort cannot go beyond you, and whatsoever you do, you will do. How can it go beyond you? How can it be transcendental? By your own efforts how can you transcend? It is not possible; you are trying to do the impossible. You can go on jumping for thousands of lives and nothing will be attained.

Accept yourself. That is the only reality there is, that is the only possibility there is. Accept yourself as you are, and suddenly everything is transformed. *Acceptance* is the word for Lao Tzu, not *enlightenment* – total acceptance, whatsoever the case is. Nothing else is possible. This is how things are. This is how you have happened into this vast universe. This vast universe wanted you to be like this – now you accept.

There are only two choices available: either you reject yourself or you accept yourself. If you reject then there are again two possibilities open: you reject in a worldly way or you reject in an other-worldly way. If you reject yourself in a worldly way it means that you would like to be more beautiful than you are, you would like to be more strong than you are, you would like to be more rich than you are, you would like to have a bigger house than you have. This is to reject in a worldly way. If you reject yourself in an other-worldly way, the religious way, it means that you would like to attain satori, *samadhi*, enlightenment, nirvana; you would like to become a buddha; you would like to possess God; you would like to live in infinite bliss. This is how you reject in a religious way. These are both rejections and both are wrong. For Lao Tzu both are equally absurd.

Your marketplace is a marketplace; your temple is also part of it. Your this-worldly desires are worldly desires; your other-worldly desires are also desires and worldly. In fact there cannot be any other-worldly desire. Desire itself is this-worldly. Desire means this world.

I would like to tell you an anecdote. It happened in a Sufi's life:

A great mystic, living silently by himself, one day was suddenly awakened by a messenger from God.

The messenger said, "Your prayers have been accepted. Now the Supreme Being, the Creator, is very happy with you. You can ask, and whatsoever you desire will be fulfilled. Ask and immediately it will be fulfilled."

The mystic was a little puzzled and he said, "You came a little late. When I needed things, when I had many desires, you never came. Now I have no desires, I have accepted myself, I am totally at ease, at home. Now I don't bother even whether God exists or not, I don't pray to him. I pray because it feels good. I have stopped thinking at all about him. My prayer is not addressed to anybody anymore; I simply pray as I breathe. It's so beautiful, whether God exists or not is irrelevant. You came a little late. Now I have no desire."

But the angel said, "This will be an offense against God. When he says you can ask, you have to ask."

The man was puzzled, he shrugged his shoulders and said, "But what to ask? Can you suggest anything? – because I have accepted everything and I am so fulfilled. At the most, go and tell God that I'm grateful. Give my thanks to him. Everything is as it should be. Nothing is lacking, everything is perfect. I am happy, blissful, and I don't know anything about the next moment. This moment is all, I am fulfilled. Go and give my thanks."

But the angel was stubborn. He said, "No, you will have to ask something – just as a mannerism. Be a little understanding."

Then the man said, "If you insist, then ask God to keep me as desireless as I am. Give me only one thing – desirelessness."

Or acceptability, they both mean the same thing. Desire means rejection of something – you would like to be something else; desirelessness means acceptance – you are happy as things are. In fact, things are irrelevant, you are happy. You are happy, that's the point. Lao Tzu says be content as you are, nothing else is needed, and then suddenly everything happens. In deep acceptance the ego disappears.

Ego exists through rejection: whenever you reject something, ego exists. Whenever you say no, ego is strengthened. But whenever you say yes, a total yes to existence, that is the greatest meditation you can enter into. In all other meditations you can enter but you will have to come out. This is the only meditation in which you enter and you cannot come out, because once you enter you are no more. Nobody can come out of it.

The third question:

Osho,
You have said that any question is violent, yet we are encouraged to ask questions. Why is this?

Because you are violent and you need catharsis. You have questions to ask; you may not have the courage to ask them, that's why you are encouraged. You have questions to ask; you have to pass through that. Ask them. I'm not saying that my answers will destroy them – no. My answers are not pointed that way. My answers have a totally different purpose. They will make you aware that all questions are useless, futile, absurd.

I would like you to come to a point where the mind stops questioning, but that you cannot do because you are full of questions. Release them, don't suppress them. Be courageous. Even if you know that they are foolish, don't hide them, because if you hide them you will never be able to get rid of them. Even if they are ridiculous – and all questions are – ask.

I'm not really answering your questions. Your questions cannot be answered. Your questions are like a person who is in a delirium, whose fever has gone very high. He is reaching one hundred eight, one hundred nine, one hundred ten, and he is in delirium. Then he says, "Everything is moving, the table is flying in the sky." And he asks, "Where is this table going?" What to say to him? Whatsoever you say will be wrong, because the table is not going at all. And you cannot convince the man that the table is not going anywhere, it is just in the room, not moving at all. That will not convince him because you cannot convince anybody against his own experience.

How can you convince anybody against his own experience? Conviction is possible when his own experience supports it, otherwise not. He is seeing that the table is flying, trying to get out of the window, that the table has wings – and not only the table, the cot he is lying on, that too is jumping and getting ready, getting ready to take off! How can you convince a man who is in a delirium? If you try to convince him you are also mad. Only a mad doctor will try to convince.

No, the doctor will say, "Don't be worried, the table will come back. We will bring it back, don't be worried. We will do something." The doctor will try to bring his temperature down; when the temperature comes down the table will come down by itself. When the temperature becomes normal the table is in its place. It has always been there – it has not moved a single inch.

That is the situation. I see, I know that you are in a delirium. And this delirium is very subtle – no temperature measuring device can measure it; it is an inner, not a physical temperature. Inside you are in a delirium. Then questions and questions and questions – like flies they go on and on. I help you to ask and even encourage you to ask, just to get rid of them. This is a catharsis, this is part of a meditation.

Listening to me, by and by you will come to a point where you will understand that all questions are futile, in fact questioning is useless. When this realization arises in you, you will have a total change of attitude. Then questions disappear. When all questions disappear, the answer arises. And remember well, there are not as many answers as there are questions, there is only one answer to all questions. Questions may be millions – the answer is one. There is only one answer, the answer, and that is self-knowledge. So I am helping you to become aware.

There is a Sufi story:

A few men were passing by a Sufi monastery; just curious, they came to see what was happening there. People were in catharsis, freaking out, screaming, jumping, going completely mad. The travelers thought, "This is a mad monastery. We always thought that people come to attain enlightenment here but these people have gone mad." And the master was sitting amidst this catharsis, this mad chaos all around him. In the midst of it he was sitting silently.

The travelers thought, "Why is the master sitting silently?" Someone from the group suggested that maybe he was too tired, he may have done this madness too much.

Then after a few months they were coming back to their town after their work was done, and again they passed the monastery. They again looked to see what had happened to those mad people. But now everybody was sitting silently, not even a single word. When they approached the monastery they became afraid: had those people left? – because there seemed to be nobody now. When they came in everybody was there but they were silently sitting.

Then after a few months they went again on another business journey. Curiosity led them again to the monastery. They looked, there was nobody. Only the master was sitting there. So they asked, "What is all this?"

The master said, "When you passed through the first time you saw the beginners. They were full of madness and I encouraged them to bring it out. The next time you passed, they had realized, they had calmed down. That's why they were sitting silently. There was nothing to do. When you passed by the third time there was no need for them even to be here. Now they can be silent anywhere in the world, so I have sent them back to the world. I am waiting for a new group. When you pass next time, again there will be madness."

I encourage you to ask – it is to bring your mind out. This will help you to calm down. My answering, in fact, is not any effort to answer your questions; it is an effort to kill them, to murder them. I am not a teacher. I may be a murderer but I am not a teacher. I am not teaching you anything, I am simply destroying your questions. Once all questions are destroyed your head is cut off – I have murdered you. Then you are completely silent, content, absolutely at home. No problem exists: you live life moment to moment, you enjoy, you delight in it moment to moment. No problem exists.

I am against metaphysics but I have to talk about metaphysics. My whole work is therapeutic. I am not a metaphysician. My work is like this: you have a thorn in your foot; I bring another thorn to take the first thorn out of your foot. The first thorn and the second thorn are similar, there exists no qualitative difference. When the first is out, helped by the second, we throw away both.

When I bring your questions out I'm not saying put my answers in the places left vacant by the questions – no. Throw away my answers also as you throw away your questions, otherwise my answers will create troubles for you. Don't carry my answers, they are only therapeutic. They are like thorns: they can be used to bring other thorns out, then both have to be thrown away.

The fourth question:

Osho,

Werner Erhard, a Western yogi, says that problems that we have been trying to change or put up with clear up in the process of life itself. How does this relate to meditation? Are the two incompatible?

Erhard is absolutely right, but you can misunderstand him because whatsoever he is saying is as profound as anything that Lao Tzu can say. You can misunderstand him.

Try to understand it. Profundities are dangerous, and listened to by ignorant people they can become very, very dangerous. Joined with your stupidity, a profundity can become a very great fall.

Yes, this is absolutely right: problems that you have been trying to change or put up with clear up in the process of life itself. That's true, a statement of fact. It happens that way. But then the problem arises whether meditation is compatible with it or not. Now your stupidity has come in.

Meditation is also part of life – you have to do it as you have to do many other things. Why take meditation as something which is not part of life? Meditation is part of life, you have to pass through it too. You have come to meditation because something in you needed it, otherwise why should you come? The whole world has not come to me, only a few people have come to me. I am as available to them as I am available to you. Even people who live in Pune have not come, and you may have crossed oceans.

There is something in you – a deep desire for it. Sex alone is not life, food alone is not life. Meditation is as much life as anything else, and it is your part in life to pass through it.

Now, what Erhard says is absolutely true, a statement of fact. Nothing else is needed, one needs only to live and everything settles by itself. But meditation is also part of life, yoga is also part of life, one has to pass through it. You cannot escape it. If you try to escape it, that part which you have not fulfilled will always remain hanging over you and you will feel that something has remained incomplete.

Be courageous and don't escape from anywhere. Wherever your inner life leads you, go. Don't bother where it leads you. Sometimes it will lead you astray, that I know, but to go astray is also part of life. Nobody can always be right, and people who try always to be right die almost absolute failures. Don't be bothered that you may go astray, if life leads you astray, go! Go happily! The energy that leads you astray will bring you back. That sojourn may be a part of the final growth.

This is my experience, that in the end one finds that everything fits together. Everything that you did, good and bad, right and wrong, moral and immoral – whatsoever you did, in the end one finds life is really wonderful, everything fits. If you look back you would not like to change anything, because if you change even a part then the whole would be changed.

This is what acceptance is. This is what the Hindu attitude about fate or the Mohammedan attitude about kismet is. The attitude is very simple, only this: whatsoever happens, take it as part of your destiny. Move into it. Don't withhold yourself.

If you have to err, err – but err totally. If you have to fall, fall – but fall like a drunkard, completely. Don't resist, because then you miss. If you have to live in darkness, live in darkness – but happily and dancingly. Why be miserable? If you are feeling hell around you, feel it. It may be part of your destiny, part of your growth.

Of course I know that when one passes through hell, it is very difficult. That I know – because growth is difficult. When one passes through a problem, a heart-rending problem, a crisis, one wants to escape; one wants not to face it; one wants to be a coward. But that way you will miss something that was going to become a part of the final whole, of the final harmony. If you have lived totally – I don't make any conditions. I say live unconditionally. If your inner voice tells you to meditate, meditate. If your inner voice tells you to go and drink, then drink and be a drunkard. But be total, because only through totality does one transcend. Only through totality is one transformed because only through totality does one start under-standing what one is doing.

People come to me and they say that they have much anger in them and they would like not to have it any more. They have had enough of it and they have suffered much for it. Their whole life has become miserable. And they repent much, whenever they become angry they repent much. They try again and again not to be angry, they decide not to be angry, they put all their willpower into it, but after a few hours they have forgotten. Again something happens, a situation occurs, and they are angry. So what to do?

I tell them don't repent, begin from there. Don't repent, at least that much you can do. Be angry and be totally angry and don't repent.

And don't feel sorry about it. You have been angry, accept the fact that you are a man with an angry nature. Okay. Be totally angry. Because that repentance is not allowing you to be totally angry, something is being withheld. That part which remains inside and has not been expressed becomes poisonous, a cancerous growth. It will color all your life, the whole of your life. Be angry, and when you are angry let the phenomenon be such that you can say, "I am anger, not angry." Nobody is left behind to look at it – you are anger. It will become a fire, a hellfire.

It will be great suffering but it has to be so. It may be that if you can be really in a hellfire only once, you will become so alert about it that there will be no need to decide against it. The very experience will have decided everything – you will never go near it again. Not that you take a vow against it, not that you go to the church and confess and repent. People start enjoying that too; they start indulging in repentance also.

I have heard that a woman came for the seventh time to the Father in the church to confess a sin. Even the Father was a little surprised because it was the same sin again and again – that she had made love to a man to whom she was not married.

So the Father said, "Have you committed the sin seven times or only once?"

She said, "Only once."

So he said, "Then why do you go on confessing it? You have already confessed seven times."

She said, "I love to talk about it. It's so beautiful just to think about it."

Even in imagination, confessing to a Father!

People start indulging in their repentance, confessions. They may even exaggerate – this has been my feeling. Saint Augustine's book, Confessions, seems to be an exaggeration; he seems to be indulging in it. The very idea of committing so many sins seems to be appealing. In India, Gandhi's autobiography seems to be an exaggeration. He goes on talking and talking about his sins, it seems he is enjoying it. And now psychologists say that there are people who exaggerate their sins because then, against that background, they become great saints – because they have not left ordinary sins, they were such great sinners, and now they have become such great saints. The distance is vast and the revolution great.

Only a great sinner can be a great saint, how can an ordinary sinner be? You smoke a cigarette – do you think you can become an Augustine or a Gandhi just because you smoked a cigarette once, or you looked at a woman and a lust arose in you, that's all? That won't do, it is not enough material. You cannot create a big saint out of small sins, you have to be a great sinner.

So people who write their autobiographies should never be believed. I must have read thousands of autobiographies, but this is my observation: that there exists no other sort of fiction which is more fictitious. Autobiography is the greatest fiction. All autobiographies are fictitious. Either one goes on praising himself or one goes on condemning himself, but both are untrue because in both ways one starts becoming extraordinary. The ego cannot be fulfilled by just being ordinary.

Somebody asked Rinzai, "What do you do? What is your practice, what is your sadhana?"

And he said such a simple thing – how could you make an autobiography out of it? He said, "When I feel hungry I eat, and when I feel sleepy I go to sleep, that's all."

How can you make an autobiography out of it? And Rinzai would not look like a great saint either. What type of a saint would this be?

After Rinzai died, his disciple was lecturing in a monastery. A man belonging to the opposite sect stood up; he was feeling very jealous because so many people had come to listen.

So he stood up and he said, "One question, sir. You are talking too much about your master. But mine is a real master, he can do thousands of miracles. I have seen with my own eyes: he was standing on one bank of the river, and it was the time of rains and the river was flooded. And on the other bank a disciple was standing with a copybook in his hand. On one bank my master wrote with a pencil and it was written on the disciple's copybook on the other bank. Can you say anything about your master, what miracles he did?"

The disciple said, "I know only of one miracle that my master used to do – every day, every minute of it."

Silence fell all over the hall. People became curious: what miracle had Rinzai done?

The disciple said, "When he felt hungry he ate and when he felt sleepy he slept. That's the only miracle that he did."

You will not think it much of a miracle but it is. It is a very profound phenomenon. It means to be completely natural. You are always fighting. When you feel hungry you don't eat because a thousand and one other things have to be done; when you don't feel hungry you eat because now is the time to eat. When you feel sleepy you avoid it because there is a dance worth going to, or a movie worth seeing. When you feel sleepy you are sitting in the movie. When you don't feel sleepy, because the movie has excited you too much, now you try to go to sleep and you have to take tranquilizers.

To be unnatural has become our natural life. Of course to be natural is a miracle, the greatest miracle: just to delight in ordinary things; in eating, sleeping, drinking, the breeze that passes you. Enjoying ordinary things, delighting in them, the whole of life becomes a celebration.

Erhard is right. He is saying a Lao Tzuan thing: "Problems that you have been trying to change or put up with clear up in the process of life itself." Live life, live in its totality, move in all its dimensions – indulge in every dimension, indulge totally, and in the end you will find that everything helped. Everything, I say – even the wife who created so much misery for you, even that; even the child that you loved so much and died early, even that; even the business that failed and you became broke, yes, even that. Everything! Failure and success, pain and pleasure, right and wrong, going astray and coming back home – everything helps.

And out of this chaos arises a harmony. But one has to live it totally. I am not saying that everyone reaches to that harmony. No, that is a possibility. One can reach, one may miss, and people who miss are those people who try hard to reach it. People who attain to it are people who don't bother much about attaining it, they simply live moment to moment.

That final harmony, that crescendo, is a cumulative effect. So enjoy wherever you are, be grateful, whatever you have. Feel deep gratitude; let that be your only prayer. Go totally wherever you go. If you go to a prostitute, go totally – and I know that even to your wife you have not gone totally. If you drink wine, drink it totally – and I know you have not even drunk water totally.

This incomplete life cannot become a crescendo; this life lived always incomplete, fragmentary, cannot create a harmony. You will die a chaos – that's why you will always die afraid of death. And when death knocks at your door you will tremble, because the life harmony has not yet been achieved, and death has come. You have not lived life, and death has come. You are as yet incomplete, in fact unborn, and death has come. You tremble.

A man who has lived his life, one who has lived his day, always accepts death beautifully because there is nothing left to be done anymore. He has done all, he has lived all and he moved in all directions. All that life could give he had accumulated in himself. He has accumulated the honey of life, now he is ready to die. There is nothing else.

Do you know, for one spoonful of honey a bee has to visit five thousand flowers? For one spoonful of honey five thousand flowers! And for one pound of honey – scientists have measured – thousands of miles have to be traveled by bees. One spoonful of honey, five thousand flowers. One spoonful of harmony and five thousand experiences, thousands and thousands of experiences...

And remember only one thing: wherever you are, be totally there, otherwise you will visit the flower and you will come away without the honey. That is the only misery that can happen to a man and that happens to almost ninety-nine per cent of people. You are in such a hurry – just think of a bee in such a hurry that she goes to the flower but never touches it because she is in such a hurry to go to another flower. Incomplete, she moves to another flower but by the time she has reached the other flower the idea is hankering in her mind to go to another. She visits five thousand or five million flowers and comes back empty-handed. Don't be that type of bee! When you visit a flower, really visit it. Forget about all other flowers in the world – there exist no others at that moment. Just be a bee – hum and delight and enjoy the flower. Be with it as totally as possible. Then you accumulate life's honey and when you die, you die blissfully, ecstatically. You lived. There is no complaint in your heart, no grudge.

And I tell you that if you have lived all moments in their totality, in awareness, at the moment of death you can bless all – your friends and your enemies. Yes, your enemies also, because without them you would not have been able to reach to this crescendo. They were part, part of a mysterious phenomenon that is life.

The fifth question:

Osho,
You once said that in the question lies the answer, so the nature of the question determines the nature of the answer. What is then the most fundamental question the mind can ask?

The mind can never ask any fundamental question because what-soever the mind asks is bound to be superficial. When the question arises out of your being, not out of your mind, it will not be verbal, it will be existential. You will be the question – then it is fundamental.

A Sufi mystic used to come to the mosque every day and he would stand there not saying a single word, for years and years. People became curious.

Somebody asked, "You never say anything, we have not even seen your lips quivering a little and we have watched you, observed you closely. We don't feel that even inside you are saying any-thing, you stand there like a rock. What type of prayer is this?"

The mystic said, "Once it happened that a beggar was standing before a palace of an emperor. The emperor came out, looked at the beggar and said, 'What do you ask? What do you want?' The beggar said, 'If by looking at me you cannot understand, then there is no need to say. I will go to another house. Look at me – naked in the cold winter, shivering. Look at my belly – it has joined the back. Look at my limbs – all the flesh has disappeared. I am a skeleton and you ask what do I want? Is my being here not enough?' The king became afraid, the beggar was right. Much was given to him."

And the mystic said, "I was passing by on the road. From that day I stopped praying, because what to say to the emperor of the world? Can't he understand what misery I am in? Have I to say it? Assert it? Have I to be articulate with him? If he cannot understand my being, what use will it be to talk? Then it is useless. If he cannot understand my being, he cannot understand my language. Silent is my prayer, unquestioned is my question, undesired is my desire. It is me, it is my total being."

That is fundamental, that is foundational, that is radical – it comes from the very roots. The word radical comes from *roots*. A radical, a foundational, a fundamental question is never asked by the mind. The mind cannot ask it; the mind is impotent about it. The mind is just like the waves on the ocean. Can you ask me which wave is the deepest? No wave is, no wave can be, because waves can exist only on the surface, they cannot be in the depth. In the depth there are no waves.

The mind is the surface, the waves. All questions raised by the mind are superficial. The fundamental question is asked when the mind has been dropped. It is a no-mind question, it is a being question. Then you stand with a question not even verbalized within you, because who will verbalize it? The mind has been put aside, your whole existence is a question mark.

And when that fundamental question is asked, only then can the master give you himself in his totality. He can pour himself into your being. When you ask a superficial question, of course a fundamental answer cannot be given, because it will fall on deaf ears, on dead hearts. When you ask a question the quality of the answer is already decided in it.

The sixth question:

Osho,
You called us the "ancient ones." If we have been with other masters in past lives, how is it possible that we could have missed them so consistently?

Because you are very consistent. Be a little inconsistent, otherwise you will miss me also.

The seventh question:

Osho,
You said that Lao Tzu was born old. How did he achieve his wisdom and maturity? Was a master necessary to bring him to the point where he could be born old?

You don't even have a sense of humor. You can't understand a joke. These are just symbolic tales, beautiful in themselves, but if you start asking questions about them they become ugly. That's how the whole mystery and the poetry of a thing is lost; and that is what has been done. The whole of theology is all about such nonsensical questions. "Was Jesus really born out of a virgin?" It is a beautiful symbol. "Was Jesus really resurrected when he was dead, crucified?" This is a beautiful symbol. "Was it a reality that Lao Tzu was born old, eighty-four years old, remained in his mother's womb for eighty-four years?" It is a beautiful Lao Tzuan joke. I suspect that Lao Tzu must have spread the rumor – nobody else could do that, it is so subtle.

If you understand the joke, you understand. If you don't understand please don't ask questions. Forget about it, because questions will destroy it completely.

It is said that whenever a joke is told there are three kinds of laughter. The first is from those who understand it immediately – and a joke has to be understood immediately, with no time gap, otherwise you lack a sense of humor. That is the whole point of it – that suddenly it strikes, suddenly it hits somewhere inside, and you know what it is. You may not be able to explain to others why you were laughing, and the more you try to explain, the more it will become a puzzle. Why were you laughing? It is a subtle phenomenon. How does it happen?

When somebody is telling a joke, the joke moves on two levels, that's how the laughter is created. On one level everything is simple and ordinary, nothing is special, then suddenly there is a turn at the end, the punch line; at the end there is suddenly a turn, you never expected that this was going to happen. That's why if you have heard the joke it is impossible to laugh again, because then the turn is not there, you already know it. When the sudden turn comes that you never expected, not even a single second before – everything was on plain ground and suddenly you are on Everest and everything has changed, and the change is so ridiculous, illogical, irrational – you explode in laughter. If you understand a joke you understand it immediately, without any effort on your part. It is just like satori or *samadhi*.

Then there is a second type of laughter. These people understand the joke, but a little time gap is needed. Then it touches only their intellect, not their whole being; their laughter comes, but the laughter is from the lips – an intellectual phenomenon. The first laughter is from the belly, the second laughter just from the head. They understand the point, but intellect always takes time, it doesn't get a very quick grasp on something. Even the most intelligent person is a little stupid, because the nature of intellect is such that it cannot jump. It moves in logical steps, it needs time, it is a progress, a gradual phenomenon – step by step you reach the conclusion.

That is the second laughter. It will be pale, not very deep, not very relaxing, not a catharsis, just an intellectual phenomenon. In the head something clicks, creates little ripples, that's all. But the first laughter is so deep that if it really happens, a joke can become a satori. In that laughter the mind can disappear completely.

Then there is a third kind of laughter – people who laugh because others are laughing. They have not understood, but not to be thought stupid because they have not understood, they laugh lastly. Seeing that everybody is laughing, they have to laugh.

Mulla Nasruddin went to France once. His wife was with him and they went to see a comic show. The wife was surprised, because whenever the man, the joker on the stage, would tell a joke or do something, Mulla would laugh so loudly that he would defeat the whole audience. People would start looking at him.

The wife couldn't understand because she knew well that he didn't understand French. So she asked, "Mulla, I have lived with you for thirty years and I never knew that you know French. How do you understand? And why do you laugh so loudly?"

Mulla said, "I trust the man. He must be saying something funny and when one has to laugh, why laugh last? Why not laugh first? And when one has to laugh, one should laugh loudly. It costs nothing and I am enjoying myself."

This is the third kind of laughter – nothing is happening to you, it is a pretension. You think that there must have been something humorous, you trust the man or you trust other people who are laughing and not to feel stupid you join in the laughter.

Whenever a joke is told you can immediately sort out these three kinds of laughter.

This is just a Lao Tzuan joke. Nobody can live in the mother's womb for eighty-four years. Even if Lao Tzu could, think of the mother also! Lao Tzu may be enlightened and could live in the womb for eighty-four years, but the mother – poor mother, think of her also.

Even nine months is too much, but eighty-four years! The mother would have been dead long before.

No, it is a subtle humor. It says that Lao Tzu was born wise. It is a symbolic thing. From his very childhood he was wise. That is the only meaning. He was so wise that the rumor spread that he was born old.

Jesus was so pure, how could he be born out of carnal desire? He was born out of carnal desire, there is no other way – life gives no exceptions. He was born out of ordinary love. But the story says something very beautiful. The story is not true and I say it is true! It is not true as a fact, but it is true as a truth. And what is a fact before a truth? A fact is an ordinary facticity of life. No, Jesus' mother was not a virgin if you go to the ordinary facts. But she was a virgin, otherwise how could such a pure, such an innocent child be born out of her? She was virgin. She must have been very, very innocent, absolutely innocent, as if she had never known any man. That is the meaning. The meaning is "as if" – as if she never knew what sex was, as if she never knew what ordinary copulation was. But those are "as ifs"; once you start forcing them as facts you are foolish. And all theologians are foolish. They try to prove that yes, she was a virgin, and God permitted an exception at that moment of history.

This is a way to say a certain beautiful thing which cannot be said otherwise. This is just saying that Jesus comes out of a virgin source, Jesus comes out of a pure innocence which has not known any impurity of the world and the body. That's all. Don't insist that it should be explained, because explanation kills the very spirit of it.

The last question:

Osho,
You said that you are merely a presence and cannot do anything. But I and everybody else feel all the time that in your compassion for us you are influencing us and events to bring us closer to your temple. Is this just our imagination playing tricks?

I cannot do anything, but my presence can. When I say I cannot do anything, I only mean that no "I" exists within me; the doer is dissolved. So without the doer how can you do anything? But things happen. And when the doer is dissolved then tremendous things happen. I cannot claim the authorship of them or the doership of them – I am not the doer. In fact I am not. I am just a presence with no label attached to it, just an opening. Much is possible if you are in my presence. If you allow my presence to move into you, melt into you, become part of you, much is possible. Even the impossible is possible – but I am not the doer, it happens. I am not specifically doing it.

I am also a watcher as you are a watcher. It is happening. If you go to the sun and tell the sun that you are very grateful because it has been destroying darkness for you on the earth for so long, the sun will be surprised. The sun will say, "I don't know what darkness is. I have never come across it. I have never destroyed it, because how can you destroy a thing that you have never come across?" But it is happening all the same: light comes, darkness disappears.

If you allow this presence that is here, much is possible. The darkness can disappear, but I am not the doer. I am not forcing anything on you because that would be a violence, and even if it were not a violence I cannot do it because the doer is no longer there. If you come into me you will not meet anybody there. The temple is absolutely vacant. A real temple is always empty. If you find a god sitting inside, then it is a man-made temple. Nothingness is the only temple.

Yes, I'm not doing anything to you, but much is happening. So don't think that this may be imagination, because this may be a trick of the mind to think that this is imagination – because then the mind can close. Thinking that this is imagination, a projection, this or that, the mind can close and then everything will stop.

Don't listen to the mind. While you are with me don't be with your mind. I am a no-mind; the only way to be with me is to be a no-mind and then things happen. Nobody is doing them, they simply happen on their own accord.

Sitting silently, quietly with me, you grow. Nobody is doing anything, neither I nor you. Just sitting silently, the existence within you grows on its own.

Enough for today.

about Osho

Osho's unique contribution to the understanding of who we are defies categorization. Mystic and scientist, a rebellious spirit whose sole interest is to alert humanity to the urgent need to discover a new way of living. To continue as before is to invite threats to our very survival on this unique and beautiful planet.

His essential point is that only by changing ourselves, one individual at a time, can the outcome of all our "selves" – our societies, our cultures, our beliefs, our world – also change. The doorway to that change is meditation.

Osho the scientist has experimented and scrutinized all the approaches of the past and examined their effects on the modern human being and responded to their shortcomings by creating a new starting point for the hyperactive 21st Century mind: OSHO Active Meditations.

Once the agitation of a modern lifetime has started to settle, "activity" can melt into "passivity," a key starting point of real meditation. To support this next step, Osho has transformed the ancient "art of listening" into a subtle contemporary methodology: the OSHO Talks. Here words become music, the listener discovers who is listening, and the awareness moves from what is being heard to the individual doing the listening. Magically, as silence arises, what needs to be heard is understood directly, free from the distraction of a mind that can only interrupt and interfere with this delicate process.

These thousands of talks cover everything from the individual quest for meaning to the most urgent social and political issues facing society today. Osho's books are not written but are transcribed from audio and video recordings of these extemporaneous talks to international audiences. As he puts it, "So remember: whatever I am saying is not just for you...I am talking also for the future generations."

Osho has been described by *The Sunday Times* in London as one of the "1000 Makers of the 20th Century" and by American author Tom Robbins as "the most dangerous man since Jesus

Christ." *Sunday Mid-Day* (India) has selected Osho as one of ten people – along with Gandhi, Nehru and Buddha – who have changed the destiny of India.

About his own work Osho has said that he is helping to create the conditions for the birth of a new kind of human being. He often characterizes this new human being as "Zorba the Buddha" – capable both of enjoying the earthy pleasures of a Zorba the Greek and the silent serenity of a Gautama the Buddha.

Running like a thread through all aspects of Osho's talks and meditations is a vision that encompasses both the timeless wisdom of all ages past and the highest potential of today's (and tomorrow's) science and technology.

Osho is known for his revolutionary contribution to the science of inner transformation, with an approach to meditation that acknowledges the accelerated pace of contemporary life. His unique OSHO Active Meditations™ are designed to first release the accumulated stresses of body and mind, so that it is then easier to take an experience of stillness and thought-free relaxation into daily life.

Two autobiographical works by the author are available:
Autobiography of a Spiritually Incorrect Mystic,
St Martins Press, New York (book and eBook)
Glimpses of a Golden Childhood,
OSHO Media International, Pune, India

OSHO international meditation resort

Each year the Meditation Resort welcomes thousands of people from more than 100 countries. The unique campus provides an opportunity for a direct personal experience of a new way of living – with more awareness, relaxation, celebration and creativity. A great variety of around-the-clock and around-the-year program options are available. Doing nothing and just relaxing is one of them!

All of the programs are based on Osho's vision of "Zorba the Buddha" – a qualitatively new kind of human being who is able *both* to participate creatively in everyday life *and* to relax into silence and meditation.

Location
Located 100 miles southeast of Mumbai in the thriving modern city of Pune, India, the OSHO International Meditation Resort is a holiday destination with a difference. The Meditation Resort is spread over 28 acres of spectacular gardens in a beautiful tree-lined residential area.

OSHO Meditations
A full daily schedule of meditations for every type of person includes both traditional and revolutionary methods, and particularly the OSHO Active Meditations™. The daily meditation program takes place in what must be the world's largest meditation hall, the OSHO Auditorium.

OSHO Multiversity
Individual sessions, courses and workshops cover everything from creative arts to holistic health, personal transformation, relationship and life transition, transforming meditation into a lifestyle for life and work, esoteric sciences, and the "Zen" approach to sports and recreation. The secret of the OSHO Multiversity's success lies in the fact that all its programs are combined with meditation, supporting the

understanding that as human beings we are far more than the sum of our parts.

OSHO Basho Spa
The luxurious Basho Spa provides for leisurely open-air swimming surrounded by trees and tropical green. The uniquely styled, spacious Jacuzzi, the saunas, gym, tennis courts...all these are enhanced by their stunningly beautiful setting.

Cuisine
A variety of different eating areas serve delicious Western, Asian and Indian vegetarian food – most of it organically grown especially for the Meditation Resort. Breads and cakes are baked in the resort's own bakery.

Night life
There are many evening events to choose from – dancing being at the top of the list! Other activities include full-moon meditations beneath the stars, variety shows, music performances and meditations for daily life.

Facilities
You can buy all of your basic necessities and toiletries in the Galleria. The Multimedia Gallery sells a large range of OSHO media products. There is also a bank, a travel agency and a Cyber Café on-campus. For those who enjoy shopping, Pune provides all the options, ranging from traditional and ethnic Indian products to all of the global brand-name stores.

Accommodation
You can choose to stay in the elegant rooms of the OSHO Guesthouse, or for longer stays on campus you can select one of the OSHO Living-In programs. Additionally there is a plentiful variety of nearby hotels and serviced apartments.

www.osho.com/meditationresort
www.osho.com/guesthouse
www.osho.com/livingin

more books and eBooks by OSHO media international

The God Conspiracy:
The Path from Superstition to Super Consciousness

Discover the Buddha: 53 Meditations to Meet the Buddha Within
Gold Nuggets: Messages from Existence

OSHO Classics
The Book of Wisdom: The Heart of Tibetan Buddhism.
The Mustard Seed: The Revolutionary Teachings of Jesus
Ancient Music in the Pines: In Zen, Mind Suddenly Stops
The Empty Boat: Encounters with Nothingness
A Bird on the Wing: Zen Anecdotes for Everyday Life
The Path of Yoga: Discovering the Essence and Origin of Yoga
And the Flowers Showered: The Freudian Couch and Zen
Nirvana: The Last Nightmare: Learning to Trust in Life
The Goose Is Out: Zen in Action
Absolute Tao: Subtle Is the Way to Love, Happiness and Truth

The Tantra Experience: Evolution through Love
Tantric Transformation: When Love Meets Meditation

Pillars of Consciousness (illustrated)
BUDDHA: His Life and Teachings and Impact on Humanity
ZEN: Its History and Teachings and Impact on Humanity
TANTRA: The Way of Acceptance
TAO: The State and the Art

Authentic Living

Danger: Truth at Work: The Courage to Accept the Unknowable
The Magic of Self-Respect: Awakening to Your Own Awareness
Born With a Question Mark in Your Heart

OSHO eBooks and "OSHO-Singles"

Emotions: Freedom from Anger, Jealousy and Fear
Meditation: The First and Last Freedom
What Is Meditation?
The Book of Secrets: 112 Meditations to Discover the Mystery Within

20 Difficult Things to Accomplish in This World
Compassion, Love and Sex
Hypnosis in the Service of Meditation
Why Is Communication So Difficult, Particularly between Lovers?
Bringing Up Children
Why Should I Grieve Now?: facing a loss and letting it go
Love and Hate: just two sides of the same coin

Next Time You Feel Angry...
Next Time You Feel Lonely...
Next Time You Feel Suicidal...

OSHO Media BLOG
http://oshomedia.blog.osho.com

for more information

www.**OSHO**.com

a comprehensive multi-language website including a magazine, OSHO Books, OSHO Talks in audio and video formats, the OSHO Library text archive in English and Hindi and extensive information about OSHO Meditations. You will also find the program schedule of the OSHO Multiversity and information about the OSHO International Meditation Resort.

http://OSHO.com/AllAboutOSHO
http://OSHO.com/Resort
http://OSHO.com/Shop
http://www.youtube.com/OSHO
http://www.Twitter.com/OSHO
http://www.facebook.com/pages/OSHO.International

To contact OSHO International Foundation:
www.osho.com/oshointernational,
oshointernational@oshointernational.com